UNIVERSITY OF NORTH CAROLINA AT CHAPEL HILL
DEPARTMENT OF ROMANCE LANGUAGES

NORTH CAROLINA STUDIES
IN THE ROMANCE LANGUAGES AND LITERATURES

Founder: URBAN TIGNER HOLMES
Editor: CAROL L. SHERMAN

Distributed by:

UNIVERSITY OF NORTH CAROLINA PRESS
CHAPEL HILL
North Carolina 27515-2288
U.S.A.

NORTH CAROLINA STUDIES IN THE
ROMANCE LANGUAGES AND LITERATURES
Number 255

DISLOCATIONS OF DESIRE

DISLOCATIONS OF DESIRE:
Gender, identity, and strategy in *La Regenta*

BY
ALISON SINCLAIR

CHAPEL HILL

NORTH CAROLINA STUDIES IN THE ROMANCE
LANGUAGES AND LITERATURES
U.N.C. DEPARTMENT OF ROMANCE LANGUAGES

1998

Library of Congress Cataloging-in-Publication Data

Sinclair, Alison.
    Dislocations of desire: gender, identity, and strategy in La regenta / by Alison Sinclair.
    p. – cm. – (North Carolina Studies in the Romance Languages & Literatures; no. 255).
    Includes bibliographical references.
    ISBN 0-8078-9259-9 (pbk.).
    1. Alas, Leopoldo, 1852-1901. Regenta. 2. Desire in literature. 3. Self in literature.
I. Title. II. Series.

PQ6503.A4E3367   1998   97-42196
863'.5 – dc21   CIP

Cover design: Shelley Gruendler
Cover photograph by Stewart Sinclair

© 1998. Department of Romance Languages. The University of North Carolina
   at Chapel Hill.

ISBN 0-8078-9259-9

DEPÓSITO LEGAL: V. 788 - 1998

ARTES GRÁFICAS SOLER, S. A. - LA OLIVERETA, 28 - 46018 VALENCIA

CONTENTS

	Page
ACKNOWLEDGEMENTS	9
INTRODUCTION	11
BOUNDARIES	35
Chapter 1. Liminal anxieties	35
Chapter 2. The gendered language of desire	59
TWOS AND THREES	81
Chapter 3. Triangles and identifications	81
STRATEGIES I: FEMALE MALADIES	117
Chapter 4. The consuming passion	121
Chapter 5. Hysteria	150
STRATEGIES II: PERVERSE RITUALS	177
Chapter 6. The force of parental presence	179
Chapter 7. Perverse rituals	196
CONCLUSION	218
BIBLIOGRAPHY	221

ACKNOWLEDGEMENTS

I would like to acknowledge the generous financial assistance of the British Academy, the Modern Humanities Research Association, and the program for Cultural Cooperation between Spain's Ministry of Culture and United States Universities, which made the publication of this book possible. I would like to thank the University of North Carolina Press for their expertise and work, and in particular for my editor Professor Carol Sherman, for her unfailingly positive support, and cheerful contact throughout the publishing process.

This is a book which has grown over time, and many exchanges, conversations and lines of investigation have contributed to it. I would like to express thanks to institutions and individuals who knowingly (and sometimes unknowingly) contributed to my work toward this book, including students in my classes, librarians, and friends and colleagues in fields both related and unrelated, including Roger Bacon, Maurice Biriotti, Lou Charnon-Deutsch, Cathy Davies, Hazel Gold, Felicia Gordon, Catherine Jagoe, Jo Labanyi, Haya Oakley, Noreen O'Connor, Enrique Perdiguero, Geoffrey Ribbans, Nicholas Round, Naomi Segal, Arthur Terry, Harriet Turner, Noël Valis. I have found the University Library, Cambridge, as ever, an incomparable place in which to work, both for its resources and its ever-helpful staff; the British Library was immensely helpful with its 19th-century sources, and the Wellcome Institute, and Professor Roy Porter, provided invaluable expertise and an excellent range of facilities. I would like to thank my husband and daughters for their tolerance while I worked on this book, and particularly to thank the former, Stewart Sinclair, for the photograph which forms the cover for this volume, and which expresses the materiality of the text that it is hard to put into words.

I am grateful to the following journals and presses for permission to reprint revised versions of the following: "The Consuming Passion: Appetite and Hunger in *La Regenta*", *Bulletin of Hispanic Studies* (Liverpool) 69 (3) (July 1992), pp. 245-261; "Liminal Anxieties: Nausea and Mud in *La Regenta*", *Bulletin of Hispanic Studies* (Glasgow) 74 (2) (1997), pp. 155-176; "Masculine Envy in *La Regenta*: the skull and the foot", *Tesserae* 1 (2) (Summer 1995), pp. 171-190; "The Gendered Language of Desire", *Journal of Hispanic Research* 3 (1994-5), pp. 231-249; "The Force of Parental Presence in *La Regenta*", in *Culture and Gender in Nineteenth-Century Spain*, ed. Lou Charnon-Deutsch and Jo Labanyi (Oxford: Oxford University Press, 1996), pp. 182-198.

INTRODUCTION

> ...a restriction of sexual activity in a community is quite generally accompanied by an increase of anxiety about life and of fear of death which interferes with the individual's capacity for enjoyment and does away with his readiness to face death for any purpose. A diminished inclination to beget children is the result. (Freud, " 'Civilized' Sexual Morality and Modern Nervous Illness" 1908a)

Somnolence, that state with which *La Regenta* opens, is one in which we are neither conscious nor unconscious. Falling asleep is the physical and mental state in which we find ourselves dragged against our volition into something other than the conscious, with a pull that is overwhelmingly appealing, and against which our struggle to resist is ultimately powerless. Yet the state of sleep, once attained, is where we fabricate the world of dreams, a world not unstructured, but with a structure and logic other than that of the waking world. In the opening lines of *La Regenta*, as we read of the apparently peaceful town and its characters in their *siesta*, a double process is set up which will continue throughout the novel. As readers we are thrust into that dizzy, uncertain world where we move back and forth over the threshold between waking and sleeping, our reading experience creating for us a direct apprehension of the uncertainties and shifting boundaries with which the characters of the novel are constrained to live. The dimly perceived struggle is smoothed over, so that we are introduced simultaneously to a surface that is distinct from the depth that it covers. If we focus our attention to the detail of the peaceful *siesta* hour, we find a backcloth that is in fact troubling not peaceful, one in which lazy movement becomes disturbing rustling, while the processes of digestion rumble on below an apparently peaceful surface.

Throughout the novel reader and character alike will struggle to establish boundaries, between sleeping and waking, between thought and action, between desire and strategic motivation, between self and other, between the psychotic apprehension of a world that is collapsing and dissolving and the desperate need to construct a framework, a bulwark against it. The acts of sleeping, waking and dreaming, thinking and acting, desiring and possessing motivation all assume some concept of a self that performs such acts, yet the novel highlights the very uncertainty of the nature of self, and the permeability of its boundaries.

In discussing the self and its relation to boundaries, whether at the level of individual character, or at the level of narrative strategy, I shall have in mind a variety of theoretical conceptualizations of the self which diverge in emphasis, but all of which have some bearing on the dynamics of what is and is not the self as revealed in the novel. These conceptualizations derive from the field of psychoanalysis. It will be seen from the ensuing discussion that I draw on theory from a variety of positions within that field. Much of my reference is to Freud and Lacan, but my framework draws also on pertinent areas of Object Relations. That is, I draw on theory both father-based, and mother-based. Furthermore, while I have not at any stage engaged in direct discussion (whether in a spirit of promotion or rebuttal) of feminist or other objections to, or reservations about, psychoanalytic theory, it will be evident that my attitude to such theory is questioning and speculative, rather than one which is engaged in adoption and application of dogma. This questioning approach I believe to be characteristic not only of debate within the field of critical theory, but also within psychoanalysis itself. Here current explorations in the clinical field demonstrate that a putting aside of such theory because of perceptions based on a narrow, or historically limited understanding of it is an action that carries a risk: that of throwing out the baby with the bathwater.[1]

In *La Regenta* there is negotiation around two types of boundary: first between the self and what is not itself, at times experienced as between the self and its collapse, disintegration or dissolution into the surrounding environment, and second between the

---

[1] A good example of a recent discussion of how psychoanalytic theory can be questioned, interpreted and understood currently is that of Rosalind Minsky (1995).

masculine and feminine, boundaries of gender. The second of these would be expected to occur between two selves, each with their own gender definition. But it of course also includes the issue of the construction of gender identity for the self as a type of defensive strategy against the dangers of collapse and dissolution experienced in the first area of boundary definition, and furthermore the struggle between demarcations of masculine and feminine within individual characters. The definition of the boundary of gender can also be regarded as defensive in that it takes the self a further stage on from the primitive demarcation of the self's boundaries with the world, and because it holds out, through the possibility of sexual intercourse and reproduction, the notion of creativity, which would be the ultimate proof of the existence of the self: not "I think therefore I am," but "I can reproduce therefore I am."

Some of the concepts of the self which portray it as most indistinct are most relevant for a reading of *La Regenta*, in that they designate that emergence of the self from the moment of birth. As I shall expand later, the occurrence of birth as such is remarkably absent from the novel, yet the whole evocation of the complex environment, physical and social, is one from which the characters, and indeed events, will have to become distinct, separate, by an act of boundary observation.

The idea of the self as being initially undifferentiated from the environment is posited by Freud, in *Civilization and Its Discontents* (1930), in his response to a query about the "oceanic" feeling which occurs "at the height of being in love." In a manner characteristic of much of his theory, Freud works back from this adult experience to posit an early source for this "sensation of 'eternity,' a feeling as of something limitless, unbounded – as it were, 'oceanic'" (Freud 1930: 251). But as he describes the feeling it is not merely that of being unbounded, but is rather "an indissoluble bond, of being one with the external world as a whole." It is perhaps significant that Freud, in responding to this query about boundlessness should begin, as he does, by affirming the clearest sense of the self: "Normally, there is nothing of which we are more certain than the feeling of our self, of our own ego. This ego appears to us as something autonomous and unitary, marked off distinctly from everything else. That such an appearance is deceptive, and that on the contrary the ego is continued inwards, without any sharp delimitation, into an unconscious mental entity which we designated as the id and for which it serves as a kind of façade [...] But towards the outside, at any rate, the ego seems to maintain clear and sharp lines of demarcation." It is this sharp demarcation which, we are told in this text, disappears in the state of being in love, and "the boundary between ego and object threatens to melt away. Against all the evidence of his senses, a man who is in love declares that 'I' and 'you' are one, and is prepared to behave as if it were a fact" (Freud 1930: 253). Freud, working backwards, extrapolates that "an infant at the breast does not as yet distinguish his ego from the external world as the source of the sensations flowing in upon him," and that to do so, he first uses his experience of sensation, and a process of separating out excitations which cause unpleasure. In summary, the theoretical extrapolation is that the task of the ego is detachment from a total environment. This consists in the external world, and "includes everything." Freud goes on to comment that "later it separates off an external world from itself. Our present ego-feeling is, therefore, only a shrunken residue of a much more inclusive – indeed, an all-embracing – feeling which corresponded to a more intimate bond between the ego and the world about it" (Freud 1930: 254-5).

In his reference to the "ego," Freud alludes briefly to the internal demarcation he has postulated as existing between ego and id. This was outlined originally in his 1895 unpublished *Project for a Scientific Psychology*, developed in Chapter 7 of *The Interpretation of Dreams*, and the metapsychological papers of 1915, and expounded most fully in his essay *The Ego and the Id* of 1923. Yet his comments on "oceanic feeling" relate primarily to that concept of the self as a singular (if complex) entity, standing in relation to the outside world. It figures as such in the 1915 essay "The Instincts and Their Vicissitudes," in which he proposes two groups of primal instincts, the ego or self-preservative instincts, and the sexual ones (Freud 1915: 120). He further differentiates on the one hand between the sexual instincts, which desire to find satisfaction with objects, and on the other the attitudes of love and hate, which "are reserved for the relations of the *total ego* to objects" (Freud 1915: 135). The definition of hate in particular is of a primitive, perhaps the most primitive, emotion, deriving "from the narcissistic ego's primordial repudiation of the external world with its outpouring of stimuli" (137).

The early sense of self implied in this essay is what will be taken up by Klein and Winnicott, for both of whom there is from the start of life some sense of the self which has to engage with and negotiate with the pleasures and the unpleasures of both the inner and the outer world. This is in contradistinction not so much with other theories of the early self, but with those theories (including Freud's later ones, and those of Lacan) which focus on the ego as emerging from a series of sedimentations and identifications with the outside and ever more social world. Recent research in infant observation suggests that a combination of both branches of the theory may fit most closely with evidence about perception and emotional response (as in Stern 1985). A simple manner of reconciling the two emphases is to think of the theories which include a sense of self from the start as encompassing the reaction to the whole environment, which in the first instance will be a primarily physical environment, and the theories which (as with Lacan's mirror-stage which has its inception at six months, and Freud's delineation in *The Ego and the Id* of the anxious, even frantic negotiations of the ego with the id and the superego) which envision the infant as relating to an environment which is ever more social, with norms, expectations and prohibitions.

Even in the theory of Klein and Winnicott, the sense of self, though implied from the start, is a self that is fragile, fragmented and fragmenting, so that another view proposed is that the infant from the start has some sense of self because it is contained by another (Winnicott 1945; 1965: 61). This is given further extension by Bick, in the idea that the skin alone may be experienced as what holds the fragments of self together: "in its most primitive form the parts of the personality are felt to have no binding force amongst themselves and must therefore be held together in a way that is experienced by them passively, by the skin functioning as a boundary" (Bick 1968: 484).

The concept of the self as having to emerge and distinguish itself from its immediate environment indicated here is extended further in Winnicott's concept of the "nursing pair." For Winnicott, there is at the first no baby, simply the dyad of infant and caregiver. This is the context in which the infant, moving towards a sense of self, has three major achievements ahead: integration, personalization and the beginnings of object relating (Davis and Wallbridge 1981: 46). The first of these is most centrally related to the idea of the emergence of the self and the establishment of boundaries. For Winnicott, even though his theory presupposes some form of the ego from the start, the newborn infant is "an immature being who is all the time *on the brink of unthinkable anxiety*," an anxiety that variously consists in going to pieces, falling for ever, having no relationship to the body, and having no orientation (Winnicott 1965: 57-8). The point at which the infant experiences himself to be a separately functioning being, within an environment, is the experience of "integration." There are, however, two possible opposites to this state: disintegration and unintegration. Winnicott (1945: 139) views the former as a defense produced by the infant against the absolute terrors of unintegration. It is "an active production of chaos in defense against unintegration in the absence of maternal ego-support, that is, against the unthinkable or archaic anxiety that results from failure of holding in the stage of absolute dependence" and although the "chaos of disintegration may be as 'bad' as the unreliability of the environment... it has the advantage of being produced by the baby and therefore of being non-environmental" (Winnicott 1965: 61). Unintegration, however, lacks this positive aspect, since it is simply a state of terror in which the self cannot experience itself as distinguished from the environment (so graphically explored in *La Nausée* by Sartre). This concept of unintegration follows on an exposition of the theory in a much earlier paper of Winnicott, "Primitive Emotional Development." As I shall explore further below, this concept is particularly apposite to the concern in *La Regenta* with the state of undefined being, and the pervasive fear that there is no safety behind or within established boundaries. That this fear is ultimately one of death, decay and annihilation, is explored in Chapter 1, through the imagery of mud and nausea.

The image of the self as presented by Freud in "The Instincts and Their Vicissitudes," and in the theories of Klein, particularly concerning the paranoid-schizoid and depressive positions, is one in which fears of persecution by external and internal forces lead the self to a series of maneuvers, reversals, introjections and projections. These maneuvers are what, in a sense, are played out in the twin neurotic modes of response to disintegration in the novel: hysteria and perversion. (Both of these I shall discuss below in relation to narrative strategy, and in Chapters 5 and 6.) There is, however, a disturbing mid-point between projection of feared objects and introjection of good or loved objects, namely the position of envy.

Envy, as defined by Klein, is a state in which an extremely confused situation is set up between the one who desires and the object that is desired. Discomfort reigns, and there is no clear-cut desire that can be permitted, because of the preponderance of guilt and fear about the desire, undercut by the feelings of personal diminishment which result from the envying self's projection away from itself of its desires (Klein 1957). The cause of the difficulty is rooted in the problems that the infant self may experience in its early practice of splitting and projection, processes which it resorts to in order to introject good objects, and project away from itself those objects experienced as bad. Since the ultimate developmental aim is to progress to the concept of whole objects, and the concern and urge for reparation characteristic of the succeeding depressive position, the splitting and projection characteristic of the early paranoid-schizoid position may come to be thought of as somewhat regrettable, but splitting does have its virtues. It protects introjected good objects from further harm. Thus, as Klein comments of the small infant, "during the first few months he predominantly keeps the good object apart from the bad one and thus, in a fundamental way, preserves it – which also means that the security of the ego is enhanced. At the same time, this primal division only succeeds if there is an adequate capacity for love and a relatively strong ego" (Klein 1957: 191). Two processes are necessary at this early stage, deriving from the capacity for love, but dissimilar from one another: splitting, and integration. The two are necessary and since "integration is based on a strongly rooted good object that forms the core of the ego, a certain amount of splitting is essential for integration; for it preserves the good object and later on enables the ego to synthesize the two aspects of it." On the other hand, this may not occur, because "excessive envy, an expression of destructive impulses, interferes with the primal split between the good and bad breast, and the building up of a good object cannot sufficiently be achieved" (Klein 1957: 192).

Once again we are faced with imperfections in boundaries drawn, in this instance between good and bad objects, and between the processes of introjection and projection. The result is that imperfect expression of desire, envy. Yet, as will be shown in Chapter 2, envy is the most characteristic expression of desire in *La Regenta*, particularly used of women and clerics, and in same-sex pairings. At the very point of desire, therefore, where one might expect a subject and an object to be clearly implied, the boundaries between the two, because of the nature of the emotion experienced, are insufficiently strong to contain and define either.

The other concept of Klein which is analogous to that of envy is that of projective identification. Here again, there is an uncertainty of boundaries, and an imperfect separation between subject and object which leads to entrenched positions, unresolved because of undeclared and/or unrecognized relationships. In projective identification as defined in her 1946 paper "Notes on Some Schizoid Mechanisms," there is a particularly injurious and impeding type of identification which results when a subject (in the case of the paper, an infant) projects into an object (the mother) parts of the self, and then identifies with them. In the course of projective identification the ego is rendered weaker, and the nature of the object relation established has a particularly aggressive quality (Klein 1946: 8). Whereas envy will be shown to be the predominant emotional bond in same-sex relations, or where women and priests are concerned, projective identification is prominent in the central dyad of the novel, Fermín and Paula, but also to be observed in some of the "between men" dyads.[2]

Theories of the self which take us beyond the first infant months, and which relate to primitive interactions between the nascent self and the external, predominantly physical world, are those in which certain internal boundaries are drawn, and in which the ego is consolidated by a series of identifications. These are the theories pertaining to the formation of the super-ego as much as the formation of the ego, and pertaining to the relations between those two and the id. Related to the developmental stage at which the identifications occur, these can be viewed as narcissistic (pre-oedipal), or hysterical (oedipal) (Lear 1990: 162-3). For some later theorists, such as Fairbairn, hysteria itself will be classed as one of the schizoid defenses of the early self (Fairbairn 1941; 1944: 122-4).

As soon as we begin to deal with the term "ego," problems and weightings arise, since for Freud the ego will become that rather beset and anxious part of the self, coming and going between the conflicting demands of super-ego and id, while for Lacan the ego will be a creature of factitious identifications that mask desire. Freud's Lecture 31 of the *New Introductory Lectures on Psychoanal-*

---

[2] On the concept of 'between men', see Eve Kosofsky Sedgwick (1985).

ysis presents the harrassed ego, trying to serve its "three tyrannical masters": "It feels hemmed in on three sides, threatened by three kinds of danger, to which, if it is hard pressed, it reacts by generating anxiety." Freud clearly derives the ego from the initial self that had to deal with sensory input from the external world, which has trained it, as it were, to be everyone's servant: "Owing to its origin from the experiences of the perceptual system, it is earmarked for representing the demands of the external world, but it strives too to be a loyal servant of the id, to remain on good terms with it, to recommend itself to it as an object and to attract its libido to itself." The ego emerges as a harried bourgeois bureaucrat, negotiating, feinting, simply trying to get the system to work, and reflecting with uncanny accuracy all those bureaucratic deceived husbands of European late nineteenth-century adultery novels (Sinclair 1993: 189):

> In its attempts to mediate between the id and reality, it is often obliged to cloak the *Ucs.* commands of the id with its own *Pcs.* rationalizations, to conceal the id's conflicts with reality, to profess, with diplomatic disingenuousness, to be taking notice of reality even when the id has remained rigid and unyielding. On the other hand it is observed at every step it takes by the strict super-ego, which lays down definite standards for its conduct, without taking any account of its difficulties from the direction of the id and the external world, and which, if those standards are not obeyed, punishes it with tense feelings of inferiority and of guilt. Thus the ego, driven by the id, confined by the super-ego, repulsed by reality, struggles to master its economic task of bringing about harmony among the forces and influences working in and upon it; and we can understand how it is that so often we cannot suppress a cry: "Life is not easy!" If the ego is obliged to admit its weakness, it breaks out in anxiety – realistic anxiety regarding the external world, moral anxiety regarding the super-ego and neurotic anxiety regarding the strength of the passions in the id. (Freud 1933: 110-111)

Dreaming and Narrative Strategy: Hysterical Flight

> Desire, like the dream, cannot be arranged, but (unlike the Proustian epiphany) the setting for its possibility can be provided. (Adam Phillips, *On Kissing, Tickling, and Being Bored*, 1993)

Sleeping and dreaming are customarily characterized as respite, escape, the permitted movement to other improbable realms. Yet dreams interlock firmly with the waking world. Žižek reminds us that for Freud, dreams were not the unconscious, and that, as Eysenck observed, it is an error to identify "the unconscious desire at work in the dream with the 'latent thought' – that is, the signification of the dream" (Žižek 1989: 12; Eysenck 1966). What the actual stuff of dreams is composed of is already a fabricated narrative, in which displaced, dislocated, repressed desires are woven into a new story, so that to follow the clues offered to the unconscious what we must do is not to read but to interpret. What matters is the form of the dream itself, the shapes that repressed desires take for the dreamer, since it is this shape, rather than those desires, which will tell us about the dreamer. But what of the dream for the dreamer? Žižek's concept of the dream-work which produces the narrative – wherever it may be – is strikingly reminiscent of the concept of the dream advanced by Bion, namely that of alpha-function theory. For Bion, the dream was a way of allowing ourselves to become conscious of certain elements (those which emerge into the narrative of the dream), while permitting us not to be aware of others. That is, he presents an idea of the dream as a type of protective membrane which simultaneously defends us against some parts of the unconscious, yet produces a screen to reveal other parts to us. Thus, for him, dreaming had many of the functions of censorship and resistance noted in Freud's original theory. For Bion, the dream-work which translates (after selection) the elements of the unconscious into the form of the dream which can be tolerated, and potentially assimilated and understood by the dreamer, resembles his concept of thinking, in that in both cases the function he refers to as alpha-function permits the self to "think about," or to be "conscious of" the unconscious. The dream thus is "a combination in narrative form of dream thoughts, which thoughts in turn derive from combinations of alpha-elements," and this process, crucially, "preserves the personality from what is virtually a psychotic state" (Bion 1977: 16).

The narrative, or the dream, thus form a protection against the intolerable chaos of the psychotic state, and a containment of those elements which, if unbounded, would be unassimilable. Thus what may be learned – and here we can take the case of *La Regenta* – is to be learned from the nature of the container, the narrative, or, as we shall see, the various competing and colluding narratives that are spun over the terrifying shapelessness and uncontrollability of experience. The dream mode characteristic of *La Regenta* is the *pesadilla* or nightmare: not a safe, comforting escape or even discharge of desire, but a disruptive reminder. The three instances of actual dream in the text, the dream of Ana, suffering the hysteric's malaise and exhaustion (II. 110, 124-6),[3] that of Guimarán after the funeral of Santos Barinaga, (II. 270), and that of Víctor, dozing fitfully in the train with Frígilis on the morning when he has had visual confirmation of Ana's adultery with Álvaro (II. 480) are more than simple nightmares. In each case they represent (within the actual form of the dream) a sense of breaking through. Ana, in an echo of Santa Teresa, whose life she has just been reading (Sánchez Martínez 1989: 57) tries to escape an infernal maze, "buscando el agujero angosto," a hole all too obviously one of sexual penetration, but then, retrospectively, connecting in disturbing manner to the "brecha" in the belly which dominates the later nightmare of Guimarán. Víctor's dream of his mockery and shaming by rows of "cuervos" is tangential on the breaking through of dishonor in his reputation, and the ultimate indignity of the fatal "brecha" which will be made in his full bladder in the duel with Álvaro.

The entire text of *La Regenta* is riddled with fissures, breaches, cracks: there is no security, no fortress that is beyond attack. These three nightmares, occurring well after the mid-point of the novel (Chapters 19, 22 and 29) simultaneously proclaim that breaking through at the same time as they indicate the desperation of the measures of the self to find containment and safety. If they are part of the fabricated dream text, they are also the sign of the breaking down of the self, or the text, that dreams. They provide the vantage point for us to observe by that stage in the text a move towards an escalation in the pace of events and a ceding to the forces of chaos.

---

[3] All references to *La Regenta* are to the 2 volume 1989 edition of the novel (ed. Gonzalo Sobejano), and will be given in the text.

For Lacan there are two questions, interrelated, and apposite to our consideration of the nature of narrative in *La Regenta*. They place in contrast the obsessional (whom we could consider as the person threatened by the proximity of psychotic chaos), and the hysteric. The obsessional lives in fear, on the edge, in an area so well depicted by Klein as the terror of the neonate: the area of the pre-verbal. The obsessional exists, as it were, already in a state of death, since, locked in a master/slave relationship, he waits only for the death of the master, believing that "when the master is dead, everything will begin" (Lacan 1988: 286). But Lacan perceives the escape, the illusory bid for freedom and freedom from fear, constituted in the question of the hysteric, who asks "Who am I? a man or a woman?" (Lacan 1993: 171). This question of the hysteric, one of "Which sex am I?" – that is of a narrative that involves difference and procreation.

Becoming involved or engaged in the question of the hysteric is, we could posit, the stuff of narrative, certainly of the surface narrative of *La Regenta*, where the web and textures of interlinking hysterical and perverse plots is the overlay to a material and spiritual world visibly and inexorably sinking into entropy.

To view *La Regenta* as a novel of adulterous desire is a misrecognition of the urges and defenses presented by the narrative. Habitually the way this confusing nature of the novel has been presented is to argue that "not only" is it a plot of adultery, "but also" a text about literature. The notion of *La Regenta* as a double narrative, or double plot, has been advanced elsewhere. But the contrast has habitually been, as in Sieburth (1990: 88), between the motion of a plot that will draw the reader into the novelistic world, and a "self-reflexive text, a continual commentary on language, representation, and literature" (see also Gullón 1983: 138-47; Rutherford 1984: 28; Sieburth 1990a: 77-97). The idea of the text of the novel as something which has a motion towards entropy is discussed at length by Sieburth in her monograph. My approach has similarities and differences. I concur with the idea of a narrative that is double, even multiply double (as suggested by her models of intertextuality and subversion). I see, however, a different distribution of elements, the most important and dramatic of which is implicitly omitted from Sieburth's model. In my reading the two parts concerned are not the surface plot, and the self-reflexivity of the novel, but rather are two elements combining in battle against a third motion in the novel, one that is towards collapse, fragmentation, decay, dissolution. This motion towards entropy, discussed not only by Sieburth but by Valis (1983), who sets up a model of the Real versus the Symbolic, is clearly a pervasive feature of the text, against which it will feel imperative to form structures of defense. The structures have their complications. The self-reflexivity, for example, undermines the concept of a knowable reality which falsely haunts the surface plot of adultery, but like that surface plot, the very self-awareness of the narrative, the level of commentary upon the act of writing, is itself an urge towards consciousness which is arguably part of a struggle against the chaos of psychotic dissolution, and as much an illusion as is the adultery plot-line.

The surface plot line is itself subdivided, and in order to understand the nature of the subdivision, one has to view it as a complex dynamic of defense. There are two prime narrative motions, one hysterical and the other perverse, the pair of them operating – sometimes in concert and collusion, and sometimes in opposition – in the face of a social, historical, political and physical context which is one of collapse, decay and dissolution. The two narratives constitute an attempt, heroic in its proportions and energy, to erect walls of defense against visible and inexorable decay, here characterized as the decay of Vetusta and its life. They are seductive because of the security and relief that they variously offer, this seduction of the reader running in parallel with the surface, novelistic seduction of the female protagonist by Álvaro, the *amante de oficio*, and the opposing seduction of the same protagonist by the offers of *jouissance* in the mystic life, whose head she misrecognizes as Fermín (Mandrell 1990).

The world of the text is less Freud's unconscious, with wishes felt and then repressed, than Klein's phantasy, which "emanates from within and imagines what is without... offers an unconscious commentary on instinctual life and links feelings to objects and creates a new amalgam: the world of imagination" (Mitchell's introduction to Klein 1986: 23).[4] As within Klein, there is the emphasis on the psychotic as disturbance, that is, on the tensions and fears of the present moment that have to be repressed, split off and project-

---

[4] The spelling 'phantasy' is used in the text when it is Klein's definition which is invoked. Elsewhere 'fantasy' is used to indicate the more generalized idea of the activity of the imagination, and the capacity to create fanciful images (as in *OED*).

ed, contrasting with Freud's original emphasis on the historic, in the trajectory traced for the hysteric. The comfort of Freud's original hysteria theory is its relationship to past trauma. However difficult to undo, there is the belief that the trauma was at some *previous point*, and that it merely has to be unpicked, unravelled, in order to be relieved.

We could view the novel as a whole through the model of a tension between a Freudian emphasis on the role of the past in shaping present experience and perception, with the view that the hysteric's tale or dislocations have their root in history, and merely wait to be undone, and a Kleinian emphasis on the terrifying, always potentially psychotic nature of our experience of the present, in which love fights with hate, and death is ever there, as our fate-to-be of annihilation, the death-drive for Klein existing from birth, in tense company with the life-drive (Mitchell 1986: 31-2).

A way of applying this distinction and tension to *La Regenta* is to contrast the concern with the patriarchal historical context of the novel, massive in its evident influence and importance, with the irresoluble given factors of the struggle to be, the struggle to differentiate, the necessity of defining oneself from the surrounding backcloth as a simple prerequisite to survival.

HYSTERIA AND HISTORY

On the surface of the narrative, the distinction between worlds, between public and private, conscious and unconscious, the natural and the law-bound, is entirely Freudian. This is hardly surprising given the patriarchal context from which Freud comes, and given what the narrative presents as its context and concern: the overwhelmingly patriarchal nature of late nineteenth-century provincial Spain, where the provincial crucible of Vetusta distills and makes more concentrated the tensions and impulses of a society in political and social turbulence.

What apparently rules in the world of Vetusta is patriarchal order, in which women are kept separate and subjugated, and in which the world of men is a private club, the Casino, where women can have no voice, their role being that of the commodity to be used in the only exchanges envisaged as possible, that is, exchanges between men (Kosofsky Sedgwick 1985; Sinclair 1993). The reader is presented with a sense that "this is the way the world is" conveyed through the masculine vision of Vetusta in Chapter 1 where Fermín surveys his domain with (phallic) eyeglass, and sees the geographical divisions of the town laid out before him. The divisions he perceives, given a physical reality by contrasts of building material, and by specific location, are social and economic divisions. There is, however, already, a troubling subtext of this social historical view which will become more and more prominent as the novel proceeds, and relates to the distinction between class and lineage.

Class in Spain at this period is problematic. Unlike any of the models of class-systems in Europe at the time, the structure of class in Spain is affected by the lack of an industrial bourgeoisie, the lack of a city-based proletariat, the paucity of a professional class which might provide the foundation of a middle class. Hence we find scholars groping for new vocabulary to mark out this class-structure as distinct and problematic: the middle classes, the *clases acomodadas*, something which is neither *pueblo* nor aristocracy. Whereas membership of the aristocracy had been a matter primarily of lineage, the *desamortización* of the earlier part of the century opened the way for the non-aristocratic to hold titles of land (as satirized in Valle-Inclán's *Ruedo ibérico*).

But however complex the issues of class in Spain at this period, they pale in contrast with deeper-rooted issues of blood and legitimacy, with the result that class-demarcation, movement and rivalry is without exception underpinned and rendered yet more difficult by attitudes relating to lineage that date back centuries, that is, to the Hispanic or Mediterranean concern with *limpieza de sangre*. Within Spanish society, nobility could be passed down through the male line, without complication, so long as public dishonoring did not occur. In cases where there was simply a claim to nobility, there was no problem in having a female antecedent of lower class. The issue of impure blood was more complex. Here the tainting of the claimed *limpieza* of a person could have its roots in the suspect blood of a relative of the female line, a tainting which could not be cleansed (Caro Baroja 1965: 102). Blood thus appears as a substance not simply thicker than water, but one which marks indelibly, whereas the social arrangements of class, in which nobility is distinct from *pueblo*, are lines of demarcation, which may move with wealth or marriage, and which are not subject to maculation: they relate to the external world of society, not the hidden, primitive substance of blood, the ultimate internal fluid which, once released from its proper container, is perceived as invasive, staining, contaminating (Douglas 1966; Sontag 1983).

In *La Regenta* we are not, or not yet, in a post-AIDS world where contamination by blood has re-awakened ancient taboos related to outcasts, stemming from the fear of a contact that will bring death in its wake. The fantasies of Don Julián (Goytisolo 1976) about the poisoning of a nation's bloodstream in a single, perverse act of revenge against the motherland are not yet with us. We are, however, in a post-Darwinian world of philosophical, biological and medical uncertainty, as evidenced by the high profile of medical discourse in the novel, and the persistent concern with roots and origins. A central question is that of whether one can know who one is (or even more vitally, who others are), accompanied by anxieties about the nature of malady, and decline.

Startlingly absent from the novel is any sense of birth, particularly of any human examples of the process. Death, however, is patently round every corner, its contagion offered with the damp of convent cells and cemeteries. Meanwhile there is continuously the sense of natural flux expressed and experienced visibly in the changing of the seasons of which the characters are so acutely aware, and which leads to Somoza's notion of the *primavera médica* (II. 110). Also absent from the novel is a sense of growth, with the exception of gross and troubling swellings that denote malady – malnutrition, infection, simple tumescence as an effect of damp and enclosure, the growth of tuberculosis which will lead to death. The prompting to physical growth is placed in the hands of Frígilis, well-meaning but ultimately bungling friend of Víctor and Ana, his matchmaking efforts moving from the arrangements of courtship to the coupling of plants.

If there is no sense of birth, there is consequently also an absence of awareness of the place from which birth might have issued. Moreover, not only is there no source, there is no context of reception after the moment of birth either. While there is no overt reference in the text to the undifferentiation of the state of the self at the point of birth, or because of the trauma of birth, we could view the widespread acute anxiety about boundaries in the novel as relating not only to death and decay, but also to the state of undefined being, or birth that has never quite been, and therefore cannot even be recollected as a moment of trauma and formation.

The absence of birth in the text gives rise to two compensating concerns, as though the gaping *hoyo* of the source of our being somehow has to be plugged. Thus we have a concern in the novelistic weaving with birth on a symbolic plane, and the seduction offered the reader in the form of the idea of birth into the Symbolic. In the face of these heavily invested desires for birth in the text, birth itself becomes mangled, twisted, unsatisfactory, in two modes which Noël Valis has labelled as monstrous (1992) and improper (1994).

Birth as monstrous, in the framework with which Valis discusses it, is closely linked to those aspects of nausea and feelings of boundlessness with which I shall be concerned in Chapter 1. In particular, her use of the concept of the "inchoate," defined as "where thought emerges from non-thought," places us precisely on that *limen* where we hover in our uncertain marking out of the boundaries of the self, and our control over ourselves and our context. Since the inchoate is the state of what is just begun, incipient, or in an initial or early stage, the word comes to carry the further meanings of "elementary," "imperfect," "undeveloped" and "immature" (*OED*). Valis emphasizes that in *La Regenta* we are placed in a mid-field where we are aware of a process that has been embarked upon, but whose end is alarmingly unclear, so that all we can focus on is that quasi-psychotic present-tense state of being, awareness and anxiety: "In *La Regenta*, things fall apart, but the terrible consequences, the sense of apocalypse in the ending, are preceded by the protracted anguish and uncertainty of *not* knowing what or how things will develop, of not knowing what the composition of that development is" (Valis 1992: 193).

This sense of the inchoate in *La Regenta*, which, as Valis remarks, takes the form of an intimate association with the body, and the bodily processes (1992: 195) is, as I shall argue in Chapter 1, closely allied to Bataille's apprehension of that spectrum which links nausea with the awareness of the processing and the natural decomposition of physical matter.

The "impropriety" of Ana's birth is fundamental in novelistic and metaphysical terms (see Valis 1994: 102, 117), but also in the more banal and widely accepted sense of "socially and sexually improper". Omitted from the novel, it is birth to the woman who comes to be characterized as a "bit of skirt," whether within the occupation of dancer or that of seamstress (Valis 1992: 205). Alas, the narrator, appears to have found it strategically necessary to confirm the "impropriety" of the birth by removing the mother as character from the novelistic scene by a premature death. This narratorial high-handed removal also operates as a strategy of convenient marginalization. Once dead, Ana's mother is in no position to redeem her own public character, which is now created in the mouths of disapproving Vetustan gossips: she cannot counterpoise the contrasting reality of her presence. Ana symbolizes the motif of improper birth on the female side, while Fermín symbolizes it in the male form, with the difference that in novelistic terms, his mother is allowed to stick her ground.

The consequences are symmetrically linked. Ana acts out in a tragic repetition the social marginalization of her mother that had been hinted at in the latter's early excision from the plot. Ana is victim, scapegoat, the necessary focalization of that aspect of Vetustan life – its idealism fused with sexuality – which has to be castigated. Fermín, meanwhile, is allowed to escape, and while his mother is characterized throughout as the presence of death, she does remain to the end of the text, all-powerful, and he escapes not only with his life, but with no small measure of his power.

If Ana's birth symbolizes the coming to being of what has to be rejected, what of her birth into the Symbolic? Valis (1994: 112) remarks that Lacan would say that Ana "has belatedly entered into the realm of the Symbolic, and has been subjected to the inescapable Law of the Father." She adds, with more precision, that "she has fallen into the sin of consciousness, expressed the only way it can be with words: in a narrative of imperfections." This suggestion I find both attractive and problematic. Whatever the degree of *caveat* that is placed upon Ana's birth into a consciousness, that birth itself is not simply improper, but arguably imperfect, as suggested in Valis's earlier (1992) paper. That is, the emphasis on what is inchoate (and therefore frightening and threatening) reflects the tenor of the novel more closely than a sense of something that is achieved. The birth is, perhaps, the ending, where Ana's reception of Celedonio's toad-like kiss is characterized by Valis as "the inert body receiving the material corruption of the world" (Valis 1994: 97). It is the final trauma of birth into the state of the material and mortal which the whole text has been set up to avoid.

If Ana herself can, despite her monstrous or improper birth, in any way be regarded as subject of a plot, or of her own narrative (which is debatable), it is the hysteric's narrative in which any one of a number of things may happen. While being the object of the perverse narratives of the two male seducers, Álvaro and Fermín, she has her own agenda, based, as is theirs, on fictions already existing, and which might give her a place in the world. But the hysterical narrative is also one of finding, or defining the identity, of making it other than those about would have it. She will grapple with the uncertain boundaries of her own identity, whether within the fiction of the adultery plot or that of the mystic's career (Labanyi 1991); she will adopt the hysterical adultery narrative offered by Álvaro but with an ultimate lack of attraction or bonding to the adulterer, denoting her seduction, typical of the hysteric, by the *idea* of sexuality and sexual enjoyment. She holds back from the incorporation of such elements into a relationship, except in the form of a packaged and submissive object, whose contours are defined by others. She will offer herself twice as sacrificial victim to Fermín, as her entry into the role of Magdalen (Chapter 26), her penitential gown designed by Doña Petronila, and in the final rejection scene in Chapter 30, redolent in its final melodramatic gesturing of the operatic motif which has trivialized the adultery story throughout by presenting it as a set-piece. Ana can even be viewed as doomed to failure as hysterical subject, in her regressive urges, in that in her collusion with the perverse plots of others she will "forever find a way to deny the evidence of her eyes and ears and surrender herself to the will of others" (Charnon-Deutsch 1989a: 99).

The other sense in which *La Regenta* can be construed as a novel of monstrous birth, aside from its own gigantic dimensions, and swelling, burgeoning plot, is in the sense of "showing," in that it constitutes a "monstrance," a putting on display, since it is on the public "showing" of Ana, in her form of her coming to a social birth, whether that of adulteress or that of religious daughter, that the main drama of the narrative hangs. In this very "hysterical" theatricality, the novel, and its hysterical protagonist, follow in the best nineteenth-century traditions of the "showing" of hysterics at La Salpêtrière (Gilman 1993; Ellenberger 1970: 95-99).

Part of the hysterical "showing" of the novel consists in the temptation offered to the reader to focus on Ana as a boundaried, and identifiable object. One can also view hysteria in *La Regenta* in the light of Lou Charnon-Deutsch's observation, namely as a transaction between male author and implied male reader by which female characters and the texts that contain them become objects, and in which what occurs is the "process of the *masculinization* of the nineteenth-century reader" (Charnon-Deutsch 1990: 14). That is, there is a close parallel between male author and his female character (and the implied male reader, or masculinized reader), and the male physician and his female patient (and the implied male reader of the case-history). Ana becomes the focalized hysteric of the novel, the character who as hysteric draws our attention, and diverts attention from others equally engaged in flight or denial. Ana is the one relegated, scapegoated, medicalized, in a way that is *convenient*, for the narrative, the narrator and for the social structures it portrays and he belongs to (Charnon-Deutsch 1989a: 94).

It has been remarked that, despite the interventions of Lacanian psychoanalysis and Derridean criticism, Ana survives as a "great subjective identity" and that she is something "critics lovingly try to reconstitute for their own and their readers' fulfillment and pleasure" (Charnon-Deutsch 1989b: 395). She is, in a sense, not merely there, waiting to be seduced, whether by Álvaro or by Fermín in the text, or by the critic trying to enclose her in a frame. In the tradition of all good Freudian seduced hysterics (the problematic nature of which is deftly discussed by Forrester [1990]), Ana is also herself seductive, since she holds so much in promise for us; she is "a different kind of plenitude, a supreme not-all in the Lacanian sense that escapes universal logic, constantly acting as a wellsource of what we believe has not been *yet* expressed in words, or is inexpressible" (Charnon-Deutsch 1989b: 395, emphasis mine). She is thus the character in the novel that readers willy-nilly find themselves drawn to adopt, hovering tantalizingly as she does with the promise of a birth which might be symbolic, and/or might be into the Symbolic, there being a degree of concern about this issue in relation to Ana which in critical texts is not habitually accorded to the other characters.

HYSTERICAL EVASION AND PERVERSE CONTROL

Alternating with Ana's flight into the career of the hysteric (see Chapter 5), and the manner in which, like a hysteric, she leads the reader on, seduces, entangles, and must ultimately frustrate (so that the reader is reduced to the bystander position of Frígilis) we have the two masculine surface motions of the plot. There is Álvaro's drive to seduce Ana, and Fermín's drive to secure her, both of these projects such that they can be construed as perverse. They move the narrative not towards birth or growth, but simply to acquisition and incorporation. Álvaro's enterprise carries all the dead weight of the sterility of the Don Juan myth (Mandrell 1990; 1992). Whatever Ana's fantasies about the growth that the move into adultery might seem to promise, for Álvaro there will be nothing beyond a further notch on the belt. Like the classic pervert, Don Juan is condemned to repeat, to perform, to repeat again, in an attempt to resolve some archaic struggle with the feminine and the insecurity of his own identity, and Álvaro carries all the significant connotations of the literary figure on which the narrative models him, and on which he models himself (as is highlighted in relation to Casanova by Roustang [1988]).

Fermín's enterprise is less clearly acquisitive. On an overt, superficial, political level, his project is no more and no less than that of Álvaro, but he also enters collusively into an unconscious fantasy with Ana that theirs is a meeting of souls, so that his private and only partly conscious fantasy is not one of acquisition, but rather of finding himself in a place where he is no longer in isolation. He remains unaware, or at least, with some convenience he periodically forgets, that his is not a place of isolation, but one of uncomfortable proximity with another: he is locked in a claustrophobic dyad with his mother. What he does is to draw Ana into a perverse plot, as object of his perversion, the replacement object for his mother over whom he can now triumph, and whose shaming he can now transfer and expose to public view. That is, the making public of Ana's possession by him in Chapter 26 is not simply the showing to Vetusta that she is in his domain, but more forcefully, it is the breaking of the code of silence and dissimulation to which his mother has held him and herself subject since his birth. Ana's shame, made public, is his mother's shame, now exposed for all the world to see.

There is a further, and more crucial level on which we need to view the motions and dynamic of the text. It exists, was written, and is read, as a whole. Thus the entire enterprise, which contains the hysterical and perverse narrative alluded to above, itself requires characterization. Here we find that the external whole of the text mirrors the internal detail, in that there is no bounded identity, no realist frame that contains it. It is itself in a sense empty, as are the characters, since its move is consistently away from its surface subject matter. It is a text of flight. The concept of narrative as evasion through an objectifying of something else so that the narrator him or herself escapes being the object of the reader's gaze and thus is an expression of power, is, as Lou Charnon-Deutsch reminds us, a view deriving from Freud. As she comments, "narrative is fundamentally voyeuristic, concerned with the veiling and unveiling of objects," the result being that narrative "satisfied the psychological need of the subject to extricate its dependency on other subjects" (Charnon-Deutsch 1989a: 93). But Charnon-Deutsch also figures the text of the novel itself as hysterical, as "a talking cure or hysterical (as opposed to historical) document, that is, the documents of a hysteric" (Charnon-Deutsch 1989b: 397). Much of her argument is a salutory *caveat* to those who are, for example, seduced into reading Ana as a subject who can be regarded as a person with a story, and it rests on a concept of the text, rather than the character, as subject. In this I would support her reading, but propose a somewhat different emphasis. Given that hysteria is a malady related to history, in that past trauma is held (theoretically) accountable for present infirmity or constriction, a reading of the text as hysterical might suggest to us that we need to search back through history. Or, as Charnon-Deutsch puts it, a reading of the text in this light would be to search for meanings deferred, a search, which, it is implied, might have an endpoint of truth. About this I remain somewhat skeptical: we cannot find the unconscious, merely the signs which point to it. Charnon-Deutsch, pointing to Lacan, reminds us that the unconscious is that part of the subject's history "marked by a blank or occupied by a falsehood: it is the censored chapter. But the truth can be found again: it is most often already written down elsewhere" (Charnon-Deutsch 1989b: 397). This is an appealing project. I would suggest rather that the truth is evasive, and if it exists, is in a psychotic present of the fear of dissolution, of undifferentiation, and ultimately, of death. That is, the text as a whole (as opposed to differing and conflicting parts of hysterical and perverse elements of the narrative) is a hysterical diversion in the face of a "hole": the Real, or psychosis.

That which is evaded is, in a sense, the end of the novel. This is the point at which the hysteric no longer has to speak, or at which, in the case of *La Regenta*, there is nothing that the text has left to say, and it is this nothing which is the ultimate center of the text.

Lacan, in commenting on the words of the subject in "The Hysteric's Question," signalled that the moment of the joining up of subject and speech, the analysis (the narrative?) would be over: "the subject begins by talking about himself, he doesn't talk to you – then, he talks to you but he doesn't talk about himself – when he talks about himself, who will have noticeably changed in the interval, to you, we will have got to the end of the analysis" (Lacan 1993: 161). The text, as subject, is thus revealed as the void, the abyss, the final fissure feared and evaded throughout the novel by the characters, who have resorted to strategies of construction, constriction and definition in order to do so.

ANXIETY AND THE ABYSS

The struggles to weave webs of narrative, whether hysterical or perverse, are enterprises that are mythical in the dimensions of their challenge, and yet, like some of those very myths of struggle and enterprise, banal in their content and process. Whether we compare them to the clearing of the Augean stables (an image of which we are constantly reminded in this novel with its struggles against filth and maculation), or the myth of Sisyphus, his desire to rise as without hope as that of Fermín, the surface narratives gain their importance and significance not for what they are in themselves (banal, well-known mouthings of the traditional narratives of patriarchy, of woman's infidelity, and man's compensating perverse and sadistic revenge). Rather, their importance derives from the enormity of their endeavor, and the fluid and uncontainable nature of existence in the face of which they are constructed. This is expressed in the material references of the text to *hoyos, pozos, abismos*, and to the shifting labile qualities of mud (see Chapter 1). But it is also evident at the level of characterization and the notable elusiveness of boundaries in relation to character.

Lacan, in commenting on the words of the subject in "The Hysteric's Question," signalled that the moment of the joining up of subject and speech, the analysis (the narrative?) would be over: "the subject begins by talking about himself, he doesn't talk to you – then, he talks to you but he doesn't talk about himself – when he talks about himself, who will have noticeably changed in the interval, to you, we will have got to the end of the analysis" (Lacan 1993: 161). The text, as subject, is thus revealed as the void, the abyss, the final fissure feared and evaded throughout the novel by the characters, who have resorted to strategies of construction, constriction and definition in order to do so.

ANXIETY AND THE ABYSS

The struggles to weave webs of narrative, whether hysterical or perverse, are enterprises that are mythical in the dimensions of their challenge, and yet, like some of those very myths of struggle and enterprise, banal in their content and process. Whether we compare them to the clearing of the Augean stables (an image of which we are constantly reminded in this novel with its struggles against filth and maculation), or the myth of Sisyphus, his desire to rise as without hope as that of Fermín, the surface narratives gain their importance and significance not for what they are in themselves (banal, well-known mouthings of the traditional narratives of patriarchy, of woman's infidelity, and man's compensating perverse and sadistic revenge). Rather, their importance derives from the enormity of their endeavor, and the fluid and uncontainable nature of existence in the face of which they are constructed. This is expressed in the material references of the text to *hoyos*, *pozos*, *abismos*, and to the shifting labile qualities of mud (see Chapter 1). But it is also evident at the level of characterization and the notable elusiveness of boundaries in relation to character.

BOUNDARIES

CHAPTER 1

LIMINAL ANXIETIES

For Tanner and Labanyi, the novel of adultery is one of broken contracts and transgression. Labanyi in particular has taken forward the original propositions of Tanner in this area to demonstrate how in *La Regenta* the spaces which are crucial to the adultery text are the transitional and marginal spaces that exist between town and country, between inside and outside, the novel of adultery thus being figured not simply as one in which there is an *adulteration* of the supposed secure and pure matrimonial contract and estate, but one in which the prime cause of disturbance is the realization that boundaries are insecure (Tanner 1979; Labanyi 1986). I propose to extend the discussion of boundaries by looking first at the nature of narrative boundaries in *La Regenta*, and then by a detailed examination of two areas where boundaries are experienced as problematic and difficult to define. These two areas, nausea and mud, can be seen as the (insecure) physical framing of a text of mimetic brittleness undermined by a dynamic of fragmentation and dissolution.

LIMINAL ANXIETIES

La Regenta is dominated by a recurrent anxiety about threshold-crossing, and its narrative lines constitute a type of armature which only with difficulty stays in place. Two of the meanings of "armature": "protective covering of an animal or plant" and "a metal framework on which a scupture is moulded with clay or similar material" (*OED*) signal for us crucial features of the surface narrative. It is designed in some way to protect, and on it hangs the physical clay of the characters and of the material world in which they exist. Clay itself is also, as we shall see, part of the expression of the framework, and subject to displacement and fissure, accentuating the frailty of the mortal beings who move in relation to it.

While, as Labanyi has highlighted, the transitions and transgressions of the novel are social and spatial, there are other transitions which have physical and metaphysical connotations. It is in the context of the latter that we can view the narrative as one of hysterical flight, provoked by liminal anxiety. Liminality, relating to the *limen* or threshold, is, as pointed out in the Introduction, close to the concept of "inchoate" as developed by Nöel Valis in relation to *La Regenta*. The difference is that the emphasis within liminality is on the transition from one state or space to another, rather than on the process of inception and expectation contained in "inchoate" (Valis 1992). In *La Regenta*, there are the obvious social *limenes* of class, wealth, profession, matrimonial attachment and social disgrace, and it is on such axes that the surface narrative of marriage, adultery and repudiation is constructed. But below the surface narrative of adultery, we are reminded throughout the novel that there is an ultimate *limen*, that of death. What occurs in the narrative as a consequence is that at the same time as there is a negotiation of transitions and transgressions around the surface social *limenes* of the text (so that marriages are arranged, the membership of the Casino is either withheld or extended, and characters such as Doña Paula, Petra and Teresina move purposefully over social and economic thresholds into more elevated strata of society), there is a further construction of a number of defensive *limenes* on the plane of identity, and even more specifically, of gender. The two patterns are not mutually exclusive, but against a background apprehension of a state of unboundedness and flux each feeds into the anxieties provoked by the other. This unboundedness is most characteristically focalized as death. While there is an absence of explicit reference to that other unboundedness of existence, the pre-birth state, there is nonetheless a sense that no form of identity or status is ever firmly established, so that no identity ever fully comes to birth (See Introduction and Valis 1994). Hence, there is a dual tension in relation to liminality, deriving from the apprehension that boundaries may never be fully or securely achieved, and then that boundaries may also dissolve. The examples of boundaries that are there to be established (the social climbing of the maids, the demarcations of

Casino life, the aspirations of Ana's aunts, the politics of the Cathedral) are relatively trivial, though not necessarily experienced as such by the characters. By contrast, concerns about dissolution and insecurity are widespread both on the plane of social plotting and planning, and on that of psychological and metaphysical anxiety, with an emphasis in the latter upon dissolution, fragility and permeability. There is a recurrent preoccupation that dissolution will be total, resulting in annihilation, a preoccupation that is reiterated through the concern with death in the novel. While actual death figures increasingly in the novel (though, uncharacteristic for adultery novels, the deaths narrated do not include that of the heroine) its presence is intimated more consistently and insidiously through the prominence of nausea, with its connotations of fainting and dizziness, and through the ubiquitousness of mud, with its connotations of the mortality of human clay, and the tainting of the sexual.

LA REGENTA AS A HYSTERICAL TEXT

As outlined in the Introduction, in considering *La Regenta* as a hysterical text, my emphasis is on the idea of entry into gender relations, or well-known gender "stories" (such as the adultery narrative), as a strategy of flight or defense rather than as a response to desire. This is an approach which corresponds to the interpretation of the Oedipus complex as found within the concept of the Law of the Father and the move into the Symbolic in Lacanian thought or in the theorizing of gender of the type advanced by Stoller, namely as a strategy to deal with the problematic nature of the pre-oedipal dyad (Stoller 1985). I shall return to the Oedipus complex, particularly as it might be understood as a cornerstone of patriarchal society, in Chapter 3.

In *La Regenta* two major patterns of personal narrative emerge – hysteria and perversion, and they do so at the level of perceptible dramatic elements in the narrative (Ana's hysteria, Fermín's perverse ritual relating to Ana and his mother). But the two patterns of narrative intertwine at a different level, in that the whole of the text can be viewed as engaging in hysterical flight from the undefinable and frightening twin phenomena of death and sexuality, while a perversely ordered ritualistic reiteration of the traditional adultery text provides a second defense against the same phenomena. Flight into hysterical narrative can be understood in two contradictory ways, in a complex relation to the Oedipus complex and the task of gender-construction. Given that hysteria is itself a narrative of sexuality and sexual difference (Lacan 1981), the flight into hysterical narrative is a move which by the construction or definition of gender is an attempt to consolidate and define the boundaries of an identity which otherwise is unclear. That is, it is a (misguided) attempt to comply with those dictates of the Oedipus complex that provoke and consolidate gender-construction. But hysteria can also be construed as an evasion of sexuality, an anaesthesia and dislocation of feeling and response in reaction to sexual stimulus, so that the hysteric characteristically moves away from the consequences of her seductive parade of sexual definition. Despite these complications, there is a high investment in gender-definition among the characters of the novel, and if there is a sense of boundlessness or unclear boundaries in *La Regenta* other than the threatened boundlessness of death and annihilation, it is the overwhelming boundlessness of insecure gender or identity differentiation within a dyad, as exemplified so powerfully in the central chapters of the novel in the relationship between Fermín and his mother, Doña Paula.

A double movement is involved. The liminal anxieties which precede and provoke defensive strategies of identity and gender formation and the establishment of boundaries within an initial dyadic relationship do not disappear. Unless boundaries are established, moreover, no relationships at all, whether diversionary, strategic, same-gender, or different-gender, can be realized. An acute loss, evident throughout the novel, is that of intimacy, since a state of intimacy requires a sense of boundary around identities in order to allow relationship. A continuous *vaivén* around the *limenes* of identity and gender is rendered more threatening and unsettling by the fact that the insecure framing of the novel in waves of nausea and mud causes the boundaries strategically engaged in during the surface text of adultery of the novel to be perceived as boundaries which are insecure, porous, permeable, shifting. Mud and nausea further indicate that the ultimate concern of the text will be with anxieties relating to nothingness and annihilation, a concern which leads to the text's hysterical symptom: the diversionary narrative of hysteria, perversion, and gender games.

Hysteria can be construed in the novel, then, not only in the characteristically hysteric behaviour of those who – like Ana – deny or repress sexual desire, but equally in those who simply resort to sexual activity as a means of denying death (Labanyi 1991; Showalter 1985). Early theories of hysteria posited that there was some initial trauma which caused a dislocation of feeling, taking physically inconvenient forms, the source of which remained totally incomprehensible to the sufferer. As a strategy, however, it also needs to be perceived as a malady which can be visited upon others, in a maneuver of domination and marginalization of the sufferer. As such it becomes a strategy to be used not just by the hysteric, but by those around her, in that it allows for the projection elsewhere, and labelling as mysterious, changing and suspect, of those aspects of our lives which do not readily lend themselves to "objective" study (Evans 1991; Gilman *et al.* 1993).

Underlying my discussion of mud and nausea, then, is the assumption that the whole structure of gender-strategy is itself a type of meta-activity in the face of what precedes gender, and that state in which identity cannot be referred to – the state of non-being, nothingness, death, the falling into nothingness which for Winnicott is the characteristic anxiety of the newborn infant (1965: 57-8). The insistence upon nausea and mud in the novel is thus more than simple metaphorical pattern, and represents large-scale processes in the novel. While the emphasis on nausea relates to the difficulties of containment pertaining to death and eroticism, elaboration on themes of mud relates to processes of splitting, projection, social positioning, purity and maculation.

Nausea

La Regenta opens in a post-ingestion state, with the "rumor estridente" of rubbish whirling round the streets as the background to the task of digesting the heavy local fare, "cocido" and "olla podrida" (I. 93). The narrative to come, an insecure membrane, will hold within itself the aspirations and longings of the displaced, the bored and the anxious, and will end on a note of denial, dislocation and projected nausea. A novel of its time, in its dialogue between the physical and the spiritual, idealism and materialism (Ife 1970), *La Regenta* is insistently modern in its denial and/or its deferral of resolution. And while the characters pose as members of other classes, another gender, as heroes and heroines, *La Regenta* poses innocently as a traditional adultery novel, within which the turbulent inner content lurks, ready to break out. Because of the posing, *La Regenta* is a novel of false or strained separations, insecure hierarchies, permeable barriers and boundaries. This results in an emphasis on the discomfort of the process of having to contain what is intolerable, and on the anxiety that, where a splitting off from what is rejected has been effected, full separation from the tainting of the physical, the material and the sexual may not have been achieved.

The process of digestion, as with the experience of nausea, is part of a mid-field. It is neither the moment of ingestion, nor is it the time at which digestion has taken place, and the food assimilated by the body. It is the period during which we may, if the process is a difficult one, be aware of what we have taken in, by dint of the discomfort to which we are subjected. Vetusta's siesta time at the start of Chapter 1 presents an image of apparently peaceful bourgeois mundanity little glimpsed elsewhere in the novel. But the opening description acts as a frail surface skin, below which the text will swell, rumble, express disquietude. The below-the-surface turbulence indicates simultaneously that something is wrong, indeed that there may be a body experienced as foreign, which needs to be cast out, vomited out of the system, and yet the nature and identity of that ingested object will remain a matter of uncertainty, until Ana offers herself for this role at the close of the novel. The step between the discomfort of difficult digestion and that of nausea preluding release through the act of vomiting is short, but no easier to take for that. The final experience of nausea at the end of the text leaves the discomfort and unease with the reader, coupled with absence of hope either that the offending object may be identified, or that it may be cast out. All that is cast out by the end of the novel is the scapegoated woman, Ana, in the characteristically rejected, indeed abject, place of woman who is co-identified with the world of the flesh and all that is uncertain (Valis 1992).

By the final page of the novel, the discomfort of digestive labors is replaced by the nausea of Ana Ozores, subjected unwillingly, and only partly in her consciousness, to the perverse, curious, and undesiring kiss from the lips of Celedonio. In this reversal of the fairytale motif by which princesses can kiss frogs and find that they have transformed the repulsive object into a handsome, desirable (and not just desiring) Prince, an act which is the beginning, so we are led to believe, of an experience of happy and fulfilled sexuality, the kiss of Celedonio reaches Ana's dim awareness as the touch not of lips, but of the "vientre viscoso y frío de un sapo" (II. 537). While Nöel Valis (1987: 800-02) has highlighted the strong local Asturian connotations of the toad, there are other, suggestive symbolic resonances. The toad itself, possessed of the inverse and infernal aspects of the positive, fertile frog-symbol (Cirlot 1962: 344), is also traditionally associated with the moon, and hence with lunar changeability and humidity. Within alchemical symbolism, it represents the dark side of nature, and its lower, but fertile dregs, and is linked to earthly matter (Cooper 1978: 174). In a sense, the return of the toad, foul though it is, may signify a necessary and fertile return to the world of matter. Harriet Turner's passing interpretation (1990: 72) that what causes the toad's underbelly to be "viscoso" is semen, not "baba" or saliva, as suggested by Valis (1987) and Sieburth (1990), confirms this link with the world of fertility.

Images of a physical *malestar* thus set the tone of the opening of *La Regenta*, and of its conclusion. By a type of reverse, or perverse narration, however, the image of the opening pages is one of the physical discomfort of what has been taken in, causing the rumblings of digestion, whereas that of the end is of a contact on the lips which has caused a feeling of nausea, and yet which relates more to the mockery of *vacío*, in that by the end all that has been taken in has come to nothing, has brought disaster, and yet has not filled the gaping void of Ana Ozores. It may be apposite here to repeat for Ana Ozores the observation made by Collas about Emma Bovary: he remarks that nausea indicates deprivation and frustration, and that Emma's retching and loss of appetite is "the immediate effect of a sudden and intolerable withdrawal of love... Nausea is here... the expression of that particular kind of moral suffering that is brought about by being frustrated in one's love feelings" (Collas 1985: 40).

The association between nausea and the experience of void is remarked upon by Bataille. For Bataille, nausea is unspecific in its stimulus, and may occur at any point in the chain of "excreta, decay and sexuality." That is, like the concept of desire, or the earlier concept of the drive as defined by Freud (1905b) it is a feeling which comes not precisely and solely in response to particular objects, but rather may simply be called up by them, so that it is, as it were, transferred on to them. Nausea, for Bataille, belongs to the area of the undefined, rather than to the precise nature of tainted objects which may have been ingested, and as such relates experientially to the imaging and portrayal of nausea in *La Regenta*: "It may look as though physical circumstances imposed from without are chiefly operative in marking out this area of sensibility. But it also has its subjective aspect. The feeling of nausea varies with the individual and its material source is now one thing and now another. After the living man the dead body is nothing at all; similarly nothing tangible or objective brings on our feeling of nausea; what we experience is a kind of void, a sinking sensation." The experience of nausea is linked to our sense of the mortal and the decaying, so that it is "the terrified recoiling at the sight of advanced decay." While Bataille associates the reaction of recoil to our sense of revulsion at excrement, he indicates the way in which we are unable to compartmentalize and marginalize aspects of our life which we reject, asserting that there is a chain by which these reactions of recoil are linked to aspects of life which denote our humanity, physicality and sensuality (Bataille 1957: 57-8).

The association made by Bataille between the experience of nausea and our fear of decay and death is curiously apposite to the thematic structuring of *La Regenta*. The emphasis on nausea or *mareo* in the novel occurs, as indicated earlier, at the margins, the edges, the boundaries of the novel's narrative. It is linked to the queasiness of uncertain digestion of the opening page, reiterated in the series of uncomfortable digestive states through the first chapter, and is the note of resolution, or rather, non-resolution by which the novel is brought to a close. It also rises and falls in the middle reaches of the novel, so that anticipation of release through the accomplishment of the act of adultery is accompanied by an undercurrent that there may be a different type of release.

As the narrative gains way, what we will come to observe increasingly in Ana is that her dis-order is not the simple physical symptom of nausea, indubitable sign that something untoward has been ingested, but rather that it is being presented as and focalized into the dis-order of hysteria, which carries with it all the social dislocation and stigmatization attached to the medical naming of "women's problems" in the context of the nineteenth-century novel (Showalter 1985). The symptom of *mareo* is of course part of the experience of hysteria, and presents as the dizziness Ana experiences in her hysterical crises. We should also note that Ana's ailments, be they nausea or hysteria, are passed to, or experienced in some degree by Fermín also. Hence in Chapter 15 his *mareo* (I. 542, 552, 564) and his *asco* (I. 555), his taking on of her *hysteria* in Chapter 14 (I. 527, and 531), where his oral urges are a point of focus, and in Chapter 30 (II. 494) his uncontained and violent experience as he tries to write to Ana.

The architectural placing of death in relation to nausea in *La Regenta* can be postulated in the following way. Nausea stands at the outer edges, and periodically comes and goes as Ana moves through her experience of (or arguably her pursuit of) the career of the hysteric in the central part of the novel. Chapter 12, where the expected demise of Rosita Carraspique is the point of discussion between Fermín, Somoza the doctor and Rosita's parents, is where the note of death is struck as a future reality (as opposed to the past deaths of Ana's parents). It is chillingly in connection with the influence of Fermín that the death is foretold, yet there is a plausible surface reason for the death in the unclean atmosphere of a convent cell that has become a *cloaca*, a sewer. The reality of physical death thus overshadows symbolic decay within the suffocating grip of the Church. Nausea resurges, as a late reaction to what appears to be Ana's hysterical "ataque" at the dance at the Casino, in Chapter 25: in fact the nausea arguably occurs in relation not to the attack, but to the religious ritual that is the alternative to the life of sexual indulgence. We might note here how it is Ana herself who in fact thus carries out the *ataque* which is planned by Álvaro, securing as hysteric the experience of the sexual without the presence of a male agent. Nausea is in a sense a part of Ana's move away from religion into sexuality, so that her un-ease comes to be in relation not just to the temptation of physical pleasure, but in reaction to what she now (rightly) perceives as the dubious nature of the religious framework within which she had sought refuge in the middle reaches of the novel.

The opening of Chapter 22 carries the gossiped news of a further threatened death, again in connection with the influence of Fermín: Santos Barinaga, commercial rival of Fermín and his mother. Don Santos' passing is eclipsed later in the chapter by the more dramatic, and more "nauseous" (because of its associations with stench and decay) passing of Rosita Carraspique in " 'la celda que era, según Somoza, un *inodoro*, por no decir todo lo contrario' " (II. 237). By grotesque association, the type of *tisis* from which Rosita dies, according to the pronouncement of Somoza, is "una tisis caseosa," in which tissues become "cheesy" in texture (Sobejano 1981: II. 237), the curious quality of cheese being that the activity of bacteria which produces it is also the activity by which it eventually becomes excessively decayed, and, as it were, "dies."

Death moves increasingly center-stage as the novel progresses. This is not the anticipated death of the adulterous heroine of a novel, brought about by the hand of another, or accommodatingly self-induced, but rather a series of deaths which signal decay through sheer physical processes, a decay awaiting all of the characters. It is, however, a series of deaths whose form reiterates the patterns of disgust, of hunger, of deprivation and of compensatory oral excesses (entailing in their turn a series of experiences of physical dis-ease) in which are articulated anxieties about being and identity in the novel. Real death continues to walk hand in hand with symbolic death, most insistently in Chapter 26, where Pompeyo's fatal illness preludes the death of Ana as public servant of Fermín in the Easter procession, itself a commemoration of a death in the service of others. The unbroken chain of death brought to the reader's attention is announced in the opening sentence of the chapter: "Desde el día en que presidió el entierro de don Santos Barinaga, don Pompeyo no volvió a tener hora buena, de salud completa" (II. 338). As Fermín goes to attend Pompeyo, he is overcome by feelings of pleasure, since Pompeyo's call to him on his deathbed is the sign of his triumph. Significantly he is ill himself, with neuralgia, his public face at this point being tested to its utmost (II. 341). The approach of death is accompanied by signs of drowning, nausea, vomiting, as though what is being taken in is more than the system can tolerate: "Don Fermín se *ahogaba* de placer, de orgullo; *se le atragantaban* las pasiones mientras don Pompeyo *tosía*, y *entre esputo de esputo de flema decía...*" (II. 348, emphasis mine). As Fermín chokes (gags) with pleasure, Pompeyo coughs and chokes in his death-throes, reminding us in the space of some twenty words that pleasure is little removed from death, and that choking (the next stage on from nausea) will tend to accompany an access of pleasurable feeling.

Pleasure and revulsion, standing contiguous to nausea, are linked in the final images of Ana. First, in her pleasure. Like Fermín, she initially takes pleasure in the sensation of being *overcome*, this time by a *mareo* of pleasure, and before the final act of adultery she has a dizzy enjoyment of the disorientation and giddiness that her "fall" provokes: "La Regenta cayendo, cayendo era feliz; sentía el mareo de la caída en las entrañas..." albeit punctuated by more bitter associations of dizziness, so that "algunos días al despertar en vez de pensamientos alegres encontraba, entre un poco de bilis, ideas tristes, algo como un remordimiento...," immediately "put down" by her through "la nueva metafísica naturalista" (II. 436-7). After the adultery, after the discovery, after the death of Víctor (made to seep in undignified manner through a perforated full bladder, symbol of the wholesale puncturing of swollen membranes), Ana emerges from her seclusion to visit the Cathedral, and to try to confess, to make, as it were, a controlled verbal outpouring, which she hopes will be received. On entering the Cathedral, her sensations are most akin to the choking of the hysteric, a choking through sheer pleasure: "sintió en sus entrañas aquella ascensión de la ternura que subía hasta la garganta y producía un amago de estrangulación deliciosa..." (II. 533). What she desires to pour out, she desires to pour out and have received: her tears, her confession. Not only is this not forthcoming, but it is replaced by its opposite in Fermín's barely controlled rejection. In this it is as if he shares her *mareo*, shown by his gesture, "cruzó los brazos sobre el vientre," a gesture that is the sign of imminent vomiting, as though there is no secure boundary between the dizziness of the two. This shared experience of nausea, encapsulated in Fermín's otherwise extraordinary gesture of digging his nails into his neck, is then cast off by him.

Mud

Mud has a number of different but inter-related connotations in *La Regenta*. Those I shall single out here are between mud and death (the link with our state as mortal clay), and between mud and tainting, social maculation (linked to the concept of *limpieza*, and the spattering of reputation by unlicensed sexual activity). The different words used for mud in the novel – *lodo, tierra, cieno, barro* – appearing most commonly, are used with considerable discrimination and point by Alas. Thus *barro* is used in the context of Biblical associations of man as mortal clay, *cieno* to denote the fouling of sin which arises from the consideration of man as sinful clay, and *lodo* and *tierra* predominantly where the text translates the concern with mud into a physical, tangible reality, although *lodo* also occurs within the context of sin. The resonance with the writings of pastoral theology here can be seen from a brief example of the *Directorio de la confesión general* by Leonardo de Porto-Mauricio, and republished by Claret in 1859 in the *Nuevo manojito de flores, o sea recopilación de doctrinas para los confesores*, where the author recommends examining the penitent first on the sixth commandment, "porque por más encenagado que esté el penitente en este pantano, camina después más desembarazado, y ya no hace aprehensión alguna de lo restante" (Porto-Mauricio in Claret 1859: 111). As with the language of desire, we can see how characters formulate and reformulate their relation to mud via a linguistic code of some sophistication.

MUD AND DEATH

If, following Bataille, the experience of nausea is linked to the interplay between eroticism and the apprehension of death, brought closer by our increased awareness of our existence embedded in physical, mortal matter, we might anticipate that anxieties relating to mud would derive principally from that Biblical emphasis on our being as clay or dust. This emphasis is placed strategically in Christian liturgy in funeral rites. Our return to mortal clay, the return of dust to dust, is commemorated in the Anglican Office "At the Burial of the Dead," *Book of Common Prayer*. This contains *I Corinthians*, 15, 20-58, where our condition as mortal clay is balanced by the news of the resurrection. In the Catholic Office for the Dead, as set out in the *Rituale Romanum* which would have been observed in Spain in the latter part of the 19th century, many of the readings come from the *Book of Job*, specifically Chapters 7, 10, 13, 14, 17 and 19, in which a strong sense of man's physical decay in death is conveyed. The atmosphere of the *Book of Job* has strong resonances with Chapters 18 and 22 of *La Regenta*. The emphasis on mud, as with the thematic strain of nausea, thus serves to undercut the diversionary tactics of gender-strategy and hysterical fictions of adultery. The reminder of our condition as mortal clay appears somewhat incongruously in the mouth of Visitación. Noting Ana's pulse quicken when she tells her of Álvaro's departure to see a previous mistress, her reaction is one of those many pre-packaged snippets of a culture that is barely possessed: "A mí con santidades – pensó – ; *pulvisés*, como dijo el otro" (II. 220), an allusion glossed later as "la teoría del *pulvisés* o sea de la ceniza universal" (II. 221). The reference here is to God's words to Adam after Eve has committed the sin of being tempted by the serpent and eating of the fruit of the tree of knowledge: "In the sweat of thy face shalt thou eat bread till thou return to the earth, out of which thou wast taken: for dust thou art, and into dust thou shalt return," translated in the Vulgate as: "in sudore vultus tui vesceris pane / donec revertaris in terram de qua sumptus es / quia pulvis es et in pulverem reverteris" (*Genesis*, 3. 19).

Part of the dynamic functioning of the motif of mud in the novel is indeed related to our condition as mortal clay. As indicated in the previous section we are brought close to the perceived horrors of the graveyard, particularly acute when that graveyard (for the impious) will be beyond the confines of the *campo santo*. The grave is characterized not as firm, warm earth (in the sense of a maternal *tierra* that might receive back its creature), but as a place where the human is relegated to the animal. This is particularly evident when the funeral in question is to be that of Santos Barinaga, who, because of his lack of belief, will not be in the *campo santo*. The horror at his fate is ingeniously conveyed through the mind of Fermín, the horror itself infected and tainted by the realization that Santos's death stands to mark him with public exposure. Chapter 22 is dominated by the expected death of don Santos. Popular hearsay has it that he is dying of hunger, robbed of a living by the simony of Fermín and his mother. Fermín's horror at his death is thus not prompted by any Heideggerian encounter with the reality of death, but by an overwhelming sense of the embarrassment that this causes: the coming death is an inconvenience given that Santos is unreconciled with the church. Furthermore, Santos's death is described in parallel with the crumbling of his premises. The emptiness of his hungry belly, the sense of implosion as he turns in on himself and drowns his sorrows, the twin disintegration of the fabric of the shop and his own guts, all provide the reader with an *exemplum* of decay worthy of a medieval moral tale, in which the vocabulary of commerce flows indistinguishably into that of alcoholic consolation: "Aquellos anaqueles vacíos representaban a su modo el estómago de don Santos. Las últimas existencias, que había tenido allí años y años cubiertas de polvo, las había vendido por cuatro cuartos a un comerciante de aldea; con el producto de aquella liquidación miserable había vivido y se había emborrachado en la última parte de su vida el pobre Barinaga. Ahora los ratones roían las tablas de los estantes y la consunción roía las entrañas del tendero" (II. 263).

Meanwhile we read of Pompeyo's horror and disgust at the experience of the funeral, under weather so foul that the cover of the coffin begins to split, revealing, with prefigurative emphasis, "la carne blanca de la madera, que chorreaba el agua" (II. 268). Santos is about to suffer the fate of the impious outcast, by receiving his burial outside the consecrated part of the cemetery. Underlying the anguish of this, however, is the fact that he is not fully outcast, or at least not safely contained in his outcast state. For Pompeyo there is, as he perceives it, an imperfect separation between Santos and the world. This escalates, first in relation to the degree to which Santos is made outcast, lodged in the animal world, on the other side of the cemetery wall, like a *perro*, and then at the fact that the civil cemetery is itself not properly enclosed, but has breaches, through which dogs and cats can come. The cortège enters the cemetery not by the proper gate, but by an "improper" gap: "una especie de brecha abierta en la tapia del corralón inmundo, estrecho y lleno de ortigas" (II. 269). In horror, Pompeyo turns over in his mind the intolerable details of the burial. Santos is not *properly* buried, but "a flor de tierra," separated from previous Vetustan inhabitants "por un muro que era una deshonra; perdido, como el esqueleto de un rocín, entre ortigas, escajos y lodo... Por aquella brecha penetraban perros y gatos en el cementerio civil... A toda profanación estaba abierto..." (II. 269). Don Pompeyo's journey to the burial leaves him with sodden feet, "encharcados," and the damp penetrates, reaching dramatic form for him in his nightmare after the burial: he is now himself no longer separate from the earth, with its enveloping connotations of shame and death: "Soñaba que él era de cal y canto y que tenía una brecha en el vientre y por allí entraban y salían gatos y perros, y alguno que otro diablejo con rabo" (II. 270) (Charnon-Deutsch 1989a). Mud is thus not only the earth to which we return, but labile, treacherous, capable of seeping through breaches, and contributing to the general apprehension that nothing in the world of Vetusta, in life or in death, can be contained, whatever the panic-stricken barriers erected against it.

Mud and Sexuality

Mud is, of course, that archetypical material of no-man's-land, of disputed territory and uncertain boundaries. It is the epitome in *La Regenta* of disorientation, of the oozing mess that at worst will be one's fate in death, and at its most benign will still spatter and besmirch. It is also the indicator, at times clumsy, of the relationship between the characters and their sexuality, while at a cultural level being the sign of the tainting that results from exposed and/or forbidden sexual activity. Thus, for example, in Chapter 9, the setting of mud to Ana's walk into the country with Petra (see Labanyi 1986). The mud that will be metaphorically ubiquitous, expressive of dishonor, depression, vulgarity, the feeling of being abject or relegated, is a mud present on the first plane of the narrative, forming real threats to the physical cleanliness of the characters, the concomitant dampness, as noted, presenting a real or imagined threat to their health.

The *desenlace* of the novel occurs from early in the second half, after the slow-paced scene-setting of the initial chapters. It is as though the boundaries which have been observed (if imperfectly) in the first half, begin at this stage to disintegrate, although at the surface level of the text the maneuvers of gender-relations in terms of the power-struggle for Ana are intensified. Thus in Chapter 1, the cat's mess (defilement attached within the Christian tradition to the animal, below-human world) is cleared away, swept into a corner (I. 121). In Chapter 15, its metaphorical significance (again with the connotations of the primitive animal world) is spelled out in detail. The mess is now that of the miners, with their craving sexual hunger. Paula has no doubts as to how to treat it: "Paula despreciaba aquella baba. Más asco le daba barrer las inmundicias que dejaban allí aquellos osos de la cueva... ...*Allí estaba ella para barrer hacia la calle aquel lodo que entraba todos los días por la puerta de la taberna; a ella la manchaba, pero a él no;* él allá dentro con Dios y los santos, bebiendo en los libros la ciencia que le había de hacer señor; y su madre allí fuera, manejando inmundicia..." (I. 556, emphasis mine). What is significant here is the internal temporal sequence, for the act of sweeping mess unhygienically into a corner in Chapter 1 is in the present tense narrative, whereas the image of Paula strenuously clearing mud into the street comes from the time of Fermín's adolescence. Retrospectively the reader is thus provided with the internal resonances that the fouling of a place deemed "pure" will have for Fermín. The dynamic of filth and purity, and the struggle for separation between mother and son, is discussed further in Chapter 4.

In this second half of the novel, it is as though the water-table rises, raising the level of the mud, endangering the characters who variously are referred to as drowning or choking. The underworld of repressed and forbidden sexuality and social relationships, of past secrets that have been kept under, now begins to surface. As Paula confronts Fermín, deep in Chapter 15, it is to point out to him the (social) danger in which he is placing them by his relationship with Ana. And yet, in the very articulation of danger, what is conveyed is communicated through imprecision, as though there can be no true speaking subject, no reference to a distinctly defined other. The rhythm of Paula's speech conveys all with its fits and starts, and sentences left unresolved. What she is saying is in a sense unthinkable, and yet, she implies, it is known by the two of them. Here the mess, the *porquerías* as she terms it (I. 545), indicates not merely the social "messiness" of a priest engaging in illicit sexual activities, but appears to allude to all the messiness of the life of physical and sexual compromise in which she has been involved. The self-interrupted, self-censored nature of her speech provides, through its ellipses, the fissures through which the mud of the repressed sexuality is intended to be glimpsed and understood. At first her speech is contained in the grammatical certainty and rotundity of a maternal interrogation of reproach, the fluency of the phrases reflecting the fact that the offenses referred to are, even if intolerable, possible to contemplate: "¡Si no hay madre que valga! ¿te has acordado de tu madre en todo el día? ¿No la has dejado comer sola, o mejor dicho, no comer? ¿te importó nada que tu madre se asustara, como era natural? ¿Y qué has hecho después hasta las diez de la noche?" (I. 544). Then the rhythms and syncopations of forbidden possibilities enter: "Fermo... a buen entendedor... Mira, Fermo... tú no te acuerdas, pero yo sí... yo soy la madre que te parió ¿sabes? y te conozco... y conozco el mundo... y sé tenerlo todo en cuenta... todo... Pero de estas cosas no podemos hablar tú y yo... ni a solas... ya me entiendes... pero... bastante buena soy, bastante he callado, bastante he visto" (I. 545). And at Fermín's challenge, "No ha visto usted nada...," Paula continues, still in oblique, interrupted reference, but getting closer to the messy *substance* of her complaint: "Tienes razón... no he visto... pero he comprendido y ya ves... nunca te hablé de estas... porquerías, pero ahora parece que te complaces en que te vean... tomas por el peor camino..." (I. 545-6). Here it is almost as though Paula is a mother talking to a child about the "facts of life" that she has never divulged, and on which he has now stumbled, running the risk of making public for the two of them what has been veiled over in familial secrecy. True to the coding of water/mud as indicators of sexuality and shame, she continues, colloquially "¿No ves que te tienen ganas? ¿que llueve sobre mojado...?," and later with a reminder of the drowning to which they had been close: "¿No nos dejó tu pobre padre muertos de hambre y con el agua al cuello, todo embargado, todo perdido?" (I. 546).

This reminder of past social "drowning" acquires weight three chapters later, in Chapter 18, in the context of the gross disintegration of Vetusta's climate, where the original text of introduction of Chapter 1 is transformed, the predominant image being no longer that of rubbish and the discomforts of digestion, but of the corpse of a "náufrago," and the falling away of flesh from bones (heralding the horrors in Chapter 22 of death in the *cloaca,* or the *inodoro* of Rosita Carraspique, and that of don Santos who goes to his ill-contained civil grave). Thus the calmness of "La heroica ciudad dormía la siesta. El viento Sur, caliente y perezoso, empujaba las nubes blanquecinas que se rasgaban al correr hacia el Norte" (I. 93), becomes violent, more agitated, with waves of furious motion as rain falls in torrents, dissolving the earth below into the various stages of decomposition of the human body after death, the reference to Job a marker of the funereal setting to come:

> Las nubes pardas, opacas, anchas como estepas, venían del Oeste, tropezaban con las crestas de Corfín, se desgarraban y deshechas en agua caían sobre Vetusta, unas en diagonales vertiginosas, como latigazos furibundos, como castigo bíblico; otras cachazudas, tranquilas, en delgados hilos verticales. Pasaban, y venían otras, y después otras que parecían las de antes, que habían dado la vuelta al mundo para desgarrarse en Corfín otra vez. La tierra fungosa se descarnaba como los huesos de Job; sobre la sierra se dejaba arrastrar por el viento perezoso, la niebla lenta y desmayada, semejante a un penacho de pluma gris; y toda la campiña entumecida, desnuda, se extendía a lo lejos, in-

móvil como el cadáver de un náufrago que chorrea el agua de las olas que le arrojaron a la orilla. La tristeza resignada, fatal de la piedra que la gota eterna horada, era la expresión muda del valle y del monte; la naturaleza muerta parecía esperar que el agua disolviera su cuerpo inerte, inútil. (II. 83)

The seeping will continue. Rosita Carraspique's lungs will continue to be invaded and eroded to form the "tisis caseosa" (II. 237), the damp around don Santos's funeral will invade the person of don Pompeyo, and the latter's dreams will be dominated by the image of fissures and seeping (II. 269). It is perhaps significant that in Chapter 22, where the two deaths are deemed to be shocking in relation to Fermín, his thoughts turn to the traditional view of man as clay. There is a massive unstated subtext here. As Ana shows herself at her most loving and solicitous to Fermín, his thoughts, though revealed fully neither to himself nor to the reader (and certainly not to Ana) appear to be on the matter of his condition of clay, for which we might read his physical or sexual incontinence: that is, he is horrified at the divergence between her view of him, and what, it is hinted, is the covert reality: "Es horroroso, es horroroso – pensaba el Magistral – pasar plaza de santo a sus ojos, y ser un pobre cuerpo de barro que vive como el barro ha de vivir. Engañar a los demás no me duele; ¡pero a ella! Y no hay más remedio." Lest the meaning of this should escape us, the images in the following sentence of puddles and mud, in contrast with her purity, convey not only the notion of his sexual adventures as seen from the confessional, but reveal, by that very terminology, his sick adoption of the confessional codifying of his behaviour: "Quería que le consolase el reflexionar que *por ella* era todo aquello, que por ella había él vuelto a sentir con vigor las pasiones de la juventud que creyera muertas, y que por ella, por respetar su pureza, se encenagaba él en antiguos charcos; pero esta idea no le consolaba, no apagaba el remordimiento" (II. 244). While "encenagar" is literally "to cover with mud," the habitual moral meaning of the word is conveyed in the phrased "encenagado en el vicio" (*New Oxford Spanish Dictionary*, 1994).

In Chapter 25, in mid-Lent, after a false and deceptive indication of spring, Vetusta sinks once more into the watery mire. Trees imprudently in blossom, caught out by spring rain and hail, are significantly figured as young women, highlighting the folly of dreams of escape into a more open and "blooming" existence: "Los árboles floridos padecieron los furores de la intemperie, como engalanadas damiselas que en día de campo, vestidas con percales alegres, adornos vistosos y delicados de seda y tul, se ven sorprendidas por un chubasco, al aire libre, sin albergue, sin paraguas siquiera. Las florecillas blancas y rosadas de los frutales caían muertas sobre el fango: el granizo las despedazaba; todo volvía atrás; aquel ensayo de primavera temprana había salido mal; vuelta a empezar, cada mochuelo a su olivo" (II. 329). The sexual connotations of the image of the storm will become more definite, in the retrospective manner so typical of the novel, during the storm scenes of Chapter 27 and 28, and will relate to the meaning for Fermín of the sudden rain in the country, and the fact that Ana and her companions are in the wood. Presumably, it is thought, they will seek refuge, the sexual connotations of which will be all too present in the priest's mind, given his own recent interlude in the *cabaña* with Petra (II. 410).

Mud, Tainting and *Limpieza*

The quality of cleanliness, fundamental to concepts of ordering and separation by which pollution is avoided, has particular connotations in the Hispanic context of *limpieza:* cleanliness with regard to lineage and blood, and cleanliness that is understood as freedom from shame, the female underside of the masculine-dominated honor code (Douglas 1966; Caro Baroja 1965; Pitt-Rivers 1965; Sinclair 1993: 97-120). Cleanliness, "freedom from mud," is thus a sign of a successful splitting between genders in the establishment of gender-identity. But there is still anxiety about the security of this splitting. Within *La Regenta*, the gaze of the reader (assumed masculine?) is forever drawn to the lower parts of the body, whether in the sexual gaze of titillation, or in the gaze that observes whether or not *other* characters in the novel are subject to tainting from mud. As it splashes feet and legs, mud is presented initially in its most prosaic, least suggestive sense, as the type of fouling which is of relatively little importance and which can be avoided. Throughout the novel there is a striking emphasis on feet, shoes, legs and "los bajos," culminating in the focus on Ana's feet in the perverse enactment of the procession in Chapter 26. Coupled with this intense interest in the *limpieza* of nether regions is a fascination with those characters who appear miraculously to be immune from the physical tainting and spattering of mud, a fascination which betrays a phantasy of the possibility of separateness from all the elements of the physical, the sexual and the ineluctably mortal nature of the human condition.

Cleanliness in *La Regenta* is, unusually, not a prerogative of the female or the feminine. In a reversal of the habitual splits of the honor code, by which honor (and moral cleanliness) is the preserve of man, while shame (and tainting) that of woman, a split which obliges woman to carry the projected-out shame and potential "filth" of the man, and simultaneously places on her an increased burden of proof and maintenance of cleanliness, we find prime male characters in the novel to be possessed of a capacity for cleanliness that is little short of amazing. Thus Fermín and Álvaro, who will become locked into rivalrous relation for the possession of virility, emphasized and brought to a head by the episode with Visitación and the swing, are both characters associated with personal pulchritude and a remarkable degree of fastidiousness. While their fastidiousness underlines their varied (and different) concerns for the maintenance of prestige and reputation, their anxiety also indicates the degree to which gender-divisions within the novel are remarkably uncertain, and are as shifting and insecure as the labile mud and earth on which they tread.

Álvaro's cleanliness is arguably more a feature of his reputation, and the phantasies that other, less skillful, males have about his ability to dally sexually without "soiling" himself, than it is necessarily a reality. It appears in the culinary foreplay of the Vegallana kitchen (Chapter 8), focalized though the envious eyes of Paco: "Mesía gozaba del arte supremo de entrar en carboneras, cocinas y hasta molinos, sin coger tiznes, grasas ni harina" (I. 324). Unsurprisingly, the effect of the kitchen encounters (presumably not just at the level of physical soiling) is a contrast between Paco and his pristine hero: "Paco se puso perdido. Mesía estaba como un armiño metido a marmitón" (I. 325). Less miraculously, and in a timorous move that heralds his final furtiveness in the adultery, Álvaro is observed approaching Ana's house down a muddy alley: it is yet another no-man's-land, echoing the non-status of the relationship: "Allí no había casas, ni aceras ni faroles; era una calle porque la llamaban así, pero consistía en un camino maltrecho, de piso desigual y fangoso entre dos paredones, uno de la Cárcel y otro de la huerta de los Ozores. Al acercarse a la puerta, pegado a la pared, por huir del fango, Mesía creyó sentir la corazonada verdadera" (I. 379). In like manner to the example of Álvaro and Paco just mentioned, the pristine condition of Fermín's shoe is viewed enviously by the minor clerics who, in their declared sexual and social ambiguity, may elevate its cleanliness to a greater degree than is the reality, linking it to the quality (*lack* of filth or shame) of a lady: "¡Aquello era señorío! ¡Ni una mancha! Los pies parecían los de una dama..." (I. 101). Fermín, as portrayed at home in Chapter 11, is a man who occupies his house in the manner of feminine space in Hispanic culture, but the status of this cleanliness is converted via the gossiping comments of the malicious Ripamilán to the level of the whited sepulcher, with a reference to "una cabaña limpia" (I. 389) that will acquire clear sexual connotations in the later episode in the hut with Petra, in Chapter 28. But Ripamilán's question about whether this pulchritude of environment is more than surface deep is posed in a manner which in its turn has disturbing echoes: "¡pero qué de trampas tapa aquella oscuridad! ¿Quién nos dice que las sillas de damasco verde no tienen abiertas las entrañas? ¿Las han visto ustedes alguna vez sin funda? ¿Y la consola panzuda, antiquísima, de un dorado que fue, con su reloj de música sin música y sin cuerda?" (I. 390-1). This recalls disturbingly the swollen, swelling furniture of the Marquesa de Vegallana (Chapter 8), whose forms are redolent of the sexual activity to which it is undoubtedly witness. Fermín, as noted above, takes the traditional Church view of the flesh as sinful, as *lodo*, as something from which he hopes to disassociate himself. Thus he thinks of the account by Renan of a "pure" love, re-couching it in the terms of the confessor who asserts the existence of places and experiences of absolute purity: "era la verdad severa, noble, inmaculada del amor místico; amor anafrodítico, incapaz de mancharse con el lodo de la carne ni en sueños" (I. 409). By Chapter 22 this detachment from mud will not be claimed even by Fermín.

No terminology of cleanliness (freedom from mud) is connotation-free. Even references to those of clean habits suchas *armiño* have their complications, given that the ermine changes its coat from white in winter to brown in summer, and that even the white is not absolute, the characteristic of the ermine being the distinctive black tip to the tail. Thus Obdulia's thought about Ana's cleanliness could be read both against the grain as well as with it: "Era limpia, no se podía negar, limpia como el armiño" (I. 164), whereas Visitación's use of the ermine is in a context already involving tainting: "Admiraba a su amiguita, elogiaba su hermosura y su virtud; pero la hermosura la molestaba como a todas, y la virtud la volvía loca. Quería ver aquel armiño en el lodo" (I. 328).

Visitación meanwhile, has an idea of her own state of cleanliness which is as complex and self-deceived as is that of her sexuality where oral satisfaction is the reward for sexual denial. It is as though she manages to persuade herself that she is in fact clean. She rehearses her domestic self-defense in Chapter 13: "era mujer de tal despacho que su ajuar quedaba dispuesto para todo el día, la casa limpia, la comida preparada antes que en otros lugares se diese un escobazo y se encendiese lumbre. Algo sucio iba todo, pero ya tranquila la conciencia, salía a caza de noticias..." (I. 486). And if Visitación's *bajos* leave much to be desired, when compared with the extraordinarily pristine ones of Obdulia, her lack of fear of the mud underfoot is a source of wonder and amazement to Ana – perhaps in itself significant, given the connotations of *humedad* with sexuality, and Ana's fearfulness compared with Visitación's certainty that she, at least, will escape staining: "No se explicaba la Regenta cómo Visitación iba y venía de casa en casa, alegre como siempre, risueña, sin miedo al agua ni menos al fango del arroyo... como pajarita de las nieves, saltaba de piedra en piedra, esquivaba los charcos, y de paso, dejaba ver el pie no mal calzado, las enaguas no muy limpias, y a veces algo de una pantorrilla digna de mejor media" (II. 89), a form of words which, as with the previous quotation, bears the mark of Visitación's sticky pretensions. Yet at this very point, in Chapter 18, where mud inexorably gains meaning for Ana in the form of a sexuality tempting, oppressive, and inevitably staining, the brief image in the quotation of the *pajarita*, with the connotations of prostitution contained in *pájara*, indicates all too clearly the possible fate of those who step in the mud. In Chapter 21, having gossiped, Visitación moves on, the image of her sweeping petticoats and their association with the dust of ill-reputation recalling Paula's energetic sweeping out of the filth from her house in the years when her activity would have given rise to most taunts of lack of *limpieza*: "Se marchó, como la marejada que se retira. Dejó los senderos blancos como si los hubiesen peinado. *La escoba almidonada de enaguas* y percal engomado dejó su rastro de rayas sinuosas y paralelas grabado en la arena" (II. 222, emphasis mine).

Visitación's dinginess in apparel provokes the reader's suspicion of a dinginess in her conduct of past affairs. Obdulia, by contrast, presents herself more convincingly as the *femme fatale*, sure of her allure, and proclaiming with emphasis her freedom from dirt. She categorizes the majority of Vetustan women as dirty, simultaneously associating the habit with a morality somehow unfreed, certainly unemancipated. In her mouth, cleanliness is associated not with narrow moral virtue, as under the original understanding of *limpieza*, but rather with sophistication in managing the world. Above all, Obdulia aligns herself with men, in a manner consonant with her secret desire, on seeing Ana in the Easter procession, to *be* a man. Hence the association she makes in Chapter 16 between lack of education in sophisticated behaviour, and lack of education in the processes of washing (the sub-text being that if you wash thoroughly enough, the taint of misdemeanour will not appear). She comments of Vetustan women: "...fingen que se escandalizan de ciertas libertades de la moda, las mismas que se las toman de tapadillo, entre sustos y miedos, sin gracia, del modo cursi como aquí se hace todo. ¡Pero qué se puede esperar de unas mujeres que no se bañan, ni usan las esponjas más que para lavar a los *bebés*... ...no sabe su cuerpo lo que es una esponja, se lavan como gatas y se la pegan al marido como en tiempo del rey que rabió. ¡Cuánta porquería y cuánta ignorancia!" (II. 34-5).

In the relationship of the different characters to mud, a code emerges that indicates their relationship to sexuality, and to its social management. In the distribution of parts available for women in the canvas of Alas's portrayal of Vetusta, bids are made: Ana and Paula both vying for the role of Virgin, in the form of the Dolorosa, while in her own confused estimation Visitación gestures towards being the *ángel del hogar*. An occupant for the role of earth mother or fertility symbol is, however, elusive, with Paula incongruously the only potential taker. In the delineation of her contact with the earth and the riches it brings, connotations of sexual exploitation rather than fertility emerge that will spread pervasively from their (geographical and historical) point of origin in her story, and seep through the fissures of the narrative of hidden sexual activity.

Ultimately, Ana's passage through the muddy streets of Vetusta will betoken her social undoing, and her (sexually suspect) subordination to the will of Fermín is made manifest. What may be at issue is not the question of whether her career as mystic forms her for the career as adulteress, or whether the career of adulteress, to which she is perhaps committed from the start, fits her perfectly, through the dislocation and the repression of desire, to the role of Fermín's *sierva*. All of this is the hysterical diversion in a text full of both sexual ambiguity and sexual ambivalence, and in the face of a reality that is seamless, or one where boundaries are breached and porous so that we have no defenses against the ultimate *limen*.

La Regenta in its final lines mouths a type of resolution, or resoluteness. A woman is spurned, the priest walks away. She is left with the nausea and has, as it were, been swept aside, like the cat's mess from Chapter 1. Yet all we know, from the preceding narrative about the permeability of boundaries and membranes, insinuates that this final relegation to the margins of Ana as spurned and scape-goated object is a gesture only, with all the impotence of Fermín's final "womanly" gesture of wrath (Nimetz 1971: 248). By this gesture nothing is in fact separated out, nor split off, nor is there the security of an enclosing and containing membrane of acceptance, merely another incipient breach.

CHAPTER 2

THE GENDERED LANGUAGE OF DESIRE

The first mention of desire in *La Regenta* is in the form of *envidia*, attributed to don Custodio by Bismarck in relation to his assertion that Fermín de Pas uses make-up (I. 96-7). This claim is preceded by a snip of dialogue, between Celedonio and Bismarck, which itself concentrates on envious comparisons with others, opening with Celedonio's "¡Mira tú Chiripa, que dice que pué más que yo!" (II. 96). This early highlighting of *envidia* is significant, as this is the feeling which will come to be seen as the most pervasive expression of desire in the novel, associated, as here, primarily with the priesthood, and with same-sex desire. The high profile of envy, however, needs to be seen in the context of other expressions of desire in the novel, with their implied connotations and attributions. What I shall argue is that within the novel there is a high degree of gender-uncertainty and gender-anxiety, and that expression of desire is used as a way of proclaiming gender-identity. This in its turn relates to the power-structures of the novel, in that the use and dynamics of gendered language highlight patterns of legitimate and illegitimate desire, with characters claiming the former, and attributing the latter to others.

In *La Regenta* we are presented with a surprising phenomenon, namely that the least obvious form of desire in the novel is that of adulterous love, and that there is a paucity of any clear-cut language of desire in relation to the projected adultery. The struggle is elsewhere, in the field of power where certain formulations of desire are simultaneously figured as masculine and legitimate. It takes place against a backcloth of those forms of desire associated with unclear boundaries between one identity and another, notably *en-*

vidia, but also other forms of desire declared prohibited by social and biblical tradition as lowly or despicable forms of desire. Most crucially of all, such forms of desire are associated both with gender-ambiguity and with the feminine, so that the notion of the feminine itself is downgraded, and hence the lack of feminine desire, or the lack of recognition of feminine desire, is explained.

Within theories of the development of the self, language – its understanding, acquisition and use – stands in that ground between the primitive formation of self and the defining of gender-identity. Oedipal theory, in the version first offered by Freud, posits the settling of gender-identity in the early infant years, yet given that the theory (more adequate for boys than girls) already pre-supposes that some gender-position has been assumed, the oedipal crisis is a formulation and crystallization – problematic in its nature and meaning, as I shall explore in Section II. Whatever the spirit in which one takes "Anatomy is destiny" (Freud 1912: 259; 1924: 320) gender difference is given strong directional impulse by physical attributes, but these strain and labor under a weight of linguistic formulations, social investments and the entrenched positions of patriarchy (Brenkman 1993).

Language is, of course, by no means neutral, and carries a burden of social, political and sexual weightings. In this chapter I shall concentrate on the last of these, but the degree to which the first two are carried along by the sexual or gender connotations attached to words and forms of language will be evident. Whereas, as proposed in the earlier parts of this book, we might, at least in the abstract, regard gender definition as a defensive move, as a further drawing of a clear boundary around the identity, gender definition becomes gender-imprisonment – at least in the patriarchal world of *La Regenta*. And the worst imprisonment of all is that of gender-ambiguity (viewed from outside) and gender-ambivalence (experienced from inside). Since the very boundaries of these types of imprisonment are unclear, it is all the harder to shake off the shackles. It is for this reason that the models of unclear boundary relating to the self that derive from Klein – projective identification and envy – are so apposite to the struggles to attain a gender definition within the novel.

La Regenta is customarily regarded as Spain's major adultery novel, comparable with others in Europe such as *Madame Bovary*, *Anna Karenina* and *Effi Briest*. Adultery there is, but we are required to wait until that space between Chapter 28 and 29 for it to occur. After 28 chapters of foreplay, there is an absent, silent moment when intercourse is accomplished, and two final chapters which move swiftly from afterglow to aftermath. The relationship between foreplay and intercourse (both as it affects the reader and as it affects Ana, the mediator, as it were, of the reader's desire that something should ultimately *happen* by the end of the novel) is such as would have placed it on the borderline of Freud's definitions of perversity, at least as outlined in "The Sexual Aberrations," the first of the *Three Essays on Sexuality* (1905b). Here Freud asserts that perversions "are sexual activities which either (a) *extend*, in an an anatomical sense, beyond the regions of the body that are designed for sexual union, or (b) *linger* over the intermediate relations to the sexual object which should normally be traversed rapidly on the path towards the final sexual aim" (italics original) (Freud 1905b: 62).

Definitions of the perverse have come some distance since that statement of Freud's, but the overall tenor of *La Regenta* is notable for an absence of the idea of legitimate pleasure, more consistent with Freud in puritanical mode than with later more liberal views, such as those of Dollimore (1991). Indeed, the attitude to sexuality in the novel, cold, detached, cynical, yet pruriently interested, is a subtle textual display of the material for anticlerical comment, presented itself through the voice of the disapproving clergy, revealing a disturbing level of fascination with sexuality, cloaked imperfectly with a veneer of disapproval. In a novel so preoccupied with the difficulty of establishing or maintaining the boundaries of identity essential to the experience of desire, it is significant that in the narrative itself there is this incomplete separation between the material provoking anticlerical comment, and the voice which speaks so slightingly of it. The attitudes and disparaging formulations of the confessional, are thus both material and mediator in this novel where the impossible priest-lover comes to take precedence over the "de rigueur" local Don Juan. It is for this reason that the novel begins and ends with images of the priesthood, in its most tortured and contorted forms, and it is for this reason that the centrally placed character of the priest Fermín is given far greater weight than either Víctor, the husband, or Álvaro, the official lover, the Don Juan, the *amante de oficio*.

In the latter part of the book I shall look in detail at masculine and feminine strategies in relation to problems of desire, whether hysterical or perverse, whether in the flight into hysterical disorder as a desperate rejection of desire, or in the perverse enactments of Fermín in relation to Ana. All of these strategies can in some degree be related to the desire, indeed the absolute necessity, of taking control in situations which seem simultaneously elusive and threatening. In the aspects of the text considered in that section there is no doubt about the problematic nature of desire, given the extremity of its coding, the hierarchies of control to which it gives form. There is a strong sense of legislation about it, of enforcement (or the evasion of enforcement), with a sense of the connotations of sexuality and power which derive from the confessional, rather than from political vision.

In this chapter, my concern is to examine the linguistic structure given to desire in the novel. Language is never neutral, and will always indicate demarcations social, sexual and hierarchical. Because of the existence of categories, and the hierarchical differentials between categories, no area of the lexicon stands in relation to either subject or object under a guise of neutrality. Hierarchies are made obviously evident within *La Regenta* by official nomenclature, whether social or eccleciastical. This is the lexicon by which the object is named, denominated, and provides a structuring of power within the novel which is easy to apprehend. Much more subtle, however, is the way in which linguistic nuance is used – both in the narrative and in the speech of individual characters – to impose and reinforce structures of power, differences of level, to differentiate between legitimate and illegitimate. The insistence with which desire is framed or articulated in particular ways, whether by characters or the narrative, expresses and indeed intensifies a sense of conflict about desire, a conflict between characters. Claims to own or to possess a legitimate and publicly recognized form of desire show that it is envisaged as the means of conferring legitimacy of identity (particularly of gender-identity) on those denoted as owners of desire. At the same time, the differentiated language of desire equally well expresses conflict or ambivalence within characters, particularly in relation to their struggle with projections, identifications and the process of being appropriated and used in relation to the desire of others.

Some consideration of the gendering of desire in *La Regenta* has been presented in a recent essay by James Mandrell (1990). His central argument contrasts the competition in Ana between the seductive, masculine or patriarchal form of desire in the Don Juan mode on the one hand, with the pull of *jouissance*, a feminine form of desire focalized in the novel around her reading of the works of Santa Teresa. The argument sets the public masculine form of desire against a female inward-turning form, and the former is declared to triumph. I would argue that while it is appropriate to give weight to the ultimate precedence accorded to social acceptance, it is crucial to see it in the context, briefly indicated by Mandrell, of tainting. The tendency to invade and stain, pervasive in the novel, characteristically at that interface of masculine and feminine which is represented by the honor code conflict between masculine honor and feminine shame, and formulated in the mobile images of earth and mud, places in question the possibility of clear conflict between parties. Further, the nature of the desire of any of the characters, whether masculine or feminine, needs to be questioned much more vigorously. That is, the surface text of the "social organization," in which conflict is embodied and played out, needs to be peeled away to reveal the degree to which characters and narrative squabble over the articulation, denomination and possession of desire in a manner which dramatizes and renders problematic central questions of identity and agency.

The generality of the questioning of desire which causes this narrative to divert from the expected adultery plot is conveyed by the fact that the recurring terms relating to desire in the novel center neither around the principals of the official adulterous triangle (Ana, Víctor, Álvaro) nor the *de facto* operative adulterous triangle (Ana, Fermín, Álvaro), in which Víctor acts not as the marital pivot, but rather as the domestic refuge (as glimpsed by Ana in Ch. 25 [II. 326] and shown in the deceptive Indian summer of the Ozores marriage in Chapter 27). Desire exists at the margins, in inappropriate places.

PROHIBITED DESIRE

Not just adulterous desire, but all desire, is presented as prohibited, outlawed. The majority of the words used for desire are weighted with Biblical prohibition: *gula, lascivia, envidia, codicia*. The pejorative associations of the words, threaded in the narrative, also convey the conceptualization of desire in the novel. If the text itself conveys the sense of disgust and disapproval of the confessor's voice when dealing with desire, so the actions of characters reveal their move to conceal their actions and motivations. Hence desire is forbidden, underhand, and, likely to be secretive, displaced, perverted. Visitación pops sweetmeats in her mouth as oral compensation for not re-engaging in flirtation with Álvaro, and Obdulia rubs coquettishly up against Saturnino Bermúdez when he shows some country cousins round the Cathedral. This visit, placed early in Chapter 1, encapsulates social and sexual behaviour in the novel, at the same time as it shows desire that is absent but assumed (the cousins have no desire to see the Cathedral, but their desire is socially assumed for the convenience of Obdulia), while Obdulia's own pleasure comes from titillating Saturnino with her perfume and rustling silk dress. She has no more designs on him than the cousins have interest in the Cathedral, beyond the perverse pleasure of arousing an excitement which she has no intention of satisfying. For Bermúdez, meanwhile, the attentions of Obdulia are substitute for his undeclared love for Ana.

The biblical terms of prohibited desire point to two areas of significance. They denote desire as just that, prohibited by the Church, the acting upon physical desire being forbidden to the celibate priesthood, and discouraged for parishioners, as evidenced in confessors' manuals. Meanwhile, and as though it were the consequence of having had that desire forbidden, at every turn desire is formulated in terms of general disgust so that desire in itself, wherever its expression, receives a baptism of contempt, a downgrading. Prohibitions against the sins and the desires of the flesh are, as indicated earlier, not contained within the confessional, but infect the narrative as a whole.

A survey of the characteristics of desire-related words as defined in María Moliner's *Diccionario del uso del español* reveals a number of particularities. Her definition of *desear* indicates that it is used always in relation to an object, eg: "tender con el pensamiento al logro de la posesión o realización de algo que proporcionaría alegría o pondría fin a un padecimiento o malestar." Words related to *desear* are *ambicionar, anhelar, codiciar, envidiar, antojarse*. Only a single line at the end of the entry refers to the sense in which we might expect to find it in *La Regenta*, and so rarely do, namely "sentir apetito sexual hacia alguien." When we consult Moliner for *ambición*, a curious feature distinguishing it from *desear* is the apparent absence of the faculty of thought, as though what is desired through ambition is desired directly, and not mediated by the mind (running contrary, according to Freud's view of the instincts and the sexual drives, to what one would have expected of the second part of the definition of "desear"). *Ambición*, a term carrying a more highly pejorative colouring than the English *ambition* is, surprisingly, the "deseo *apasionado* de ciertas cosas" (italics mine), the quality of passion being offset, perhaps, by the banality and the materiality of the things desired: "riqueza, poder, honores o fama." Passion enters again in the second definition of "pasión o estado de ánimo del que es ambicioso," borne out by the example given of "dominado por la ambición de poder." Moving through the letter *a* we see that *antojo* is decidedly lightweight (and therefore, in this patriarchally languaged world, suitable for denoting the passing alimentary desires of pregnant women). Not only that, but the *antojo* is associated with a stain left on the infant if the desire is not satisfied. While this is a popular belief that we might recognize from our culture as well as that of Spain, the associations of *antojo* and the recommendation from Fermín to Ana in Chapter 9 that she use *anhelo* instead will be significant. *Anhelo* is a "deseo vehemente de algo, particularmente inmaterial," and the use of it instead of *antojo* thus marks a move away from the material world into the spiritual. Similar to the *antojo/anhelo* tension there is the need on the part of Fermín to separate himself linguistically from the world of his mother in the differentiation between his *ambición* and her *codicia*. The problems of differentiation between Fermín and his mother will be discussed further in Chapters 4 and 6.

Terms related to desire which have a distinctly pejorative impact are those habitually deriving from the condemnatory language of sin, and we thus might simply signal them as being part of the confessorial narrative. But underneath these terms – *lascivia*, *lujuria* and *codicia* – lie some interesting associations. In Moliner, *lascivia* is simply related to an excess of sexual desire, so that *lascivo* is applied "a la persona habitual y exageradamente *dominada* por el deseo sexual y *que lo demuestra en sus palabras, gestos etc* (italics mine)." Although the original definition of *lascivia* is relatively neutral in terminology, the later cross-references are clearly pejorative: *ardiente, deshonesto, desvergonzado, disipado, impúdico, indecente, inmoral, lujurioso, malicioso, obsceno, pecaminoso, provocativo, sensual, verde.* Meanwhile two concepts in the initial definition are central to the text of *La Regenta*: domination, and the relationship between *lascivia* and language. First the idea of domination. In a system where women are habitually referred to as prey, where one of the signs of Víctor's assumed masculinity is his taste for the chase (albeit one in which he is involved in oiling and fiddling with ever more complicated mechanical devices – a code for masturbation?), the issue of whether one dominates or is dominated is central. More interesting is the relation of *lascivia* to language. The word *lascivia* is characteristically used with reference to *lascivia* in a woman, not a man, so that a sense of impropriety in relation to sex and speech is located within the feminine. Thus we have the classification of Doña Camila as "grosera y lasciva" (I. 193, Chapter 4), in relation to the way she speaks of Ana, while Ana's aunts demonstrate verbal *lascivia* (Anuncia with her mouth so watering that she constantly has to spit into a spittoon) in the following chapter (I. 218), and Visitación in turn demonstrates her capacity for *lascivia* in her verbal pornography with Álvaro (I. 330) and with the shop-assistant (I. 355). *Lascivia* used of women but not specifically related to language is found in the classification of the behaviour of Ramona by Álvaro (this time to excite his audience at the Casino [II. 176]), and is used by Víctor to Álvaro of Petra (in a complaint about her "provocaciones lascivas" [II. 429]) – again a use that we can see shaded with desire to pronounce his masculinity against her despicable femininity. A striking exception to the use of *lascivia* to describe woman's desire is that of the priest whose appetite is suddenly awakened by Paula. In this example, the suggestion is of an account filtered through the language of a puritanical confessor, conveying obliquely, through the narrative voice, an attitude of prurient interest and observation: "Y una noche, reparando al cenar que Paula era mal formada, angulosa, sintió una lascivia de salvaje, irresistible, ciega, excitada por aquellos ángulos de carne y hueso, por aquellas caderas desairadas, por aquellas piernas largas, fuertes, que debían de ser como las de un hombre" (I. 500, Chapter 15). A second exception is that of Álvaro in a moment of wishful self-perception in the Casino ("en su rostro correcto los vapores de la gula no imprimían groseras tintas, sino cierta espiritualidad entre melancólica y lasciva; se veía allí al hombre del vicio, pero sacerdote, no víctima" [II. 172]). While in this example "sacerdote" is used by Álvaro to convey to himself his domination and not his passivity in relation to his desires, it is the very term which in the course of the novel is to be linked to the illegitimacy and non-consummation of desire. Significantly, in a mirror-image moment, when Fermín, the man who is indeed priest, wrestles early in Chapter 25 with the conviction that he has been betrayed by Ana, he tries to dissociate himself from this sinful and femininized form of desire, and longs desperately to know that "el amor no era todo lascivia" (II. 316).

Lujuria (used much less frequently in the novel), denotes excess, but also indicates viciousness, since it is "deseo sexual exagerado o vicioso." Again here we might note the emphasis in Spanish which increases the pejorative tone, in that *vicio* denotes an obduracy and determination in wrong-doing, rather than a simple propensity to wrong-doing. Further down the list of the capital sins, *codicia* is again a form of exaggerated desire, this time related (as are *ambición* and *deseo*) to the desire for precise things, objects. *Codicia* is the "deseo exagerado de poseer o de tener mucho, de dinero o de otras cosas." In the novel, we find that *codicia* is used only of women or priests, with the implication that it is a forbidden desire, or rather that it is forbidden for people in these two classes to desire *things*.

The vocabulary of desire in the novel is, then, such that we encounter "good" words and "bad" words, coinciding neatly, or so it would appear, with "masculine" words and "feminine" words. As we can see, a number of these signal words for desire which are redolent of prohibition and censure, are strongly attached to the feminine. It is not casual that the notion of either excessive desire, or the excessive desire of *things* should be thought of as inappropriate for the feminine in a patriarchal society. We are, however, left with two fundamental questions about desire in the novel. Firstly, does this excessive desire that is so much talked about really exist (or is it merely talked about, forming a type of verbal pornography, or one suspects, verbal masturbation)? Secondly, if this desire does exist, is it concealed by a process of habitual dislocation which moves it from a prohibited sphere into a permissible one?

There remain the terms least and most commonly used for desire in the novel: *deseo* and *envidia*. The word *deseo* itself rarely appears. It is used at the moment immediately before the adultery occurs, in relation to Álvaro: "oía la voz del deseo ardiente, brutal" (II: 441) – and one wonders whether, rather than this being the reflection of any direct experience, this might be a slice of *style in-*

directe libre indicating Álvaro's formulation of the experience to himself to fit the phantasies of the Great Lover. That is, the consistently ironising text deflates, along with everything else, the image of Álvaro as the locus of brute physical desire. The word *deseo* reappears, signficantly, in the final two chapters of the novel, linking the three male principals in the surface adultery text, and centering around the desire, or lack of it, for revenge. First Víctor, as ever, is classed for us as the man whose desire is a desire *not to*: faced with the evidence of his wife's infidelity he longs to opt out, and become a part of nature, "Vivos deseos sintió Quintanar por un momento de echar raíces y ramas, y llenarse de musgo como un roble secular" (II. 483). Like his cuckold predecessor, Carrizales in Cervantes' novella, *El celoso extremeño*, Víctor at this point feels grief and weariness. The liveliness of desire in relation to revenge has to be presented to Víctor by Fermín who wants the legal husband to commit the act of vengeance that he has no legal (or other) right to exact. In *style indirecte libre* we learn the advice uttered by the priest's forked tongue, in which he declares he understands and forgives in Víctor desires which in fact Víctor does not entertain, "sus deseos de pronta y terrible venganza," his "deseo de vengarse, hasta para poder vivir entre las gentes con lo que llama el mundo decoro" (II. 503). Here the notion of desire rings hollow, in this final foisting of it on a man who is emotionally unwilling by one who is socially impotent.

Envy, however, the most pervasive indication of a type of desire, is not related in the first instance to issues of gender-association, although it comes to exercise that function in the text. Envy, or *envidia* as Moliner indicates, is founded on the Latin *in-videre*: the baleful, resentful look that we throw at the possessors of what we envy. It is related to the suffering of lack, not to a sense of the appetite of desire. The experience of envy is akin to being an existential, resentful black hole: "Padecimiento de una persona porque otra tiene o consigue, cosas que ella no tiene o no puede conseguir." It is only as a secondary (and we might say, consequent) process that *envidia* comes to mean desire, and it is related to what another person does or has, in that it is a desire to replicate: "deseo de hacer o tener lo mismo que hace o tiene otro." The gender-neutrality (on the surface) of envy, coupled with its gender-specific associations (below the surface) is precisely what renders it the obvious fighting ground of gender and desire in the novel.

The first mention of desire in the form of envy occurs in the context of a conversation of comparison and assertion, in the exchange between Celedonio and Bismarck about power, about who is the best *delantero*, about how either of them compares with anyone else, and about the comments of Don Custodio about Fermín de Pas: everything said is with reference to (and implied deference to?) everything else, the aim being that of defining of self and self-value. At this point the occurrence of *envidia* is in its absolute and theological sense, whereas later in the novel, it will appear as a form of desire, a never-to-be-fulfilled longing.

Envy comes to be all-pervasive, existing between Celedonio, Bismarck and Fermín, between Víctor and Frígilis, between Glocester and Fermín, between Álvaro and Paco Vegallana (I. 278, Chapter 7). Víctor envies Perales, the actor (II. 44), and envy is part of the package of "celos, envidia y rabia" felt by Álvaro in relation to Fermín. It is what Obdulia feels in relation to Ana for her tiger-skin rug (I. 164, Chapter 3) and for her plan to be a Nazarene in the Easter Procession (II. 355, Chapter 26). It can be felt not only across class-boundaries, but within them, as between Petra and Teresina (II. 192, Chapter 21). Ana recalls it as the feeling she perceived in Doña Agueda in the early days of her marriage (I. 376, Chapter 10). In a contorted manner Olvido seeks to be the object of envy for her dress (I. 473, Chapter 12). Envy even exists (in posthumous form) between Doña Camila and Ana's dead mother (I. 189).

All of those examples are of same-gender. Envy across the gender divide is much more rare, and relates notably to the experience of Ana. Thus it denotes the feeling of Ana to Víctor for his freedom to go hunting (II. 88), her feeling of longing for the type of existence of Frígilis as an example (to her naive mind) of uncomplicated love (II. 137). In these cases, it would appear that we have Ana's simple desire to be other than she is (that is, a man not a woman), and for the identifiable advantages that men patently enjoy in the patriarchal society she lives in. She represents, perhaps, that Freudian old chestnut, penis-envy.

La Regenta, however, in its mapping of desire, contains far more striking and complex issues than this. *Envidia* is generally represented in the novel as being unworthy, so that Fermín despises the envy of Celedonio because it comes too close: "la envidia de aquel pobre clérigo le servía para ver, como en un espejo, los propios méritos" (I. 120). For that very reason, that is, because it comes too close, and has to be defended against, envy within this patriarchal novel may also be regarded as feminine. But envy is not only itself regarded as feminine. It can be perceived as relating to being feminine, so that when we encounter examples of envy between men, it suggests either a sense of their lack of possession of masculinity, or that they are involved in a deprived (because feminine) form of desire. Put another way, this articulation of their desire, displaced and resentful, is a sign of their uncertainty relating to gender. And here we might return to comment on the link between *envidia* and baleful looks. The baleful looks of envy, such as commented on by Bond (1984: 31) may become that "male gaze" so prominent now in discussions of gender issues, and which we could now construe not as evidence of possession of power (and knowledge of that possession), but rather a defense against powerlessness.

What, however, is envy, this feeling that seems to be about in the novel, a sign of what characters long for in relation to others? The finding from both theology and psychoanalysis is that envy has little or nothing to do with desire, and everything to do with emptiness, lack, feeling diminished. The theological view is above all that envy is fundamental, a root sin. The book of *Wisdom* 2.24 reminds us that Satan's envy brought death into the world, a conceptualization of envy in relation to the devil reiterated in the characterization of the priest in "El diablo en Semana Santa" (1880), the short story which provided the basis for *La Regenta*. Satanic links with envy and death were articulated in the 4th century AD (Petruccione 1991: 333), and Prudentius, an early Christian, characterizes envious activity as "the corroding, darkening, or soiling of the bright, the pure, the clean" (Petruccione 1991: 334), an interesting characterization given the emphasis on staining and *mancha* in *La Regenta*. Predominantly, theological commentary focuses on envy as the state of lessening of the person who experiences envy (*Dictionary of Moral Theology*). Envy is, in a sense, a reverse form of *schadenfreude* (one's pleasure at the misfortune of another), since, according to Aquinas, "the envious person is saddened not precisely because he feels his exclusive right is violated when another possesses the good he envies, but because he feels lessened and humiliated when another is more favoured than himself" (Aquinas *Summa* 2a 2ae 2 36.1).

If envy is to do with personal diminution, what relation does it bear to desire? Lack experienced becomes desire to cancel that lack, and hence a form of desire. But envy is more complicated, in ways outlined by Melanie Klein, and as already noted in the Introduction. Within Klein's theory, envy belongs to primitive, two-person relationships and is characteristic of those relationships where boundaries between the two people involved are unclear, as a result of which a dynamic of envy is established in which contempt and destructiveness alternate with attempts to offset the feelings of destructiveness with praise. This dynamic, conceived of as that between mother and infant, is one in which the infant, faced by something good which he wants and cannot have, is overcome with "an impetuous insatiable craving, exceeding what the subject needs and what the object is able and willing to give." The feeling of envy derives from the consequent destructive impulses that arise in the infant, and which are projected out. This has the double effect of contributing to the infant's ability to create a good internal object, which would compensate for his lack of the thing he desires, and, because he has projected elements of the self out (the bad feelings), literally feels diminished in relation to the desired object, or the object that contains the desired properties (Klein 1957: 180-81). Thus my desire leads me to discomfort, I project out the feelings of discomfort, and feel yet more diminished in the face of the possessor of the good that I desire.

The state of the envying being is thus linked to lack of defined identity. If boundaries between the self and the external world are unclear, then the nature of the identity itself is similarly ill-defined, as observed by Brennan (1992: 80), and as represented by Dante in the Thieves' Cantos (Ellrich 1984: 62-3). It is significant also that Brennan reports Freud as believing that envy or jealousy were of the characteristics of femininity (the others being passivity, masochism, narcissism or vanity, a weaker sense of justice, less social sense and an inhibition in knowledge) (Brennan 1992: 178). Whether or not we would be persuaded now to agree with Freud on these points, they are arguably those of his society, and arguably those of the society portrayed and reflected in the narrative of *La Regenta*. On another front, we might observe that the approach of Klein to envy is consistent with the concept of desire as one in which desire cannot be experienced without there being a sense of being a subject. Anything less will place one in the no-man's-land of being no more than the used and manipulated object of the Other, and even desire itself is necessarily linked to the notion that one is in a constant state of being either unsatisfied or defrauded (Copjec 1989: 238).

LANGUAGE, GENDER, AND POWER

In the final part of this discussion I would like to highlight how language relating to desire is used in conflicts of power and gender. First, there is the lengthy battle undertaken by Fermín to class his form of desire as masculine and not feminine, and indeed to extricate himself from the relationship with his mother. Secondly, there is the way in which certain characters, most significantly Álvaro and Fermín, "up the stakes" in the use of language, and, by their selection of words with particular resonances in their attempts to establish dominance in a same-gender situation, or in a cross-gender situation. A third and different phenomenon can be observed when the notion of language and desire is at its most powerful, when desire becomes actually unnameable (perhaps because of an essential need in the characters to de-contaminate the notion of desire from gender-attributes). In this last situation when there is finally a precise naming of a situation relating to desire, that naming is utterly simple yet so devastating as to be pivotal in the action.

First the battle of Fermín for the requisite classification of his desire. This takes the form of negotiations within himself as priest for ownership of valid desire. As priest he is denied the outlet of sexual desire, and thus the type of masculine desire he envisages for himself is limited to its non-sexual forms. Given that his vocation of priest (the social, maternal choice of Doña Paula) was imposed not chosen, he perceives ownership of masculine desire as a means of asserting himself as masculine in relation to his mother, and in relation to that maternal institution, the Church. His concern above all is his struggle to detach his masculinity from the staining mud of Doña Paula's femininity (and all the stain of ignoble origin). I shall give one example here from Chapter 1.

The initial situation is one of extreme narrative complexity. The liberal use of the *style indirecte libre* in this key first chapter of the novel renders fluid the motion between action perceived or described, the interior monologue of Fermín, and perceptions or thoughts that could be attributed to Fermín. The first survey of Fermín's desire surfaces in the wake of the display of the perversity and *envidia* of Celedonio, some of the significance of which has been discussed by Rutherford (1988: 58-73). The appearance of Fermín has been preceded by the envious comments of Celedonio about whether or not the former uses make-up. The description that ensues indicates some gender-ambiguity in Fermín, for example, in the colour of his cheeks, which links him to shame, and a susceptibility to language that draws him to passion (signalled as *sangre*) at the same time as it is the sign of the feminine (always linked to shame within the honor-code): "era el rojo que brota en las mejillas al calor de palabras de amor o de vergüenza que se pronuncian cerca de ellas, palabras que parecen imanes que atraen el hierro de la sangre" (I. 102). Entering where he does in the novel, Fermín comes into the narrative against the backcloth of illegitimate or dislocated desire as embodied in Celedonio. He is thus associated, by a pre-figurative shadowing, with Celedonio, the minor clerical character of markedly unclear gender. Celedonio is also presented within the framework of prostitution, which will refer not only to himself, but to the priest-protagonist whose shadow he provides. Celedonio's entry under the sign of prostitution thus signals the public stereotype given to Fermín and his mother and for which in the middle reaches of the novel they come under attack from the Casino-based supporters of Álvaro. The image provides the means of reading both the private and figurative prostitution of son to mother, in which he has been prostitute to her desire, and the public and real (though concealed) prostitution of his mother with the miners in the attainment of her desire for elevation through her son. At this early point in the narrative, Celedonio's gaze of desire to Fermín tells all, most poignantly indicating the sadness that such prostitution entails: "una intención lúbrica y cínica a su mirada, como una meretriz de calleja, que anuncia su triste comercio con los ojos sin que la policía pueda reivindicar los derechos de la moral pública" (I. 100). This background of desire in the narrative gives rise, dynamically, to Fermín's attempts to assert not his prostitution as a fake woman, but his independence and masculine desire as a man of power, the seamlessness of the narrative, as it moves from phenomena perceived to inner thought, being characteristic of the unclear boundaries of the novel as a whole. Thus where we see Fermín next is in his survey of Vetusta. The assumption of the position of the male gaze, the "placer voluptuoso" (I. 104) he experiences on looking at his domain, is a substitute pleasure, and at the same time one signalled as masculine, since Vetusta is his "pasión y su presa" (I. 105). As the text continues to elaborate how Vetusta stimulates him to "gula," he is still in the position of consumer, and therefore masculine. He thinks back over the past, and turns his thoughts to his *ambición* (a form of desire for *things* that would have been an acceptable trade-off, one imagines, for the loss of his freedom as a priest). This, however, is rapidly replaced by *codicia* (a less worthy, and certainly in the context of the novel, a less masculine, or legitimate form of desire). It moves down the scale to a point where his desire is on the animal level more closely related to the animal prey than to the masculine hunter: "era el hambre que no espera, la sed en el desierto que abrasa y se satisface en el charco impuro..." (I. 106). Having reached these depths, Fermín now tries to climb back up the scale to masculine possession of desire. He turns again to think of what he terms his *ambición*, the prey more oblique, in that he dominates the Bishop, he is "el amo del amo" (I. 107). He compares himself to those of the Encimada. What have they done? "Heredar," whereas what he has done is "conquistar." That is, linguistically, and imaginatively, he has worked his way back out of the "charco" to a recognizably masculine position of conqueror. Tellingly, the image that then fills his mind is of the town "que se humillaba a sus plantas" (I. 108), shocking prefiguration of the final image of himself and Ana.

Later in the novel, the tension between his *ambición* and the *codicia* of his mother becomes yet greater, since in this relationship power is less easily held. It surfaces after the first appearance of Doña Paula in the text and the vocabulary of desire underpins Fermín's consistent effort to distinguish himself, and indeed to extricate himself, from the dyad of private and public life in which he exists with his mother. Here it is made yet more explicit than at the start of the novel that *ambición* is to be read as a masculine, and therefore (for Fermín) acceptable desire, whereas *codicia* is a feminine, disempowered and taboo form of desire for that which is not properly ours (and forbidden by the Old Testament to boot), and which is associated with his mother. Thus *ambición* is associated with approvable masculine aims such as *conquistar* or *dominar* (I. 419, I. 423) whereas *codicia* is feminine, the domain of Paula (I. 419). The *ambición* which will lead to domination will of course also eventually lead to Fermín's perverse aim of making Ana his "sierva" or "esclava," terms which indicate her participation in the act of perversion, or, as Masud Khan (1979) would have it, her willingness to act as accomplice.

These examples of Fermín reveal the constant negotiation in his mind about the nature of his desire, set against, but not entirely separate from a shifting, invasive text, so that on the one hand he is perceived as trying to distinguish himself from the associations with his mother, but on the other is shown as trying to emerge from the troubling connotations of the text which surrounds him. The desire to pull free from the ties of surrounding text is manifest further, and arguably more dramatically, when characters themselves take on the task of manipulating and shaping the linguistic context in which they are seen, a task which takes the form of "upping the stakes," as the urge is always to move the register of desire upwards to what is more socially impressive. Two characters are noted for upping the stakes in language. Unsurprisingly they are both men, and both contenders for Ana: Fermín and Álvaro. A brief example of this is the instance mentioned earlier when Ana's use of *antojo* is followed by Fermín's shift to *anhelo*. When Ana speaks to Fermín (I. 341, Chapter 9) of how "en la adolescencia había tenido antojos místicos," her lexical choice of *antojos* downgrades her desire. This echoes the manner in which her concept of mystical desire was downgraded in her adolescence by those about her, the downgrading being a defensive vilification against the threat posed by a mystical, literate, or indeed, sexual woman. At the same time, the use of *antojos* is associated with the banal, feminine "papel" of marriage and childbirth for which her aunts had destined her, and indicates if not the antidote to the dangers of mystical excess of desire, at least society's mode of containing it. Fermín, whose words are quoted directly, wields the transforming wand of a linguistic fairy-godmother, declaring "Hija mía, ni aquellos anhelos de usted..." and thus elevates her urges in a single phrase. Behind this advice we should remain aware of Fermín's lengthy history of trying to detach himself from the stain of feminine shame that his mother marks him with. He is speaking as much to himself as to Ana. He is speaking from a position of assumed linguistic (and hence social) power, and therefore a more highly invested one.

The most notable contribution of Álvaro to the raising of the language of desire occurs in the swapping of sexual exploits in the

Casino. Álvaro has held back, smoking his cigar, a symbol by this point in the novel that is redolent of sexual potency and masculine agency. Finally, as though to bring this occasion of verbal sexual display between the men gathered in the Casino to a type of story-teller's orgasmic climax, Álvaro tells the story of his own exploits, culminating with the three-day struggle with Ramona (remarkably reminiscent of the battles we are told took place with Fermín's mother, Doña Paula). Prime features of Álvaro's characterization come to the fore here. Throughout the novel he is the icon of the material, whereas Fermín is a (self-proclaimed) icon of the spiritual. Álvaro is also, as it were, the Freudian of the novel, or perhaps his biological forbear, in that he projects (at least in what he articulates for others and for himself) a view of desire that is rooted in a concept of drives, or the sexual instincts (Freud 1915). In this novel concerned with performance and not with being, what Álvaro enacts is the role of the reader's unmediated libido-man, associating an active libido with a generally healthy physical state (both brought severely into question as we observe his own physical decline in the course of the novel). Thus we have had earlier his view of the need to restore Ana to health by getting her to eat red, even raw meat – this detail hinting that for him the experience that woman has of sexual passion is necessarily related to her being not just healthy, but in a primitive, uncivilized state.

Álvaro's telling of sexual activity in the Casino (Chapter 20) is relayed as a *tour de force* of seduction (although, significantly, we are not initially given the direct speech that he uses, merely an account of it). The placing of the episode is pivotal, and fulfils two functions. First, it is in a sense a re-play of the type of struggle I have just outlined in the case of Fermín at the start of the novel, since Álvaro's verbal seduction of the other men (seduction based on their *envidia* of him, and using his account of a super-human, super-masculine conquest of a woman) occurs shortly after he has been brought to the realization that his competition with Fermín from Ana is on a physical basis, that on those grounds he is likely to lose to Fermín, and that therefore he must operate through politics rather than through his physical self. The motive of the telling is thus linked to his own uncertainty about gender-strength: we learn that he has become subject to "celos, envidia, rabia" (II. 164), moving along a scale of helplessness in relation to desire, from the acceptably masculine *celos*, through the ambiguous *envidia* to the infantile impotence of *rabia*. In the experience of *celos* he suffers the shame of failing to attain a state of legitimate *celo*, allowed by Aquinas as potentially proper, whereas *envidia* cannot be (Sinclair 1996b). A telling confirmation of this is given in the comment before his main speech: he exposes himself, but it is to have his existence as Don Juan confirmed: "Mesía se dejaba ver por dentro, más que por complacer a sus oyentes, por oírse a sí mismo, por saber que él era *todavía quien era*" (II. 174, emphasis mine). This much on the personal level. But the second function of his telling is that this is the start of his political campaign. That is, the telling of his story of sexual triumph to the others in the Casino is part of his campaign to gather other men around him, in an opposition to Fermín. Yet, ironically, in his telling, Álvaro presents himself as the *priest* of passion. He is "el hombre del vicio, pero sacerdote, no víctima" (II. 172). One could view the whole of the novel perhaps as a type of psychological musical chairs, in which no-one wishes to be left with the role of victim, until Ana first of all conveniently adopts it in Chapter 26, then has it foisted irrevocably upon her by Fermín's rejection of her in Chapter 30. Álvaro appears to flaunt before his audience all the dangerous and traditional associations between love and death. The gazes of his listeners show that the correct effect has been achieved: "Entre la admiración general serpeaba la envidia abrazada a la lujuria: las tenias del alma" (II. 174). In that reference to "tenias," tapeworms, we see how the phallic gaze has become a corrosive turning inwards, so that the *envidia* becomes unsatiated desire: "los ojos brillaban secos." In Álvaro's account of himself and his exploits he actually uses the word "deseos," outlining an omnipotent fantasy in the figuring for the other men of an impossible vision of feminine passion which responds to his mastery and violence. Thus he comments how he approached Angelina, "la llenaba de deseos de él," that her "pasión" (another "good" word being appropriated here) reached the state of "paroxismo," before he, the "favorito de todos" slipped away from the scene. In the subsequent account of the conquest of Ramona, this time in direct speech, he is yet more assertive: "Mi deseo era más poderoso," and this power existed, he says, because he knew that she was enjoying it. The two are portrayed in a primitive, sensual fight beyond all belief (II. 176-7). Significantly the struggle is in a *panera*, a grain-store on legs, remarkably like the place where Paula lost her virginity, and one of those liminal places signalled for us as central to the adultery theme by Labanyi (1986).

The text of *La Regenta* displays, then, the struggle of the principals for linguistic domination as much as they struggle for sexual domination. But ultimately there is the question of whether this is all performance, or rehearsal even, and that when language is placed correctly in relation to desire, the characters find themselves in a situation which is too terrifying to endure. That is, while characters go through the surface motion of demarcating desire along gender lines, ultimately the plot requires them to face the mode of desire prohibited in the text, and which is arguably the only one which is seriously in question in it: not just adulterous desire, but the desire to break celibacy. At the point where this is realized we enter the general reluctance of any of the characters to articulate or recognize desire for themselves, since it is either entirely unattainable, or, even if attainable, absolutely unsanctioned.

DESIRE UNNAMEABLE

Early examples in the novel show that one of the commonest ways in which desire is experienced as unnameable is in its somatization. Thus Bermúdez, for example, somatizes his desire into stomach-ache (I. 126). Ana, after her walk in the country, has her attention caught by poor children staring at the sweetmeats in a shop window, the sexual significance of the "golosina" being already familiar to us from the practices of Visitación. What the children do is to name the desire that they cannot have in a way which is painful to Ana as onlooker (a thumbnail encapsulation of what goes on at large in the novel everytime that desire is given a name but cannot be experienced). The *pillos* "discutían la calidad y el nombre de aquellas golosinas que no eran para ellos, y cuyas excelencias sólo podían apreciar por conjeturas" (I. 353). Ana is moved to tears, and suddenly realises, through this impotent naming, that somehow she and the children are kindred. The sweets "no eran para ellos; esto le parecía la más terrible crueldad de la injusticia. Pero, además, ahora aquellos granujas discutiendo el nombre de lo que no habían de comer, se le antojaban compañeros de desgracia, hermanitos suyos, sin saber por qué" (I. 354). Fermín, in an analogous state of uncertainty, is even more articulate about being unable to put a name to things. In Chapter 14, realizing his state of disarray in thinking about Ana at El Vivero, he meditates: "Era enemigo de dar nombres a las cosas, sobre todo a las difíciles de bautizar. ¿Qué era aquello que a él le pasaba? No tenía nombre. Amor no era; el Magistral no creía en una pasión especial, en un sentimiento puro y noble que se pudiera llamar amor; esto era cosa de novelistas y poetas, y la hipocresía del pecado había recurrido a esa palabra santificante para disfrazar muchas de las mil formas de la lujuria" (I. 527). His use of "bautizar," and "palabra santificante" reveal the way in which, ironically, the legitimating terms of the Church are used by him, so that he clings desperately to the authority of the language of the institution that imprisons him. His next thought shows the urge to somatize, or to interpret within the habitual framework of physical illness: "Lo que él sentía no era lujuria; no le remordía la conciencia. Tenía la convicción de que aquello era nuevo. ¿Estaría malo? ¿Serían los nervios? Somoza le diría de fijo que sí" (I. 527). Later, Ana, in the confessional with Fermín, finds herself unable to articulate what she feels. She is able to say the standard thing – that she does not love her husband in the way that she should. But there is more than this, she feels unfocused, dizzy, there are – "gritos formidables de la naturaleza, que la arrastraban a no sabía qué abismos oscuros, donde no quería caer; sentía tristezas profundas, caprichosas, ternura sin objeto conocido; ansiedades inefables" (II. 19), all of this making her seize the Church as defense (just as Fermín has done in the example previously cited). In response Fermín is not able to ask the question of whether *he* is the object of her desire, simply to think "¿seré yo?" (II. 21).

Essentially the two of them pussy-foot around the recognition of what is involved, until the point at which it becomes evident, and simultaneously impossible. Suddenly the text moves into simple, awful clarity. In Chapter 23, Fermín finds himself in a Freudian slip, relating to Ana how someone else had referred to him, Fermín, as the "rival" in relation to her. The cat is out of the bag, and he realizes how this conveys what he had not said: "yo soy hombre, tú eres mujer, el mundo juzga con la malicia" (II. 289). Ana, however, misses this statement of the truth, continues to offer to grovel as victim. Realization comes in her inner thoughts in Chapter 25 when Fermín, repeating his transferential tantrum habits with his mother, flounces out of the room, having realized that he was a man, she a woman, and that she had betrayed him, "Todo era verdad. Le engañaba; era una mujer" (II. 321), and more than that, she occupies a place in his affections illegitimate in the priesthood: "Es mi mujer, la mujer de mis entrañas." Ana meanwhile is left with the social shock: "¡Aquel señor canónigo estaba enamorado de ella!" (II. 321), a devastating realization. Fermín, in Chapter 27, comes likewise to realize his feelings, and his situation, the first unnameable, but recognized, and the second absolutely recognized. He still places it all under the accepted guise of hatred of his rival Álvaro, however, and realizes his own sense of personal diminishment in relation to "el arrogante mozo a quien aborrecía": "Don Fermín ya no se lo ocultaba a sí mismo. No daba nombre a su pasión, pero reconocía todos sus derechos y estaba muy lejos de sentir remordimientos. 'El era cura, cura, una cosa ridícula, puestas las cosas en el estado a que habían llegado.' Había comprendido que Ana sentía repugnancia ante el canónigo en cuanto el canónigo quería demostrarle que además era hombre" (II. 396). There stands the novel in a nutshell. The impasse of desire is reached, articulated, and all that can ensue is the diversion of the duel (with, as it were, the wrong man), and the speechless final encounter of the two unrecognized principals of the adultery drama, Ana and Fermín.

TWOS AND THREES

CHAPTER 3

TRIANGLES AND IDENTIFICATIONS

Envy, as is evident from the preceding chapter, is the dominant mode of desire in *La Regenta*. It is the illegitimate form of desire, prohibited in the strongest terms by the Church, and yet revealed in the novel to be one of the most characteristic emotions of the clerics of the novel. In addition, it is felt predominantly *between* men, and *between* women.

In developmental terms, envy belongs not only to the dyad, but to the dyad at an impeded moment of development. In the state of envy, splitting and projecting are imperfectly achieved. This has the double result that it becomes impossible to preserve or consolidate good objects in the self, and that there is not the gradual sedimentation of the self through a series of successful identifications and introjections which will lead to a sense of boundaries around the self (Klein 1957). As a result, the establishment of the capacity for relationship is severely impeded, since there is neither a sense of self, nor a sense of where one self ends and another begins. Furthermore, what sense of self exists is dogged by the feeling of being inferior, lessened. The definition of envy, in theological terms, already sets out for us the dramatic parameters of the state Klein describes. It is one of the gravest of the mortal sins, and has a bearing on the diminution of the self: it is about feeling lessened, feeling diminished, as outlined by Aquinas in his *Summa Theologica*: "another's good may be reckoned as being one's own evil, in so far as it conduces to the lessening of one's own good name or excellence. It is in this way that envy grieves for another's good..." Aquinas continues that "Since envy is about another's good name in so far as it diminishes the good name a man desires to have, it follows that a man is envious of those only whom he wishes to rival or surpass in reputation," and comments that envy is thus found between people whose *condition is comparable* (Aquinas 2a 2ae 2 36.1). Envy, thus construed, is passively painful, and encapsulates that absence of agency, that impotence and implosive tendency which in *La Regenta* is the condition characteristic of clerics and women in the novel. It is evaded only mechanically by men, in their acting out of the roles of hunters and gatherers (of sexual objects), collectors of items, each object acquired part of the shoring up of identity against the tides of self-lessness, while women have no strategy of evasion available in this particular social and historical context. Envy is, furthermore, primitive and early in onset. We may evince no surprise on reading that Klein associates it with the child in the throes of early development, and that she traces the feeling of envy to the child's envious relationship to the breast. It is striking, however, to encounter the observation of envy in a small infant in the *Confessions* of St Augustine, quoted by Aquinas: "I myself have seen and known even a baby envious, it could not speak, yet it turned pale and looked bitterly on its foster-brother" (Aquinas 2a 2ae 2 36.3).

To escape from the trials and vicissitudes of envy, an obvious route would appear to be the establishment of possession. This is an emergency strategy, and has no link with the observations of Klein about the way that envy may be abated as a sense of security about the self and the concomitant development of a capacity for gratitude and concern that emerges. In speaking of the adoption of the strategy of possession as the solution to envy, my thought is that this is the mechanical way out of envy that occurs to the envying self. Possession will, in a sense, be apparently all. It will be proof of existence, of agency, and hence of identity. In this this chapter I propose to focus on the struggle for possession, as proof of the existence of the identity of the one who possesses. Furthermore, concern about possession, in the form of *celo*, will be the uncontestable sign that the envying being has moved on a developmental stage to the jealous being, protagonist of the three-person relationship, contrasting with the prisoner of the two-person relationship. I shall argue that the act of possession, or the desire to take possession, is as crucial in the effort to construct boundaries of identity and gender as is the attempt to make such legitimizing delimitations through the use of language which is coded and culturally valued. Underlying this argument is the assumption that the move into a situation of threes rather than remaining in the situation of a dyad is understood and experienced as an advance, a step forward which will free, enable, and open up the path to identity and desire.

OEDIPAL GEOMETRY

The paradox of oedipal theory is that it denies possession (the incestuous, forbidden possession of the mother by the child), in order to open out the possibility of a new, legitimized possession. Furthermore, it postulates an affirmation of boundary through limitation, and this limiting is one which simultaneously curtails desire, in order to free the subject from impossible desire. At the same time, at least by the Lacanian formulation of the theory, it exposes the subject to the experience that desire must forever be unsatisfied, must forever be constituted as a type of lack. The move through the Oedipus complex is thus a confrontation with reality, a coming to terms with the fact that the subject is not alone in the world, but must confront a world in which others relate to others, and not necessarily to him or to herself. This perception, which confirms his state as isolate is the one which also declares him free from the imprisonment of the dyad. Thus, as Caldwell resumes the impact of oedipal theory, it gives us "Freud's fundamental expression of human limitation, the eternal discrepancy between what we want and what we are capable of; a discrepancy which turns the child away from his first sexual love and is reformulated in every act of sex thereafter, and which may be generalized as the conflict bwetween the pleasure principle and the reality principle. The paradox of our existence is that our continual restless search for immediate instinctual gratification is continually resisted by the inhibiting factors of reality; happiness is always, at best, a fragile compromise between these essentially irreconcilable principles" (Caldwell 1974: 213).

Since Freud's initial postulation of oedipal theory in a letter of 1897 to Wilhelm Fliess (Gay 1988: 100; Britton 1985: 34), and further elaboration of it in the *Interpretation of Dreams* (1900: 363-66), much theoretical water has passed under the bridge. At one extreme there is Kleinian oedipal theory which posits the oedipal stage as belonging to an age well before the four or five-years watershed envisaged by Freud (Klein 1928). The Kleinian formulation lays emphasis not on a desire that is predominantly or exclusively sexual, but on the epistemophilic instincts of the infant, and on the progress of the infant towards the depressive position. For her, the move towards the oedipal triangle is something which runs alongside the move towards an increased sense of the self as subject, and of the existence of others as objects. A different emphasis occurs in Lacanian theory which postulates the oedipal experience as one necessarily visited upon the child in the process of patriarchal socialization. Moving on from the Lacanian position, already for some extreme and saddening in its affirmation of a Symbolic that – for woman at least – is a structure which necessarily does not include her, there is the formulation of Brenkman that oedipal theory is "integral to a process of socialization-individuation whose goal is for young men to adapt to the symbolic-institutional configuration made up of male-dominated monogamy, the restricted family, capitalist social relations and patriarchal culture" (Brenkman 1993: 29). According to this model, the father as source of prohibition of desire is also the model for it: "the father's 'No' makes the mother the object of a taboo, but it is also from the father that the son learns what it means to desire her. The father furnishes the voice of the taboo and the scenarios of transgression" (Brenkman 1993: 57). As ever, woman's desire, we may note, is placed on the margins of what cannot be defined, or perhaps there is no wish to define. The response to Freud's famed "What does woman want?" with its evasive "Who knows?" (a phrase that does not foreclose explicitly Freud's interest in the possible answer) is replaced with greater honesty, within the patriarchal formulation of desire, by Lacan's "Who cares?" (Mandrell 1990: 7).

Within the inter-character dynamic of *La Regenta* different aspects of the above formulations come into play. As outlined in the earlier part of this book, the text is one of negotiation around two types of boundary. There is first the boundary between what is the self and what is not the self, or between the self and its possible or impending collapse, disintegration or dissolution into the surrounding environment. Then, in the maneuvers of defense to establish the boundaries of the self, come the preoccupations about the boundaries of gender. These are defensive in two ways: by the definition of gender, as opposed to merely the definition of the self, there is the erection of a bulwark against nothingness. But the definition of gender also promises, through the establishment of difference, the possibility of creation, of reproduction, the issue at the heart of Lacan's hysteric's question (Lacan 1981). Hence, having postulated the power to reproduce, the differential establishment of gender promises a further guarantee of the self: if it is capable of creativity, the capacity to reproduce itself, it *must* be deemed to exist.

The assumption of oedipal theory is – in a sense – that the rest of the world exists. Whether we believe or not that negotiation of the Oedipus complex is central to gender-construction, or operative in our relations with the outside world, or whether we believe oedipal theory a to be yet another erection of the defenses of patriarchal society, it provides a formulation of something more fundamental for us: the fact of having to assimilate emotionally the existence of not just one other, but a plurality of others, in the world we inhabit. In my discussion of triangulation and identification in *La Regenta*, I shall take as a central assumption this fundamental formulation of the Oedipus complex as one which informs us that we do not live as isolates. At the same time, the interplay between characters in the novel is consistently at the level of the surface preoccupations with possession or not of a stable gender-position, with the result that the traditional Freudian reading of the Oedipus complex, with its emphasis on the incest taboo, and on identification with a more powerful parent as the key process in the acquisition of gender identity, comes to the fore.

Some triangles are made (oedipal), some are foisted upon us (variations on the oedipal), some we construct (adulterous), some we are driven to create in order to resolve problems on an ancient dyadic agenda (perverse). The problem with the triangles in *La Regenta* is their number, their complexity, and their unstable geometric integrity. As a result, it is unclear who is relating to whom, with what feeling, and – where there are alternates, or substitutes – whether it is expected that the original or the substitute subject at the corner of a triangle should act. At each of the three levels of triangle outlined above, we encounter multiplicity and confusion. Fathers, mothers, lovers, all have substitutes, figures who are imagined in place. Within the oedipal triangles both fathers and mothers have substitutes and alternates, not to mention the number of sexual partners who adopt the role of, or are accorded the role of phantom not-parents who exercise a shadowy impact as quasi-oedipal figures. Thus, as a type of the oedipal model, extended to five terms by Brenkman, building on Lacan, the real father and mother are accompanied by the imagined or ideal father and mother (Brenkman 1993: 204-22). The oedipal triangles of the novel show a range of family-romance speculations about figures who could serve for identificatory purposes, with the issues of *real* mothers and *real* fathers all too evidently still in the picture.

THE OEDIPAL TRAJECTORY IN *LA REGENTA*

I commented in the Introduction on those critical readings of *La Regenta* that perceive a double motion in the narrative: the plot that draws us into the novelistic world, and the self-reflexive narrative that stands apparently aside to comment upon it. I further suggested that the two in conjunction may form a defense against the dangers of a third motion, which would consist in a falling into dissolution, annihilation, nothingness. At this point, a different way of viewing the structure of the narrative can be essayed, which focuses on a dynamic of twos and threes. Turner, commenting on the detailed summary of chapter sequence and content laid out by Alarcos Llorach draws out the clear geometric lines of the narrative. Whereas we know of the clear double nature of composition of the narrative (the first part, predominantly descriptive narrative, took a considerably longer time to compose than the second, action-packed dénouement), a breakdown of chapters and locations shows a reiteration of the motif of three, and the narrative falls in "strict numerical sequences, structuring parts in multiple, interrelated clusters of three: each volume consists of fifteen chapters, divided into three subsections. Within these subsections the action of the plot turns also repetitively and reductively on the number three – three days, three years, three main characters, three major settings – *catedral, casa, casino*" (Turner 1990: 69-70; Alarcos Llorach 1976).

This persistent, consistent orientation towards the motif of three provides a background structure built upon internal orientations of characters towards the motif and the structure of three. At the same time, and particularly in relation to the major settings – *catedral, casa,* and *casino* – the three-cornered narrative reminds us of those triangles which are visited upon us, in contrast to those whose angles we may choose to occupy.

If we analyze the sequence of thematic emphasis in the novel, we see that it moves from a preoccupation with twos to a perception that a triangular structure is not one of escape, but one of social and personal impasse. The narrative opens with the exposure of clerical envy, characteristic of the two-person relationship, beset with one-up-manship. Then we learn of Ana's feelings of being tempted to adultery (barely admitted) sketching out, even, at this stage, the triangle formed by the fantasy of adulterous desire. Though conceived as a flight from a dead dyad to something that might attend to unmet and scarcely formulated need, the "adultery desire" is a phantasy because so closely bound – in this case – to Ana's experience of flawed and absent parental relations. The narrative then exposes the phantasy nature of this desire by the excursion into Ana's past, at the same time as revealing that the desire of Álvaro is, it is hinted (I. 235), as much bound up with matters of moving among class strata as with any desire orientated to one person in particular. Thus, in relation to Álvaro, Ana is downgraded, at the inception of the novel, to a useful object. There is an uncanny twinning between the two. We are told that he has never approached her, since they are "dos orgullos paralelos," but they are also bound together in a relation of sameness by their socially ambiguous position. Álvaro, patronized at this point by the (presumably socially secure) narrator, who refers to him as "Álvarito," is one who lives in the interstices of society, "entre plebeyos y nobles," while a parallel interstitial position is foisted on Ana by her birth, and by her father who moved precisely between "plebeians and nobles" in his search of a mate. The following section of introductory narrative (Chapters 6 to 8), shows Álvaro's strategy to acquire position and authority, namely by taking on the role of alternate oedipal father to Paco Vegallana (and other Vetustan males), displacing the aristocratic Marqués, father to numberless and nameless illegitimate offspring. The strategy of becoming alternate oedipal father is then shown also to be that of Fermín (Chapter 12), but with the twist that his strategy is to substitute for fathers of weak, uncertain masculinity, and the offspring in relation to whom he is father are sickly, aristocratic girls. In both cases, however, the urge to become involved in the "parentesco" of the aristocracy is a strategy of social placing, which has underlying sub-strategies of gender-identification and/or differentiation. Chapters 14 and 15 then unpick the integrity of Fermín's desire, shown with images of his *vergüenza*, uncertain masculinity, contrasting with the phallic image of his mother, the background of the miners, and the sexual ambiguities of his upbringing. From Chapter 16 onward, adulterous triangles are set up in earnest, weaving in and out with one another, with the emerging clusters of jealousy (glimpsed briefly by Ana in Chapter 9 as the gaze of *celucos*, and qualified by her as "una belleza infernal, sin duda, la de aquellos ojos, ¡pero qué fuerte, qué humana!" [I. 353]), and thoughts of revenge desired and perceived as required. The establishment of the adultery triangles (with the running subtext of a variety of perverse triangles of desire, or triangles of perverse desire) is thus posited as the response to the uncertainties of desire, both masculine and feminine, and hence the certainty of the motivation of desire within the characters involved in the adultery triangles is placed in question.

The trajectory thus runs from the dyad to the triangle, from envy to jealousy, from non-possession (in envy) to the loss of possession (in jealousy). But since the final two principals of the drama, Fermín and Ana, have no social permission to make the move from envy to jealousy (neither can be permitted to possess, and hence to lose the other), the final motion of the novel is read as a strategy undertaken by Ana and Fermín, from which the adulterous triangles involving Víctor and Álvaro are a diversion, resulting in a reiteration of the impasse of the original dyad.

TRIANGLES: THE SPACE FOR CHOICE?

The fullest exposition of oedipal forbears is produced for the two characters readily identified as principals in the novel, Ana and Fermín. Ana is brought to Fermín by Visitación, the ubiquitous Celestina, in a desired *cita* for confession which forms the incident of note in Chapter 1, and it is to the relationship of Ana with Fermín that the narrative will unfailingly revert, only periodically displaced by the "official" adultery narrative with Álvaro. In the following discussion, I shall therefore comment on these three occupants of the points of the central effective triangle of the novel, Ana, Álvaro and Fermín. In each case I shall begin with the obligatory triangles, and then move to those of choice, a choice which at times may be construed as a strategy.

ANA

There are deficiencies in Ana's natural oedipal triangles, and in the substitutes for them. In the first, there is the social shame attached to her natural mother (a shame which, in Hispanic honor tradition, will taint the line indelibly – [Caro Baroja 1965]), and in the later ones the substitutes are hardly promising in terms of the development of her desire, with the possibilities of her sexually repressed aunts (their desire converted into their desire to fatten her up for the sexual market), and Doña Camila, "grosera y lasciva, anafrodita," uttering "Improper!" and behaving "improperly" throughout. At no point is Ana's father sufficiently present to give her an inkling of desire, and his preferred company is that of other "liberal" men. Eventually his place in the oedipal triangle is to be taken by Víctor, Ana's husband, whose envy of masculine desire in the form of Álvaro produces a variation on the Girardian triangles of desire.

The timing of the triangles is significant. Ana has a natural mother, who dies at birth, and a father who is absent for crucial periods of her upbringing: it is on his death that she reaches puberty. This significant timing presents an early suggestion that Ana is son rather than daughter (since she "replaces" him on his death) or that the parent/child relationship is one in which it is paradoxically the *absence* rather than the *presence* of a father which accompanies the final confirmation of sexual identity of the offspring. In the social re-writing of Ana's family, the mother comes and goes, and changes profession, through the gossip of others, from the slightly suspect *modista* (I. 185, 190), to the less reputable *bailarina* (I. 190, 232, 244), to "una perdida, corriente" (Marquesa de Vegallana, I. 215). Social shame is attached to her natural mother, a social shame which is not one of blood, but of profession, and, it is implied, the shame of a profession to which women are driven through some sort of initial moral lowliness or defect. Her mother is clearly constructed and reconstructed from the initial gossips' perception that she is the father's "bit of skirt," the "bit on the side."

It is clear from the narrative that the re-writing of Ana's mother is an invested re-writing of a society which at a number of levels has social anxieties and preoccupations. First the narrator gives us what we might regard as a framed, literary account: "Loco de amor se casó don Carlos Ozores a los treinta y cinco años con una humilde modista italiana que vivía en medio de seducciones sin cuento, honrada y pobre" (I. 185). Ana's mother is thus presented within the set frame of a popular love-story, of exaggerated (and therefore improbable) virtue, in the midst of a dramatically unspecified set of dangers: the "seducciones sin cuento" suggest seductions of others around her, but do not exclude the possibility that she also has come under siege from seducers. In a sense, what the masculine narrator is doing is to formulate the introduction of the mother in a way that is flattering, gratifying to Ana's father – she becomes the impossible repository of virtue, as in a fairy-tale, and by the association of his choice, he is redeemed as an ideal figure. The narrator also rehearses for us here the "idealized" version of Ana's natural family that would be characteristic of Freud's family romances (1909), and which at the age she might have such romances is made impossible by force of circumstance. Two factors differentiate Ana's story, or the story of Ana's mother, from the fantasies of family romance. Unlike the child protagonist of Freud's account, Ana does not present the reader with visions of a "real" mother superior in class and ability to her natural one, although her reiterations to herself of the ideal nature of the mother she has lost have some resonance with that idea. Secondly, while Freud comments that the child "comes to know the difference in the parts played by fathers and mothers in their sexual relations, and realizes that '*pater semper incertus est*,' while the mother is '*certissima*' " (Freud 1909: 223), what happens to Ana is that her mother's reputation is changed as it is passed from mouth to mouth, whereas her father's reputation is not made to undergo such public devaluation.

There is no uninvested speech in *La Regenta*, and this applies particularly to public utterance which may shape the public selves of others. The first substitute mother for Ana is the *aya*, Camila, of noble birth, but apparently reduced means (since she needs to work as a governess), and prime agent in the transformation of the image of Ana's mother. Since, Camila reasons, don Carlos has been prepared to marry below him ("que era un hombre que se casaba con la servidumbre," [I. 189]), she should be able to "seduce" him. Essentially she takes the same attitude towards him as does doña Paula for the first priest she works for, but with singularly less success. Dominated by "un culto de envidia póstuma a la modista italiana," Camila sets about destroying Ana's reputation by casting aspersions on that of her mother, linking the "uncertain" social origin of the mother to potential excesses of sexual appetite in the daughter. This is well before the Germán episode, and the aspersions cast upon the sexual proclivities of Ana are made when she is of the classically oedipal age of four: "El aya afirmaba en todas partes, entre interjecciones aspiradas, que la educación de aquella señorita de cuatro años exigía cuidados especiales. Con alusiones maliciosas, vagas y envueltas en misterios a la condición social de la italiana, daba a entender que la ciencia de educar no esperaba nada bueno de aquel retoño de meridionales concupiscencias" (I. 189-90).

Ana's tender years, and the term "concupiscencias," alert us once again to the degree to which the narrative, whether the point of provenance is the narrator, or some other character, carries the disapproving yet salaciously interested tones of the confessional. The shorthand form of Camila's destruction of the character of Ana's mother is to indicate her profession, while her lowered voice, as with the "alusiones maliciosas, vagas y envueltas en misterios," conveys as much as does the hint that "tal vez antes que modista había sido bailarina" (I. 190). Camila, her envy and thwarted desires for social advancement as the source of her verbal portraits of the *modista/bailarina*, goes on to be the cause of the further disintegration of Ana's mother's public persona. She is the source of the aunts' suspicions about Ana's sexual precocity, given the letter, whose contents are not divulged in the narrative, that she sends to them after the Germán episode (I. 194). Still this information is coded in terms of the mother's profession, and brought to mind by the aunts after the "scandal" of the discovery of Ana's writing of poetry to the Virgin: "Por allí asomaba la oreja de la modista italiana que, en efecto, debía de haber sido bailarina, como insinuaba doña Camila en su célebre carta" (I. 232). The force of the *bailarina* reference, considered in the context of the whole novel (running parallel to historical context, in which it is a profession little removed from the oldest one of prostitution), is that it highlights the public spectable of legs, an object of specific and recurrent curiosity and fixation throughout the novel. Dancing is equated with showing the legs, and the multiple references to *bajos*, and the masculine gaze directed to feminine *bajos* (plus, in the case of Ana, the gaze that dare not fix itself on the legs of Álvaro, merely on his extremities), so that the verb *bailar* comes to have the same force as *prostituirse*, as in the angry thoughts of the aunts about the "ungratefulness" of Ana in refusing don Frutos: "No le faltaría a la hija de la bailarina – ¿quién dudaba ya que la modista había bailado? – no le faltaría una cama en el palacio de sus mayores; pero ellas, las tías, no tenían qué poner a la mesa; todo lo había comido la niña" (I. 244). In these thoughts of envious recrimination, of desire disowned and unappeased, we note, as in the subtext about sexuality and control surrounding Ana's relationship to food, the aunts' unconscious adoption of the same idiom: Ana has eaten too freely, or is in a position to do so, at the table of sexuality, provisioned by the aunts, at the cost of their own denial. That she has done so and has thus served as their vicarious agent of desire, is the additional cause of their envious rage, since she has turned her back on the consummation of that sensual and sexual preparation in which they had had so much investment. All of this feeds into their re-creation and demotion of her mother, or rather their ready adoption of what Camila conveys about the mother – none of which is based, of course, on any knowledge. Further fuel is added to their adoption of this pejorative image by the degree to which their attitudes contain denial of the sexual – whether in masculine or feminine form. In the horrified discussions that result on the finding of Ana's poetry to the Virgin, horror is felt at what is viewed as a breach of class that is simultaneous with an aberrant sexuality. Because what she has done – to write creatively – is construed as masculine (on her bedside table the "phallic" pen that will dip into the "feminine" inkwell being the visible evidence of her aberration) their horror stems from the belief that what they witness is a perversion as shocking for its crossing of class barriers as for its adoption of an illegitimate form of sexuality: "Aquello era una cosa hombruna, un vicio de hombres vulgares, plebeyos. Si hubiera fumado, no hubiera sido mayor la estupefacción de aquellas solteronas" (I. 232). The shock expressed in the image of a woman smoking will inevitably come to the reader's mind on the appearance of doña Paula, with her habit of smoking (I. 414), and her indubitably emancipated and calculating history of the manipulation of the sexual weakness of others. The attitude of the aunts to Ana and her sexuality is as complex as is their attitude to her as a figure of uncertain social placing, and in their engagement with the gossip about her antecedents, and presumed resultant sexual career, they are enveloped in a movement of projective identification. This relationship, as outlined originally by Klein (1946: 6-12; 1952: 68-9), is what occurs when the self projects into another an aspect which is felt to be intolerable, and yet retains a lively interest in it, indeed an identification with it, when placed within the boundaries of the self of another.

In the final account of Ana's parentage on the maternal side, in one sense Freud's comments about the mother being *certissima* ring true. The story of the social questionability of the mother is repeated so often that it becomes gospel. What is certain is that the mother, as antecedent, is dubious, and what is of most import is the "impurity of lineage" that her marriage to don Carlos constitutes. Thus Glocester reiterates in Chapter 5 the Vetustan judgment that the marriage was an "abdicación abominable," and further qualifies it as "una alianza nefasta en que la sangre, a todas luces azul, de los Ozores, se mezcló en mal hora con sangre plebeya; y lo que es lo peor... según todos sabemos, representa esa niña la poco meticulosa moralidad de su madre, de su infausta...," a slandering verbiage which is cut through by the Marquesa de Vegallana's clear, dismissive, but untroubled separation between the reputation of the mother, and the evidence of the daughter: "sí señor, su madre era una perdida, corriente; pero la chica se presenta bien, según dicen sus tías; es muy dócil y muy callada" (I. 215).

It will be noticed that Ana's first substitute mother, Camila, is instrumental in the production of a flawed social identity of her natural mother, motivated explicitly in the first place by envy of this parallel lowly creature who nonetheless has managed to marry into the nobility. But Camila is aided and abetted, as it were, by the narrator. The first moment of intimacy in which Ana appears in the text of the novel is in her preparation for the "confesión general" which Fermín has suggested would be appropriate in the inauguration of their new confessional relationship. There is no need for the hints Camila or the aunts will later drop about Ana's sensual potential given the portrait that moves through hint and innuendo to suggest her abandon not only of garments but of all restraint about sensual contact. After the initial indication that she is not, at this stage, completely naked ("Después de abandonar todas las prendas que no habían de acompañarla en el lecho"), the narrative hints heavily that indeed she is: "Jamás el Arcipreste, ni confesor alguno, había prohibido a la Regenta esta voluptuosidad de distender a sus solas los entumecidos miembros y sentir el *contacto del aire fresco por todo el cuerpo* a la hora de acostarse" (emphasis mine). Should this be insufficient, we are then told that "La deleitaba aquel placer del tacto que corría desde la cintura a las sienes" (I. 165). Moreover, we might bear in mind Padre Claret's advice on how to avoid *impureza*, which begins with comments on abstinence in food and drink, and ends with "Si durmiendo se toca, se pondrá una camisola de mangas cerradas y atadas al cuello que no... [sic]" (Claret 1862: 84). Thus, whatever society will say about Ana's forbears, and their or her morality, the implied masculine voyeur-reader is already informed that she has the capacity for pleasure and the implied negation of mind of woman as object of the gaze, conveniently relieved of her instincts of modesty, in that she seems "una impúdica modelo olvidada de sí misma en una postura académica impuesta por el artista," the woman who will be the object of pornography (Charnon-Deutsch 1989a).

Ana's luxuriating on the soft sheets of her solitary bed is a childhood substitute for maternal softness and comfort, adopted in desperation, given her treatment by Camila, all the reverse of those expected maternal qualities: "Una mujer seca, delgada, fría, ceremoniosa" (I. 165). Deprived of her natural mother, Ana falls into a perverse oedipal triangle, consisting of Camila and a character initially referred to as simply the "hombre que le daba besos" (I. 171). Carlos has been substituted for by a man who now becomes not a paternal figure of the prohibition of incest, but the future abusive masculine figure of what becomes an infernal triangle. From the first mention, Camila and "el hombre que la daba besos" are a couple experienced as separate from Ana, yet a couple to whose sexual activity she is obligatory and involuntary witness. As a primal sexual scene, their relationship is shadowed by veils of prohibition, secrecy, and yet an openness that leads Camila to urge restraint on the man "Delante de ella no, que es muy maliciosa" (I. 169). Camila blames "el hombre" for the supposed sexual aberration of Ana with Germán in the boat, declaring that he has enlightened her sexually with his "imprudencias" after which Ana becomes the object of his expectant gaze. His role is that of an abuser-to-be, one who has already coloured her perception of sexual life: "Desde aquel día el hombre la miraba con llamaradas en los ojos, y sonreía, y en cuanto salía de la habitación del aya le pedía besos a ella, pero nunca quiso dárselos" (I. 172-3). Thus the narrative of what will be the investigation of Ana's supposed misdemeanors by a priest is overshadowed by knowledge she has been made privy to, but that she can understand no more than she can understand the priest's questions after her night in the boat with Germán. The presumed intensity of this can be construed from Claret's admonitions to parents in his *Llave de oro* when commenting on their duties. Under the discussion of "Honor thy father and thy mother," children are presented as easily given to sin, and Claret recommends that they be not allowed to sleep with one another (Claret 1862: 46). He further comments (139) on the greater propensity of girls to sin, especially that of masturbation.

All of this information about the perverse parental triangle that succeeds the natural one for Ana is relayed before the recounting of the marriage of don Carlos to his *modista*. Ana has become an object of interest in the text, of pornographic seductive qualities, and has also appeared as the innocent, but not totally unsullied victim of the adult relationships and insinuations about her. It is insinuated, briefly, that Carlos is the subject of *lujuria*, in a reference to his indulgence in the "delicias de Capua." This is one of the many instances where a brief allusion by Alas carries a whole weight of meaning. Capua, by the account given in Livy, in his history of the war with Hannibal, was a city of wealth, where life had always been luxurious. Livy describes how social instability (especially within the ruling classes) meant that "all control went to the winds, no extravagance spared, no sensual pleasure unindulged" (Livy Bk 23.4). Carlos is thus, by a brief allusion, tarred with the same brush of moral and sensual laxity as the Vegallanas. Notwithstanding, the text is relatively uncensorious of him, and strategically the narrative moves away. Any disrepute that could arise from this reference to Carlos has already been offset by the preceding seductive portrayal of his daughter when adult, and the determined re-construction of the sexual and moral character of his unfortunate wife. Should any doubts remain about the intended freedom from sexual culpability of Ana's father, there is the detailed description of the *lujuria* of Camila, the *aya* who will take over the safe-guarding, supposedly, of Ana's development. Camila above all represents the horrors of compromise, a compromise that will be repeated in the extraordinary doctrine of "ten con ten" which is advanced by Ana's aunts in Chapter 5 (I. 228). Her hypocrisy *is* her ambiguous sexuality, constructing her to fall somewhere between the *beata* and the unbeliever, and finding its sexual form in what we must construe as autoeroticism (the vice, for confessors, most likely for the female sex to be prone to): "La hipocresía de doña Camila llegaba hasta el punto de tenerla en el temperamento, pues siendo su aspecto el de una estatua anafrodita, el de un ser sin sexo, su pasión principal era la lujuria, satisfecha a la inglesa: una lujuria que pudiera llamarse metodista si no fuera una profanación" (I. 188). Claret's suspicions about the depravity of the female sex are confirmed.

We might note in passing the ambiguous import of the term "estatua anafrodita," given that *anafrodita* is used either for those who have no sexual appetite, or for those who abstain from sexual pleasure (María Moliner). The use of the term, therefore, in relation to characters becomes complex and suggestive. Ripamilán, for example, is characterized as having "instintos anafrodítocos," but these are "awakened" by the smell of Obdulia's perfume that he notes in the Cathedral air. While the narrator comments on his "pasión desinteresada por la mujer, diríase mejor, por la señora" (I. 143) (a remark that reiterates the concern for class-status which so pervasively overides sexual desire in the novel), the notion of disinterest coupled with the preceding evidence of Ripamilán sniffing for the presence of woman produces a gap of credibility. This sense of gap will be reinforced by other examples where "sniffing" is clearly linked to scandals relating to honor and class being "sensed" out by those who are all too aware of the vulnerability of others through their sexual apetites. Thus Paula's examination of Fermín's room, and of Teresina's person, in which "parecía olfatear con los ojos" and in which she subjects Teresina to a body-search of the gaze which knows no barriers: "le preguntó cualquier cosa, haciendo en su rostro excavaciones con la mirada, como quien anda a minas; se metió por los pliegues del traje, correcto, como el orden de las sillas, de los libros, de todo" (I. 424). The same association between "sniffing," and discovering dishonor through sexual misdemeanour is made with the equally suspect Petra, who, on suspecting the coming infidelity of Ana, takes pleasure in the possible power that may lie in her role – "con una delicia morbosa, la rubia lúbrica olfateaba la deshonra de aquel hogar" (I. 387) – a dishonor in which her *lubricia* will have its place. And while the girls of the catechism class in Chapter 21 *may* rightly be referred to as "anafroditas" (though their budding bodies, showing their move to sexual maturation, are not without impact on the narrator's eye at least), there is, through the novel, other contexts in which the word *anafrodita* occur remove it from innocence. Thus Fermín's thoughts about the "purity" of his relations with Ana in Chapter 11, characterized as "amor anafrodítico, incapaz de mancharse con el lodo de la carne ni en sueños" (I. 409) will be detached only with difficulty from an effect of self-deception, while Fermín's raging and impotent jealousy in Chapter 29 will carry a note of credibility in his perception of his "ludibrio de hombre disfrazado de anafrodita" (II. 464).

Camila, then, is the compromise that avows purity (or at least decorum) of action, but that carries an underskin of contorted or perverted sexual desire. As substitute mother for Ana, she brings with her a substitute father in the person of Iriarte, "el hombre" who so haunts the waking and sleeping hours of Ana. Iriarte's impact on Ana will be that of disquiet, the unease produced by the man who waits for a sexual opportunity. But he also represents that capacity for plotting signally present in the social underclass, waiting for its opportunity to take advantage of the social stratum above. It is Iriarte who recommends Camila to Carlos as a governess, Iriarte who then sells his country house to Carlos, and Iriarte who then takes up occupation of the same house with Camila (I. 188-9).

Camila and Iriarte join in projecting what will be the tarnished public image of Ana's sexual purity. This they do with enthusiasm after the Germán episode, creating for themselves by this the impure child they need, rejecting the innocent child who will be of no use or interest to them. Camila labels Ana as "*Improper*" (I. 193), and her version of the nature of her impossible task in bringing up such a child is seamlessly merged with the narrator's account, so that her possible images and self-presentation become part of the narrative proper:

> – ¡Como su madre! – decía a las personas de confianza.
> – *¡Improper! ¡improper!* ¡Si ya lo decía yo! El instinto... la sangre... No basta la educación contra la naturaleza.
>
> Desde entonces educó a la niña sin esperanzas de salvarla; como si cultivara una flor podrida ya por la mordedura de un gusano. No esperaba nada, pero cumplía su deber. (I. 193)

Meanwhile, Iriarte comments on her presumed sexual precocity with pleasurable anticipation: "Lo que es desarrollada lo está y mucho para su edad... decía el hombre de doña Camila, que saboreaba por adelantado la lujuria de lo porvenir" (I. 193).

Yet more troubling than the construction by her stand-in parents of Ana's precocious or aberrant sexuality is the ambiguous and shifting stance of the narrator. In the first telling of the Germán episode, Germán himself takes the initiative, proposing the adventure in the boat. This is, of course, the incident as remembered, indeed, as re-created by Ana in her preparation for the "confesión general." Later, the account of her writing of epic contains a level of detail that suggests – conceivably – some sense of sexual awareness and possible arousal, in the detailing of the "ejércitos de bravos marineros de Loreto, de pierna desnuda, musculosa y velluda, de gorro catalán, de rostro curtido, triste y bondadoso, barba espesa y rizada y ojos negros" (I. 191-2). As with the contamination of "anafrodita" from its strict meanings by particular use elsewhere in the text, the references to the sailors' legs here will scarcely be without impact and sexual suggestion. In this account of Ana's imaginative exploits it is clearly she who is the instigator in the episode with the boat, repeating once again an initiative in the games with Germán (I. 192). Coming later in the text than the account of the construction of her by Camila and Iriarte as a precocious perverse being, yet previous in time, this framing shows how that perverse construction now becomes part of the narrator's view of his "improper" heroine.

The effect upon Ana of her confused and confusing upbringing is one of castration. The Germán episode, even when forgotten by Vetusta, remains with her, tainting her former innocence, so that she loses all desire, or, defensively, has to repress it: "Cuando ya nadie pensaba en tal cosa, pensaba ella todavía y confundiendo actos inocentes con verdaderas culpas, de todo iba desconfiando." She submits to what amounts to the prohibition of her impulses:

> Creyó en una gran injusticia que era la ley del mundo, porque Dios quería, tuvo miedo de lo que los hombres opinaban de todas las acciones, y contradiciendo poderosos instintos de su naturaleza, vivió en perpetua escuela de disimulo, contuvo los impulsos de espontánea alegría; y ella, antes altiva, capaz de oponerse al mundo entero, se declaró vencida, siguió la conducta moral que se le impuso, sin discutirla, ciegamente, sin fe en ella, pero sin hacer traición nunca. (I. 195)

In the wake of this enforced sexual enlightenment of Ana, there is more than a little irony in her father's education of her which avoids "sólo aquello que el rubor más elemental manda que se tape" (I. 197). Despite the knowledge which she perforce has, and which has been foisted upon her, she retreats from sexual knowledge, and "cuanto hablaba de relaciones entre hombres y mujeres, si de ellas nacía algún placer, por ideal que fuese" she treats with distrust (I. 199). At the same time she is also subjected to a separation from men, in the guise of an inflammable material that has to be kept from the flame. She retreats to a world of men, somehow deemed sexless, the world of her father, where she is given an "educación neutra" (I. 200). Her father's friends are presented as asexual, constituting an oddity themselves in that they have rarely spoken with women. Tellingly, a reference to these asexual companions hints much about the sexual defensiveness of other male characters in the novel: "Eran de esos hombres que casi nunca han hablado con mujeres. Esta especie de varones, aunque parece rara, abunda más de lo que pudiera creerse. El hombre que no habla con mujeres se suele conocer en que habla mucho de la mujer en general" (I. 201). One is minded of the heated, competitive exchange of stories about women and sexual conquest that takes place among the denizens of the Casino (as in Chapter 20).

On Carlos's decision to live all year round in Loreto, an alternative – and apparently preferable – oedipal triangle is formed for Ana: her father is restored to it, indeed her father comes to break into the perverse triangle of Ana, Camila and Iriarte. Ana adopts St Augustine as mother (I. 204), an interesting link since it is from Augustine she learns that all children are born sinful, with "perversión innata," an impression she may well also have learned from the comments of others about her natural mother. Later the Virgin comes to supplant Augustine as a maternal figure (I. 207), but troublingly, rather than completing a positive oedipal triangle for Ana, she appears to represent, by the close of Chapter 4, the option of merging with a maternal presence, rather than the resolution of identity and the stimulus of desire.

What happens in terms of Ana's oedipal geometry is, then, catastrophic. She is deprived of a mother, who is transformed and denigrated in the mouths of others, in particular by the speech of those who, like Camila and the aunts, have been obliged to renounce at least the public satisfaction of their sexuality. Then she is imprisoned in a solitary condition by the very person, her father, who theoretically would act as a third term to break an initial dyad, and who would represent the possibilities of desire. She is then consigned *by him* to a place in the triangle where her own sexuality will be unable to be formed, since she is placed under the care of a "ser sin sexo." The emergence into a further oedipal triangle is one into imaginary relationships, or indeed, in the case of the Virgin, relationships that may be of the Imaginary, or even of the Real. This last triangle brings no boundaries and makes no contribution to settling the limits of identity and the possession of desire.

Carlos's death, narrated at the opening of Chapter 5, coincides with Ana's confused coming to sexual maturity. She is precipitated, however, into a boundless state in which the grief is not at the loss of an object, but at the more total sense of "su abandono, que la aterraba" (I. 212). The implication is, perhaps, that she has not yet been in a state where possession of an object, or relationship to one, has been a reality, and thus loss cannot imply self. There is no gap in the narrative, other than a chapter-break, between her sense of merging with the Virgin (an experience with all the connotations of a desire to return to the refuge of a maternal membrane) and the trenchant, social *cut* formed by the opening of Chapter 5, a point at which the death of Ana's father *has already occurred*.

This handling of narrative sequence heralds Ana's role as an inconvenient object, a left-over of family business who will have to be picked up, dealt with, cared for. It is small wonder that at the dissolution of the final, fragile oedipal triangle that she had constructed (a false one, given her move towards merging with the Virgin), she has no sense of self. In a general sense there is some credibility in this in that, unlike the model of the masculine subject who comes through the oedipal crisis, no such emergence takes place, nor is there a sense of agency as a result. In addition to the more characteristic, even consistently confused feminine passage through that crisis (Olivier 1989) there is an identity given her by external circumstance. What is thrust upon her, in the role of inconvenient object, is the identity of impediment. Unfortunately, she is then appropriated as the agent of desire of those who care for her.

The tutelage of Ana by her aunts is of a complication to rival the perverse domestic situation of Camila and Iriarte. As in the latter situation, much emotion surrounds her "origins," the mother no-one will let her forget (in terms of social and moral culpability, an inheritance of explosive instability), but that no-one thinks to replace in terms of affection (with the exception perhaps of Frígilis).

Her mother is officially replaced by the aunts in the eyes of Vetustan society, but this paradoxically only serves to reinforce awareness of the gossip surrounding her mother. Two systems work at odds with one another, confusing in the extreme for Ana who is at the center of each. On the one hand, there is the relentless apprehension (with an admixture of interested excitement and relish) that Ana may, as it were, revert to her true stock. On the other, there is the conviction of the aunts that Ana's only future is in social establishment by marriage. Here there is yet another *bifurcación*. For if they believe that Ana's future is to marry well, or rather that it must necessarily be to marry well, if she is to cease to be a burden to them, then they also patently believe that what they have on offer is "damaged goods." As a result, their philosophy of "ten con ten," by which fondling and fumbling are permitted when not in clear public view, is partly a philosophy based on what is generally done in Vetustan society. But they are dealing with a particularly risky form of merchandise.

In this Ana's aunts are not, of course, in the minority. In Vetusta, most goods may be presumed to be damaged, as will be hinted three chapters later by the Marquesa de Vegallana when musing on the decency or otherwise of what takes place in her house: "'Buenas son mis nenas; si alguno se propasa, las conozco, me avisarán con una bofetada sonora... y lo demás... niñerías; mientras no avisan, niñerías.' En efecto, sus hijas se habían casado y nadie se las había devuelto quejándose de lesión enormísima. Si había habido algo, serían niñerías" (I. 310). The Marquesa's following thought is a troubling one for the reader inclined to believe that "nothing happens." It would appear that plenty does, and the talk of death, and the Marquesa's willingness to act swiftly and decisively, suggests that either abortion or birth may lie behind untoward outcomes: "Y la otra había muerto porque Dios había querido. Una tisis, la enfermedad de moda. Cuando se había tratado de sus hijas, al notar algún síntoma de peligro, siempre había puesto con franqueza y maestría el oportuno remedio, sin escándalo, pero sin rodeos" (I. 310-11). Damaged goods are likewise passed off by Paula to Zapico when she gives him as a bride a maid who formerly served Fermín, yet in terms of knowledge Zapico retains the upper hand: "es claro que jamás dijo a doña Paula el secreto de aquella noche en que hubo sorpresas muy diferentes de las que suponía la señora" (I. 563). The narrator remains one up on Paula, hinting that while she was aware of the goods being damaged, they were nonetheless of a nature she did not imagine – the dealings of her son with the maids is thus a secret almost unveiled to the reader, and yet – it is implied – one which is not fully known to Fermín's mother. Thus are the tables turned in the matter of suppositions about sexual innocence.

Ana, however, is more than a burden to be married off. She serves as a vehicle for the revival of pleasures and longings now renounced. The text of the campaign to make Ana plump and attractive to suitors thus carries with it a subtext of a troubling existence of the aunts' repressed, deferred but not renounced *lascivia*.

Age here, as throughout *La Regenta*, is of prime importance, and calls to mind that other feature of the Oedipus complex, namely that while the initial version tells of the prohibition by the father of the son's sexual longings, there is a further element in that at some point the son will come of age, will supersede the father. Thus, accompanying the general backcloth of anxiety about the dissolution and crumbling of the world of the flesh through age, central characters are portrayed as being either at the cusp of their powers, or already on the slope downwards. There is a twin urgency in the ages of Fermín and Ana, the former in the classical prime of life of the mid-thirties, the latter at the point where sexual activity must begin if she is to join the life-cycle of the sexually-mature female. Carlos, we might note, married in his mid-thirties (I. 185), the age of Fermín at the inception of the novel. Visitación, screeching and excessive in her show of social vitality, maintains at close to thirty-five the *aturdimiento* for which she was renowned at the age of fifteen (I. 316). Álvaro, with his "cuarenta años y alguno más" (I. 289) is clearly balancing on the edge of his powers before an inevitable decline, and the characterization of him as substitute father for Paco Vegallana reinforces the vision of him as a father who, sooner or later, will have to leave sexual pickings for the more vital son. And lest we fail to notice the potential anxiety about aging in Álvaro, it is spelled out for us by his "son," whose dominant "duda" in Chapter 7 is how to reconcile the need for experience, for "aventuras" with the need to marry. Paco sees himself, in the relation of marriage, as condemned to an unpalatable partner. Calculation here, as elsewhere, is all. True to the Mediterranean double sexual standard, Paco thinks of his own need for sexual experience, and anticipates a bride of virtuous reputation: "pensaba que el buen casado necesitaba haber corrido muchas aventuras. Él estaba destinado a cierta heredera tan escuálida como virtuosa, y había puesto por condición, para comprometer su mano, que le dejaran muchos años de libertad en la que se prepararía a ser un buen marido" (I. 290). His calculations are precise, and he puts them to Álvaro: "¿Debo casarme pronto para que mi mujer no llegue a mis brazos hecha una vieja? ¿Debo preferir tomarla vieja y ser libre más tiempo para disfrutar de otras lozanías?" (I. 290).

Whereas Paco, and to some degree Álvaro, can calculate about how much activity they may fit in before their powers decline, and, in the case of Paco, social dues have to be paid, the aunts have a more severely circumscribed set of possibilities. Their lives are lives of deferment, of opportunities lost. Hence their particular investment in that unsolicited object, Ana. Anunciación, we are told, significantly just before Ana becomes her "object for disposal," is forty-seven: well over her prime, but not so far as to have lost her longings, and desires which will be realized vicariously. Ana, ill, orphaned, is taken on – a signal act of charity, but one which fortuitously serves as a sop to desire. She is characterized as a burden, in the representation which the aunts give of it to public consumption: "Había echado sobre sus hombros una carga bien pesada: mas ¿quién no tiene su cruz?" (I. 212).

An apparent aspect of the burden constituted by Ana is her moral fragility. But the description of the aunts as they discuss the Germán episode reveal how Ana, for them, is the vehicle of otherwise prohibited excitement. Whereas Anuncia is able to feign distaste at the doctor's outspokenness on the matter of Ana's arrival at puberty, with her sister, an immense physiological expertise is displayed as they discuss "como dos comadronas matriculadas" the credibility of various interpretations of the Germán episode. Both have their memories: Agueda of a plumpness acquired (after some unnamed experience, indicated by the *puntos suspensivos*, and which causes Ana to blush [I. 218]), while Anuncia is left with memories of "unos amores románticos rabiosos" (I. 219).

Ana's place is, once more, in a triangle. This time, however, it is a triangle in which the other two angles are either identical or complementary, and, instead of promising the option of the experience of difference, the aunts work together in a covert enterprise to convert Ana into what they themselves were unable to become. A telling, but unglossed verb is slipped into the account of Anuncia's thoughts about Ana in relation to her own ill-destined loves: "*ella quería utilizar*, si era posible, la hermosura de Ana, que si se alimentaba bien sería guapa como su padre y todos los Ozores, pues lo traían de raza" (I. 219, emphasis mine). In terms of class ambition related to marriage as a means to rise, Ana holds out the possibility of a union, if difficult, which was denied to the aunts, given their untouchable (because noble) status as Ozores and untenable prospect as undowried spinsters.

Ana's only route of escape from the triangle of her aunts is to follow the course laid out for her by them: to become the fattened object of their desires which will attract the desires of others. What Ana wants is, thus, reduced to a submission to *anything* in order to escape: "quería fuerzas, salud, colores, carne, hermosura, quería poder librar pronto a sus tías de su presencia" (I. 220). What her aunts want, it would appear, is for her to bear the vicarious experience of sensuality. Encouraged by them to lie in (a habit continued after marriage) her dreams are again of the Germán episode, now imbued with a sense of the sensual: "Para ella su lecho no estaba ya en aquel caserón de sus mayores, ni en Vetusta, ni en la tierra; estaba flotando en el aire, no sabía dónde. Ella se dejaba columpiar dentro de la blanda barquilla en aquel navegar aéreo de sus ensueños." The swing, leit-motiv of Western European art, as a sign of female sensuality, as is the boat cast on the waves (location of the scandalous journey of Maggie Tulliver in *The Mill on the Floss*), signals the dislocated satisfaction of her aunts' desires. She enacts for them the luxuriating in the pleasures of the body. Should the link escape the reader, it is made more obvious by the next detail of Ana's daydream – one of preparing exquisite meals for others, just as her aunt Agueda, two paragraphs later, is shown as expressing her sensual potential in the art of cookery: "Y mientras los personajes de su fantasía se decían ternezas, ella les preparaba un suculento almuerzo en un jardín de fragancias purísimas y penetrantes. Ana aspiraba con placer voluptuoso los aromas ideales de sus visiones turgentes" (I. 222). This is followed by a detailed account of Agueda's investment in the art of cookery, in which Ana's role, as required object that will consume and appreciate the food offered is one in a dyad of vicarious gratification of Agueda's desires: "Doña Agueda con unos ojos dulzones, inútilmente grandes, que nadie había querido para sí, miraba extasiada a la convaleciente que iba engordando a ojos vistas, según las de Ozores. Mientras la joven saboreaba aquellos manjares tributando un elogio a la cocinera a cada bocado, doña Agueda, satisfecha en lo más profundo de su vanidad, pasaba la mano pequeña y regordeta con dedos como chorizos llenos de sortijas, por el cabello ondeado entre rubio y castaño de la sobrinita de sus pecados, como ella decía. El artista y su obra se dedicaba mutuas sonrisas entre plato y plato" (I. 223). Ana acts *for* her aunt, whose tender looks have been left without her own object, and colludes in a duo of gratification which, as Agueda acutely perceives by the nickname of "sobrinita de sus pecados" is the gratification which was denied to Agueda.

I have referred earlier to the backcloth of pastoral theology against which we can read *La Regenta*. If we return to Claret's *Remedios contra la impureza* in *La llave de oro*, where he has been addressing himself particularly to matters concerning girls as confessional daughters, the first six points in the order of recommendations run:

1. Comer poco.
2. Comer vegetales, poca carne, y aun poco pescado.
3. No beber vino, cerveza, ni licores.
4. Cenar poco.
5. Baños frescos de río, o mar, aires del campo.
6. Cama dura, o a lo más un colchón, no de lana, sino de clin, o jergón de paja de maíz, si puede ser, y evitando en cuanto pueda el calor de la cama por la noche. (Claret 1862: 84)

Given the received view within Vetustan society that Ana is sexual and moral dynamite, the regime provided for her by her aunts of luxuriating in bed and indulgence in the delicate pleasures of the table is noteworthy to say the least, and the comment to Vetustan society of Anuncia – whose part in the fattening campaign is to do the marketing – that "Yo me desvivo por la niña" (I. 224), if read literally as an account of giving one life for another, is pregnant with the burden of transferred desire.

With Ana's role of being object for the realization of her aunts' desires, and her only hope of escape from that role being to be an object, yet again, to further their desires, by being married off, it is no surprise that she is mild in her protest against the regime to which she is subjected. Perversely, in order to escape, she must submit to her regime. As will be evident later (and discussed further in

Chapter 5), her only options are to retreat, and to stop eating. The triangles of her varied oedipal relations may affirm to her that the rest of the world exists, in that she becomes an object for others to manipulate, but fail to release her into any autonomy as subject.

ÁLVARO

The difficulty with family members is that we do not normally choose them: they are visited upon us, and while we might (misguidedly) entertain illusions about the degree to which we might shape and influence our children, the relationship of child to parent is of such intractability that the only room for maneuver is through the finding of substitutes.

As is evident from the resume of the sequence of thematic concerns in *La Regenta*, there is a dynamic concerning the resolution or non-resolution of desire. Alleys are explored: some are found to be blind-alleys (as with Ana and her aunts), some open up possibilities. Between the exploration of the ways in which Ana's desire is blocked, diverted, or used by others, and the central chapters of the novel which set the scene for Fermín's equally complex and difficult path to the owning of his own desire, sit the sketches of two patterns of relationship, each of which details the production of a substitute father for an unsatisfactory oedipal constellation.

The two patterns relate to the idea of the father as a source of power. In the first, however, the context is the masculine competitiveness of which sexual exploits are reckoned to be the hard currency, while in the second, the power of the father is concerned with its exercise over women, in particular, with their seclusion from men.

Following on Chapter 5, full of the contorted maneuvers and covert calculations of Ana's aunts, in which Ana can never be agent, only object or mediator, and in which there can never be a sense of her possession of things, Chapter 6 moves us into the apparently more powerful realm of masculine desire, the location being that masculine realm of the Casino. The move from *casa* to *casino* is one that opens up the illusion, at least, of choice and agency. Instead of waiting for suitors to come, or engaging in ploys to lure suitors to the *casa*, the Casino is – overtly – a place of freedom for men (away from the constraints of *casa*), of knowledge, of those activities

– smoking, drinking, gambling – demarcated as the indubitable signs of the masculine sex. The Casino is furthermore the location of masculine descent (in terms of authority) as much as it is of masculine dissent (against the third realm of the *catedral*). The dead weight of paternal tradition is declared in the opposition of "el elemento serio y de más arraigo" in contrast with the desire of the "socios jóvenes" to move away from the old *caserón* (I. 249). What is masculine and the source of authority is thus coupled, from the outset, with the perception of what is lifeless, boring. If masculine presence in the Casino initially seems to be well set in the tradition of prohibition, it is far removed from the concept of the masculine as the agency or model of desire: "Tres generaciones habían bostezado en aquellas salas estrechas y oscuras, y esta solemnidad del aburrimiento heredado no debía trocarse por los azares de un porvenir dudoso en la parte nueva del pueblo, en la Colonia" (I. 249).

That entry into the Casino is associated with the step through to masculinity is intimated through the ironic description of the inner sanctum. The physical threshold of the *gabinete del tresillo* is viewed as one of significance: "Los más bulliciosos muchachos al entrar en el gabinete del tresillo se revestían de una seriedad prematura; parecían sacerdotes jóvenes de un culto extraño. Entrar allí era para los vetustenses como dejar la toga pretexta y tomar la viril" (I. 251).

What is posited here, amid all the irony, is a model by which the acquisition of masculinity is through a rite of passage within a masculine world, rather than through the resolution of the oedipal triangle of the family. If there is an oedipal sense to the relation between youth that passes into maturity, and a body of men that certifies their entry, then what is troubling is the dead weight of that source of authority. Founding members gather: "Hablaban poco. Ninguno se permitía jamás aventurar un aserto que no pudiera ser admitido por unanimidad. Allí se jugaba a los hombres y los sucesos del día, pero sin apasionamiento; se condenaba, sin ofenderle, a todo innovador, al que había hecho algo que saliese de lo ordinario" (I. 263). There is to be no risk, no waves can be permitted. Yet more troubling is the complacency, and the avowed interest in family line, descent, inheritance ("El derecho civil también les encantaba en lo que atañe al parentesco y a la herencia"), while they take pleasure in the confusing observation that everyone is family:

> Ese es hijo de [...] nieto de [...] que casó con [...] que era hermana de ...
> Y como las cerezas, salían enganchados por el parentesco casi todos los vetustenses. Esta conversación terminaba siempre con una frase:
> – Si se va a mirar aquí todos somos algo parientes. (I. 264)

The assertion that "todos somos algo parientes" is one which removes precisely that apprehension of difference which theoretically comes from the experience of the oedipal constellation, and which lies at the root of the tensions and creativeness of sexual desire.

The complacency about inter-relation and the lack of difference that it makes, while here apparently a cause for celebration, is one which could give us pause. The boundaries which, by their absence, failed to protect Ana from the attentions of Iriarte, or from her awareness of Camila and Iriarte as a pair (just as Fermín, as it is recounted in Chapter 15, will have to block his ears to the audible evidence of the relationships of his mother with the miners), are also lacking as the customary social markers of difference and decorum. Ana's aunt Anuncia, painstakingly outlining to her the basis of the "ten con ten," puts it to her as a series of familiarities which are permitted because "everyone is family":

> – Como todos somos parientes – continuó – de cerca o de lejos, nos tratamos como tales; y ni porque se te acerquen mucho para hablarte, ni porque hagan alusiones picarescas, y siempre llenas de gracia, a la hermosura de tus hombros, a lo torneado de lo poco, poquísimo de pantorrilla que te hayan visto al bajarte del coche; por nada de eso, ni aun por algo más, con tal que no sea mucho, debes asustarte, ni escandalizarte, ni darte por ofendida. (I. 228)

The underlying Mediterranean assumptions about kinship are those which require exogamy, and which declare a sexual impasse within family kin, including the adopted kin of *padrinos* (Pitt Rivers 1954: 107-10). What happens in *La Regenta* is that this state of asexual relationship, which permits a degree of inter-sexual familiarity not licit in formal circumstances, is affirmed as existing in the most incongruous of situations. Visitación demonstrates her intimacy with others (not family, but considered as such, since they all fall happily under the naming by the Marquesa de Vegallana as *niños*) by outrageous and noisy behaviour; the cooking party at the Vegallana house ends with Álvaro and Paco accompanying Obdulia and Visitación as they retire to tidy themselves after their labors: "¿por qué no? Se conocían demasiado para fingir escrúpulos" (I. 326), and if eyes are averted it is not to protect the modesty of the other sex, but to leave in peace lovers of old (I. 327); finally, an enforced and humiliating familiarity is threatened for Ana by the Marquesa at the start of Chapter 10, when she threatens "¡Ea! arriba; o aquí mismo, delante de estos señores te peino, te calzo y te visto" (I. 367). While it could be argued that there is excitement, a *frisson* of the prohibited, in this flagrant breaking of social convention, and in the high jinks of Vegallana society, one of the results is precisely that removal of difference and prohibition that will goad Álvaro on, and which will be the ultimate cause of savour, as much as of frustration, in the relationship between Ana and Fermín.

The Casino, however, is the place of an all-male society. Difference, if it is to be established, is therefore to be based on the results of competitiveness, rivalry. Action is minimal (apart from card-games and gambling), so that language becomes the public arena for competition. Whereas in Chapter 13 the episode of the swing provides the opportunity for a public competition of male strength (and in which the triumph of Fermín provokes the disquietude of Álvaro), the confines of the Casino in Chapters 6 and 7 set up a situation in which stand-offs and challenges can be linguistic only.

Álvaro occupies a singularly pivotal position in this society. The broad division, as noted above, is between a dead authoritarian older section of the membership, and the youthful members: a division between "venerables" and "alborotadores" (I. 264-5). Álvaro is the only member of the Casino who is able to introduce a sense of difference, in terms of his recognition by others, and yet paradoxically he is the force who is recognized by the two sides of the Casino population. Before we are told of this (I. 265), a clear signal of his importance is given through the reaction of the Casino "porteros." In relation to most of the members, they exercise their own show of power by denying recognition, by failing to greet them. Ronzal, coming with minimal experience from outside, is able to exact a vestige of recognition from the *porteros*, who move on to a carefully differentiated scale of greeting which declares the status of the various members. Álvaro is at the top of this scale: "si era un individuo de la Junta se levantaban de su silla cosa de medio palmo, si era Ronzal se levantaban un palmo entero y si pasaba don Álvaro Mesía, presidente de la sociedad, se ponían de pie y se cuadraban como reclutas" (I. 250). But he is also given recognition by the "venerables" who note that, precisely, what he brings on his visits to the Casino, is difference:

> – Únicamente cuando viene el señor Mesía.
> – Oh, es que el señor Mesía... es otra cosa.
> – Sí, es mucho hombre. Muy entendido en Hacienda y eso que llaman Economía política. (I. 265)

The arena in which Álvaro makes such an impact is primarily one of competitiveness rather than desire. If there is identification, it is in the area of display of power, rather than identification of one who will be the agent of desire. That these are all inter-linked is the point articulated by Jessica Benjamin. For her "the father is not powerful simply because he *has* a phallus, but because he (with his phallus) represents freedom from dependency on the powerful mother of early infancy. In the preoedipal world, the father and his phallus are powerful because of their ability to stand for separation from the mother. The phallus, then, is not *intrinsically* the symbol of desire, but *becomes* so because of the child's search for a pathway to individuation" (Benjamin 1988: 95). The point at which the *socios* of the Casino stand, however, is the first of the two outlined by Benjamin: they compete, and compare themselves with one another, in order to assess power in relation to the women from whom they have set themselves apart. The very tautness of the lines of social separation, evident as much here as elsewhere in Hispanic literature, derives from the splits, projections and demarcations that underlie the honor code (Sinclair 1993: Chapter 4).

Male relations at the Casino are beset with anxiety. Joaquín Orgaz is presented as one whose mating and marriage plans are predominantly social and class-based: "su propósito era casarse cuanto antes con una muchacha rica. Ella aportaría el dote y él su figura, el título de médico y sus habilidades flamantes" (I. 269). Pepe Ronzal is a climber, son of a "ganadero rico" (thus not dissimilar, one could note, from Fermín). His class-anxiety is conveyed by his unfailing use of gloves – not only because, for him "siempre había el guante sido el distintivo de la finura, como decía, del señorío, según decía también," but for the more vital reason that he suffers from sweaty hands, associated, one infers, with the following comment on his hatred of "lo que olía a plebe" (I. 272). He has all the anxieties of the social-climber, all the investment in removing himself from leaving tell-tale signs of his origins. The sensitivity to smell he shares, of course, with Paula, and Petra, also set on social climbing.

In Chapter 7, Álvaro could be viewed as doubling as father to Ronzal and to Paco Vegallana. But in the relationship with Ronzal, competitiveness takes the form of envy, so that there is never sufficient separation between the two to allow Ronzal fully to identify with his model. Ronzal copies Álvaro in dress, always lagging one step behind, imitating style and speech with imperfect skill (I. 278). Ronzal has "soberana envidia" of Álvaro, the only one who he judges his superior. It is an envy that dominates his moves, so that each appearance of the two is characterized by Ronzal's awareness of his model, leading to a relationship not of identification merely, but of servile and laughable mimicry. In a grotesque dependence, Ronzal looks to Álvaro for cues as to what recognition *he* should give to others: "Miraba a Mesía Ronzal, y si aplaudía su modelo aborrecido aplaudía él, pero pausadamente y sin ruido, como el otro" (I. 279-80). And while he pays continuous, obsessive attention to his model, he also denigrates his powers to others, hallmark of the one who envies (Klein 1957: 217).

Running parallel to this envious dyadic relationship is the more conventional, and clearly more gratifying adoption of a father/son relationship by Álvaro and Paco Vegallana. It is clearly of import and pleasure to both parties, in some measure because of the degree to which they pretend to be – on the basis of age – not in the classical relationship of a son whose vigour and youth will necessarily triumph over the waning powers of the older man, but in a companionship in which there can be similarity and comparability: "Aquella amistad era como la de un padre joven y un hijo que le trata como a un camarada respetable y de más seso. Pero además, Paco veía en su Mesía un héroe. Ni el ser heredero del título más envidiable de Vetusta, ni su buena figura, ni su partido con las mujeres, envanecían a Paco tanto como su intimidad con don Álvaro" (I. 289). Significantly, Álvaro, aware of Ronzal's apish imitation of him in dress, warns Paco against it – taking the role of adviser and model – a role frequently cast upon him, not least by Víctor (Sinclair 1993: 204-10).

If the situation is ripe for identification between the two, other features of the oedipal relationship are somewhat disturbed. Álvaro, for example, rather than act as the paternal figure who prohibits, and deflects the desire of the adopted son from his own sexual objects, instead passes them on to him. What is yet more crucial is the feminine form the narrator adopts to express this type of inheritance: "Como una dama rica y elegante deja vestidos casi nuevos a sus doncellas, Mesía más de una vez dejaba en brazos de Paco amores apenas usados" (I. 291). There are two hints here. First, the relationship is one in which both members are feminine, not masculine. Second, and more crucially, it is one in which the class-relationship is reversed, since Álvaro lives in the interstices of society, in which his possible gain is to clarify his position of being "entre plebeyos y nobles" (I. 235), and his implied class-position here is clearly above that of Paco, heir to the most ancient local family. Lest we should forget the feminization of the text's *ex officio* lover and the way he acts, it is repeated in the way Álvaro treats Paco, not now in a woman to woman relation, but in a pastiche of Álvaro as the seducer of a woman easy to seduce. Paco has caught Álvaro in a moment of weakness, with regard to Ana. Microcosmically the narrative keeps Álvaro in the position of father and model of masculinity, even down to the classic motif of the cigar:

> Una mano de Mesía tembló ligeramente sobre el hombro de Vegallana.
> El Marquesito lo sintió, y vio en el rostro de su amigo grandes esfuerzos por ocultar la alegría. Los ojos fríos del *dandy* se animaron. Chupó el cigarro y arrojó el humo para ocultar con él la expresión de sus emociones. (I. 292)

From this position of assumed superiority, Mesía goes on to "deceive" Paco about love, in a way that reduces the masculine status of Paco within the narrative, and is the sign not of Mesía's regard for him, but rather his contempt – a contempt, we may infer, which operates also with regard to women:

> Mesía explicó a Paco lo que sentía. Le engañó como engañaba a ciertas mujeres que tenían educación y sentimientos semejantes a los del Marquesito. La fantasía de Paco, sus costumbres, la especial perversión de su sentido moral le hacían afeminado en

el alma en el sentido de parecerse a tantas y tantas señoras y señoritas, sin malos humores, ociosas, de buen diente, criadas en el ocio y el regalo, en medio del vicio fácil y corriente. (I. 292)

The following chapter shows a yet more complex aspect to the relationship, as we see that not only is Álvaro father to Paco, but that Paco's father, the Marqués, acts as father to Álvaro. Not only is this spelled out with utmost clarity, but once again the troubling characterization of Álvaro is made in feminine guise, and lest our attention should wander, it is done twice: "Don Álvaro era al Marqués en política lo que a Paquito en amores, su Mentor, su Ninfa Egeria. Padre e hijo se consideraban incapaces de pensar en las respectivas materias sin la ayuda de su Pitonisa" (I. 302). Figured thus as wife (the Ninfa Egeria was wife and counsellor to Numa Pompilius), and as priestess (Sobejano 1981: I. 302), Álvaro is placed in the role of feminine adjunct, albeit a relatively powerful one. And if the Marqués could be considered as a good masculine model (aristocratic, politically powerful, and sexually potent, as will be revealed in Chapter 18 [II. 90]), his only option to avoid the power of his liberal and scandalous wife is to retreat to an upper floor, making his own "sala de recibir" which will be distinct from her scandalous "salón amarillo" (I. 312). Its kinship with other places of retreat is revealed in his name for it: "Mi celda!"

Fermín

A full discussion of Fermín and his natural oedipal triangle will be given in the following chapter. There it will be seen that his attention is necessarily divided between his natural father, Francisco, and his father as patron, Bishop Camoirán, with the possible mirage of the miners as fathers unnameable, and yet suggestively possible. Here, however, I would like to outline his presence in two oedipal triangles where we see him situate himself, as does Álvaro, in pride of place as substitute father. As with Álvaro there is more than a little class-consciousness in this, and it is arguably a strategy that he adopts since it allows him to rise through society through his *own* agency, rather than through that of his mother which made him adopt the career of priest in the first place.

If Ana has a mother whose nature and identity are changed by the accounts given of them by others, none of the transformed constructions being socially acceptable (the *modista* [I. 185, 190] who becomes *bailarina* [I. 190, 232, 244] and then *una perdida, corriente* [I. 215]), there is a comparable level of difficulty for Fermín in relation to his fathers. He is the son of Francisco de Pas, a local wastrel who combines proof of exceptional virility with a general temperament of weakness and dissipation. His achievement is to overcome the "virtue" of Paula where numerous others (so we are given to understand) have failed, but he then spends his life in gambling and other pursuits "deemed" masculine. In this he is not, of course, dissimilar from the men of the Casino. Fermín will think of his natural father as a symbol of "real" masculinity, through the image of the *cazador* (when encountering the frustration of not being able, as priest, to act within the role of jealous husband). Paula finds a substitute father for her son in Camoirán, the bishop. The bishop, however, does not provide an obvious model of sexual masculinity, and significantly Fermín, once priest, disassociates himself from the emotional "feminine" style of Camoirán, too closely associated with sensuality (see Chapter 12, eg. I. 439, where the furniture, as in the Vegallana household, conveys all). No-one, to my knowledge, has speculated about the possible negative family romance (Freud 1909) that Fermín might have spun about himself, given the information we are provided with in Chapter 15 about his undoubted adolescent awareness of his mother's relationship with the miners. All we are told is that he is required to keep himself separate from them and that "cuando el estrépito era horrísono, tapaba los oídos y procuraba enfrascarse en el trabajo hasta olvidar lo que pasaba detrás de aquellas tablas, en la taberna" (I. 555).

Fermín, of multiple and elusive fathers in the original oedipal triangle, moves in adult life to be himself the substitute father in a number of triangles. The two about which we are told in detail, in Chapter 12, have clear significance in relation to his sexual definition, and not just to his social power within Vetusta. He stands in place of Olvido Paez's weak father Francisco (I. 473), and in place of the father of Rosita Carraspique (Chapter 12).

There is complex investment from all parties in the placing of Fermín in the Paez household. Olvido like Ana has no mother. Like Ana she moves into a fantasy world, troublingly similar and symmetrically complementary. She throws into relief the possible negative readings that one might make of Ana with her concept of her desperate, forlorn, orphaned state. Thus, Olvido, who has been spoilt all her life, decides at eighteen "que quería ser desgraciada, como las heroínas de sus novelas" (I. 473). To this end she creates a contorted perverse scenario for herself. She assumes she will be loved only for her money, and will therefore have to reject all her suitors. More and more her attention is drawn by the detail of the scenario she has chosen, namely her wealth, and she dedicates herself to it. Her next move, again running parallel to Ana, is to take to religion, and become "devota" (I. 474), but moreover to "enamorarse místicamente" (Olvido's phrase) of Fermín. Ostensibly Fermín is drawn to the Paez family because he would like to exert power over the father, and he sees his channels to so doing in the love of Olvido's father for her, and Paez's "manía del buen tono." There are two possible further agendas. Francisco Paez is presented as weak, as uncertain, and Fermín's place is arguably to supplant him, being the triumphant oedipal son (though loved by the daughter of the triangle, not the mother). But there is also a possible attraction *to* Paez, a type of identification, in that here is an eminently successful social climber and who, moreover, has got where he has without being pushed along by a powerful mother. In relation to Fermín's feelings about *envidia*, in controlling the daughter as well as the father, he is arguably able to experience himself as agent, however elusively, over one in whom *envidia* is housed, and who, like himself, is the *object* rather than the avowed *subject* of *envidia* (Sinclair 1995).

Paez's subservience to his grasping daughter (whose perverse source of pleasure has been to create envy in others [I. 473]) is but one sign of his implied weakness. The Hotel de Páez has a shield on it dated 1868 (I. 471), date of the revolution which dethroned Isabel II and her consort Francisco de Asís, a figure who is much around in the structure of the story. It seems not by chance that Carraspique's full name was given at the start of Chapter 12 as Don Francisco de Asís Carraspique, or that Fermín comes to be preoccupied (II. 20) by what might have happened on the excursion to El Vivero on the "día de San Francisco de Asís." The local implication of the reference is not to St Francis of Assisi, but to the consort of Isabel II. That Francisco de Asís, whose wife was dethroned by the revolution of 1868 was renowned for his homosexuality, and for *not* having fathered the children who bore his name. The trail leads back to the casting of doubt on Fermín's own parentage. If the name Francisco is consonant with uncertain masculinity, where can he turn to for the task of identification with the masculine?

The answer, it appears, is perhaps to *be* the father, rather than to identify with him. He becomes the substitute for the Francisco of uncertain masculinity. Furthermore, there is a subtext of Fermín's roles in these alternative oedipal triangles which is related to the subjection of women who otherwise are powerful and destructive forces for him. Paez is under the thumb of his daughter; Don Francisco de Asís Carraspique is dominated by his wife (I. 425), fuelled in her anti-liberal feelings by the fact that the *cristinos* hung her father in the Carlist wars. Further underscoring of the parallel with the original Francisco Asís is made, in the reflection of his neo-catholicism which takes the form in Carraspique of his Carlism coupled with his weakness: "la debilidad de su carácter, sus pocas luces naturales y la mala intención de los que le rodeaban, convertían su piedad en fuente de disgustos para el mismo don Francisco de Asís, para los suyos y para muchos de fuera" (I. 425).

Fermín steps into Francisco's place. The unfortunate agent who is to prove his supremacy over Francisco's wife is their daughter, Rosita, whose lingering illness to death is the background to the adultery plot from Chapter 12 through to Chapter 22. Re-named Sor Teresa, she is clearly emblematic of a sexuality that is disowned and punished, through to death, in the body of another. Her significance as the symbol of sensuality and sexuality is conveyed, quite simply, through her name, and hence through the allusion to the mystico-erotic writings of Santa Teresa, and the heavy hints about the non-platonic relationship between Fermín and his maid Teresina.

Agency, it would seem, the extreme form of proof of secure identity, is proven through control, or impact, on others. It appears not to be sufficient to be possessor, though Fermín will make great efforts to exert power over others, and hence to "possess" them. Having agency may entail, in fantasy, and chillingly in the reality of Rosita, left to languish and die in a cell that is little more than cesspit, *overcoming* the Other by annihilation. Destroy so as not to be destroyed: a motif taken up, and played out in complex fashion, as shown in Chapters 5 and 6.

STRATEGIES I: FEMALE MALADIES

> *Ubi irritatio, ibi fluxus* (Boerhaave)
>
> C'est toujours la chose génitale (Charcot)
>
> Who am I? a man or a woman? ...Am I capable of procreating? (Lacan, *The Hysteric's Question*)
>
> Whether she knows it or not, and however obliquely metaphorical the language of her symptoms may appear, the anorexic is trying to tell us something, and something quite specific about herself and the context in which she exists. We know, from the outside, that it is something of tremendous importance because some anorexics would rather die than stop saying it. (Macleod, *The Art of Starvation*)

In a novel where communication is through and in surface signs, it comes as no surprise that the presence of malady is material ripe for interpretation, and that both its presence and its forms will be perceived as text variously to be constructed and read within the narrative. In Chapter 1 we saw the degree to which the framing of the novel is weighted down by the clay and decay of the human condition, the nature of which is ever ready to break through to the surface of experience, rending apart the frail web of social *mores*. That prominence of the physical is what is brought to our attention in the opening lines of *La Regenta*, where even in a state of physical repose, there is considerable evidence of physical (and concomitant mental) malaise. There are problems (rumblings) with what has been taken in, while what has been cast out (the "migajas de la basura" – glossed, lest we fail to read their import, as "aquellas sobras de todo" [I. 93, emphasis mine]), is liable to get lodged and stuck anywhere, out of its proper place, frozen in incongrous and inappropriate relation to its surroundings, yet – as figured in the example of the "arenilla" – clinging ("agarrada") to its new surrounds, for fear, as it were, of falling. Thus it will be with the characters of *La Regenta*, clinging to social position uncertainly held, out of place, feeling trepidation about the fate that would ensue from letting go, the "cayendo" of Ana's eventual fall into adultery.

In the Introduction, I suggested that Ana follows the "career" of the hysteric, a career into which she moves as a flight. Typical of the hysteric she appears not to know what it is that she does, and yet she retains some level of consciousness (awareness of the symptoms of the *ataque* and of the strategy of convenient *jaquecas*). Similarly she appears to know, and yet not to want to know, of the narratives of seduction and adultery, in which she is offered a part, and to which she offers herself. And just as she embroils both Álvaro and Fermín in complex projects of control and capture, while entangling her husband in the net of unspoken resentments and desires of their domestic life, she also leads the reader on, seduces, entangles, and ultimately frustrates. Or, *mejor dicho*, and more accurately, she is so presented to us by her narrator, creation of the author, as to frustrate, so that we as readers react to her as do the puzzled members of the entourage of the hysteric.

Whereas in the Introduction and Chapter 1 prominence was given to the narrative as a whole as a type of hysterical flight from annihilation and chaos, a performance of defiance and attempt to establish some known demarcations of territory and action, my emphasis in this chapter will be primarily upon the strategies engaged in by individual characters, and which play out in a microcosmic and relatively contained way, the major motions and dynamics of the narrative as a whole.

Although the discussion in Chapters 4 and 5 will center on the two disorders primarily associated with Ana Ozores, anorexia and hysteria, the assumption throughout is that these are the disorders distributed, as it were, to the female characters, occasionally breaking out in male characters, but always carrying with them the social coding and stigma reserved – true to the time and place of the action of the novel – for the sex regarded unfailingly as the weaker, periodically as degenerate, and one whose disorders are intermittently dangerous or contagious. The very lack of a secure boundary around the maladies designated as female is yet another example of the imperfections of separation that exist throughout the novel, whether in the fissures of the cemetery wall, or the demarcation of subject and object in the experience of jealousy, or in sexual identity that suffers deficits and failures because of faulty oedipal structures and experiences.

The link between the two disorders associated with Ana is a simple one, in which the question is not that of their origins (though these could indeed be explored), but in the manner of their symptoms. We could apply equally to the two conditions the outlines of Szasz's reading of hysteria, here summarized by Porter:

> Properly speaking... hysteria is not a disease with origins to be excavated, but a behavior with meanings to be decoded. Social existence is a rule-governed game-playing ritual. The hysteric bends the rules and exploits their loopholes. Not illness but idiom (gestural more than verbal), hysteria pertains not to a Cartesian ontology but to a semiotics, being communication by *complaints*. Since the hysteric is engaged in social performances that follow certain expectations so as to defy others, the pertinent questions are not about the origins, but the conventions, of hysteria. (Porter 1993: 234)

The two conditions can be contemplated, within their converted or dislocated symptoms as a struggle about either the confrontation of power (anorexia) or the attempted evasion of power (hysteria). They are also a coded communication, so important for the anorexic that she is prepared to die in the attempt of making it (Macleod 1981: 11), so precious to the hysteric that she is as likely as not to follow Dora in her angry flight from Freud's consulting room.

The issues of power and control, central to social relations in general and gender-relations in particular within the novel, are played out most overtly in issues of the table, so that characters have to choose to consume or to be consumed, to prepare others for the (sexual) feast, or to suffer – or enjoy – the fate of the consumed morsel. In *La Regenta* there is a clear and frequently public enactment of the relationship to food, and an apparent clarity about the coding of alimentation as the language of love, sex and sexual consumption. This potential clarity of meaning, which will permit us to read the signs of behaviour as communications about appetites other than those of the stomach, is one which is more emphatically hidden in the converted language of the hysterical symptom. Eating, or not eating, is a form of behaviour which is visible, habitually public – a detail over which it will later be appropriate to pause – and thus the oddities and vicissitudes which go to make it up are readily observed, drawing comment from other characters, and arresting the attention of the reader. Most of all, engagement in the act of eating, or not eating, is a strategem which far from being unconscious (in the way that the hysteric would have us believe her maladies have unconscious roots), entails an act of will. In moving, therefore, from the strategy of anorexia to that of hysteria the discussion will move from the conscious and the clearly observable to the unconscious (or the feigned unconscious). Both strategies are experienced as disruptive, both summon up attention and activity from others, both reflect the female condition of the time.

Chapter 4

THE CONSUMING PASSION

Eating as a metaphor for sexual activity has a long history, the connection between the meeting of the two different appetites expressed in ways as diverse as superstitions about the aphrodisiac properties of certain foods, or beliefs about the appropriate food for weddings, the savouring of a meal between Tom Jones and his mother as a prelude to unknowingly committing incest – a case in which the breaking of bread together is the establishment of an intimacy where it is not known whether this is the family table, or the table of lovers-to-be. The majority of traditional associations between food and sex follow one of two paths: either there is a link to the pleasure represented in the the alimentary metaphor or to the pleasure in the underlying sexual reality. But at the least it appears to be anticipated that there will be pleasure on the part of those participants who can be classed as consumers. Galdós, however, in displaying the horror of Fortunata shortly before her marriage to Maxi Rubín as she watches him devour the "arroz" she has so carefully prepared for him, highlights the possible negative connotations of the association: as he consumes what she has offered him, her future fate as consumed morsel is made evident to her (Galdós 1884-6: 188-9). In *La Regenta* there is a surface rehearsal of the pleasurable associations between the consumption of food and sexual activity, but the connection between the two is highlighted in a way that emphasizes the unpleasurable and the perverse. This is communicated by Alas's examples of displaced or jaded appetites, by the examples of those who consume under duress, and by his perception of what it is to be consumed rather than consumer.[1]

---

[1] The very public nature of food, and its function as intended adjunct to cel-

In the memorable opening paragraphs of *La Regenta* key motifs concerning the process of digestion are introduced, and the atmosphere – one of nausea and unease, as discussed in Chapter 1 – is set. We read of somnolence, of rubbish, and an uneasy and sluggish post-prandial digestion. Then, the description of the cathedral, following directly on this evocation of physical heaviness and unease, itself uses images of the physical to suggest the building's shape and proportion. The keynote of the cathedral is one of delicate balance (just as there will be a delicate but shifting balance between forces in the course of the novel). The tower first is outlined in terms of a rejected image of the physical, one that prefigures some of the perversity and pretentiousness to come: "no era una de esas torres cuya aguja se quiebra de sutil, más flacas que esbeltas, amaneradas como señoritas cursis que aprietan demasiado el corsé" (I. 94). The reality is other: the stone is solid, robust, and is presented as – by contrast – an apparently masculine structure, full of exciting physical tension and potential: "Como haz de músculos y nervios, la piedra, enroscándose en la piedra, trepaba en el aire" and goes on and up to end in a perilous-seeming balancing act: "y como prodigio de juegos malabares, en una punta de caliza se mantenía, cual imantada, una bola grande de bronce dorado, y encima otra más pequeña, y sobre ésta una cruz de hierro que acababa en pararrayos" (I. 94). If Alas is intentionally producing a masculine, phallic "reality" to counterpoise the initial dismissed image of the pretentious and absurdly laced *señoritas* it is an image undermined not only by the precariousness of the equilibrium described, but also in the excess of the statement – an excess and over-protestation that in general will surround the nature of masculinity and its possession by the male characters of the novel.

The novel thus announces succinctly, but in complex manner, two of the poles around which the narrative will turn, and which will serve as background both for the maladies discussed in this chapter, and the male strategies of perversion discussed in the following one. On the one hand there is the awareness of ill-regulated and over-controlled nourishment (indicated in the girls who lace

---

ebration, has been explored by others. Valis (1981) considers feasting in the novel within the classical traditions of lasciviousness and irreverence, and the banquet specifically is commented upon by Paulino Ayuso (1989), Mazzeo (1968) and Weber (1966), while Labanyi (1986) has suggestive comments to make about the importance of food in the novel.

their corsets too tight), suggestive of the discomforts and weaknesses produced by excesses of control. This signals one simple model, which is that the girls do so in response to some perceived view of desire or concept of the acceptability of an hour-glass figure which comes from society as a whole, and a belief about what pleases men in particular. The more complex model, which will be explored here, is that this is an activity produced not in order to please men, or indeed society, but rather to evade control by either, even if at the expense of health and freedom. Nonetheless, the image of the girls also announces the concept of woman as sexual object, whether she likes it or not, a being who either makes herself enticing at the expense of her own comfort, or has to resort to equal discomfort in order to escape from the social-sexual nexus that oppresses her. It is as object that Ana will emerge as the one to be "eaten" at the sexual table, rather than herself be a consumer. The contrasting masculine system, announcing the emphasis on energy, muscle, meat and power, is, as already indicated, undermined by its own over-statement.

THE WORLD OF THE FLESH

Other oppositions within the novel which pertain to the role of the flesh have been outlined elsewhere: the material versus the spiritual, the natural versus the civilized, and, by extension, the town versus the country (Ife 1970, Rutherford 1974, Weber 1966, Labanyi 1986). Implicitly, in the discussion of the material versus the spiritual, there is the suggestion that the *carne* which represents the material flesh may have the more solid connotations of the flesh that one eats in order to stay alive. It is significant in this connection (and what will be seen below of the diets that are offered to Ana in her "illness") that for Pedro Felipe Monlau, whose works on hygiene, public, private and family health were an authority in Spain in the latter part of the nineteenth century, a diet of meat was linked to the life of passion and sexuality. In his *Elementos de higiene privada* (1857) he outlines first how "la *alimentación animal* es muy reparadora y substanciosa. El régimen animal exclusivo aumenta la tonicidad, la firmeza de las carnes, la contractilidad de los tejidos y la fuerza física; activa todas las funciones, dispone al amor, a la cólera y a las demás pasiones llamadas *exaltantes*" (Monlau

1857: 184-5). The link between a diet of meat and sexual activity is outlined further in the definition of the "dieta fibrinosa": "Es la más nutritiva y excitante de todas las dietas, debiendo no poca parte de estas propiedades al osmazomo. Los alimentos fibrinosos aumentan el calor animal, enriquecen de fibrina la sangre, aceleran el curso de ésta, aumentan el volumen y la fuerza de los órganos, activan las secreciones glandulares y las exhalaciones, dan aptitud para los sacrificios que exigen los placeres de la reproducción, y fomentan las pasiones más vivas, como la ambición, la cólera, etc." (Monlau 1857: 191). The other sense in which we might understand *flesh* is, of course, in the theological context, whereby flesh forms a member of a triangle with the world and the Devil. This aspect of the flesh, explored in the context of religion by Valis (1992), overshadows the presence of flesh in the mundane contexts of sex and the activity of eating. The risk is that by focusing on the opposition flesh/spirit, we may fail to see that parallel that is as important as the opposition – that the idea of the life of the flesh, which is epitomized and understood in terms of sexual activity, is echoed throughout the novel by the idea of the life of the flesh which is involved in the appetite for food, and the consumption of food. Alas uses the language and the substance of food to highlight for us sexual processes in the novel. This comes to constitute an overt text understood and acted upon by the characters, and for the reader (if not for all the characters) provides a way of understanding the much more dramatic and vital subtext of the struggle for personal definition, control and independence which forms the core of the novel.

Some of the significance of food as an indicator for sexual activity has been highlighted by Labanyi. As she points out, noting the location of Ana's adultery in Vetusta, "Adultery does not represent the abandoning of the city for the country... but the taking back of the country into the city," a comment which encloses the idea (and the problematic nature) of ingestion. The blocked manner of nutrition, so crucial to an understanding to the dynamics of social exchange and sexual behaviour in the novel, is encapsulated in her comment that Vetusta is "suffering from the effects of indigestion, suggesting that it has problems in digesting the natural ingredients which sustain it" (Labanyi 1986: 62-3).

Hunger, whether experienced as hunger for food or hunger for sex, is a pressing need, an urgent reminder of what we must do if we are to survive. If we do not eat, we will die of starvation; if the members of the human race fail to engage in sex, the race will die out. In this last parallel we may note an implied division: we all of us need to eat in order to live, but we do not all need to indulge in sex for the race to survive. The division rests on a particular understanding of the meaning of "survival" as being a collective issue. Society will only survive if at least some of its members indulge in sex for procreation. Alas, however, looks at the individual, and by his overwhelmingly negative examples, might appear to suggest subscription to a more Reichian view: that full human survival for the individual in the sense of participation in life, rests on the foundation of a satisfying and satisfactory experience. He does not exemplify this (just as few, if any writers who treat of the difficulties and frustrations of marriage give examples of happy ones), although there are hints of it in his portrayal of the robust Petra. Far more prominent in the novel are examples that suggest that if sexual activity is perhaps a necessary condition for the overall well-being of the individual, it is far from a sufficient condition. Ana above all bears this out. When we are introduced to her at the start of the novel she is lacking that experience. When we see her at the end, overcome with shame and nausea, we are perhaps invited to conclude that while sexual appetite requires to be met, it is not necessarily the case that feasting at the sexual table results in well-being and growth.

APPETITE AND PUBLIC CONSUMPTION

One of the paradoxes about eating is that it is indulged in to meet intimate and individual appetite, so that one might suppose the act of eating to be an intimate and private act, whereas it is most frequently social (beginning with the first social pair of mother and child) and the preparation and cooking of food one of the fundamental signs of civilization. Helena Michie has argued, however, that the image of the young lady in the nineteenth century was habitually incompatible with the possession of a healthy appetite which demanded proper feeding. It is again the link between sex and food that explains this phenomenon: "The portrait of the appropriately sexed woman, then, emerges as one who eats little and delicately. She is as sickened by meat as by sexual desire" (Michie 1989: 17). Curiously, what happens in *La Regenta* is a type of shocking reversal of the image of the Victorian miss evoked by Michie, in that what Ana will be urged to do by her aunts is to eat, to be fattened, and then urged by her husband and would-be lover to eat, indeed, to feast. But *La Regenta* takes place in a social milieu where not only is everything in the wrong place, but it is somehow all inside out as well. Thus Michie's comments that "the aesthetics of deprivation forced eating to become a private activity and abstemiousness a public avowal of femininity" and that "eating is typed as a bedroom activity, something too personal to survive the public scrutiny of the dinner table" (Michie 1989: 20) may simply present us with a cultural difference between Spain and England at the period. Conversely, it may alert us to an openness and public enactment in relation to food in *La Regenta* which is both shocking and confusing in relation to gender-norms.

Sex, meanwhile, is normally considered an intimate act (even though in *La Regenta* many actions of sexual approach and touching are necessarily made under the cover of public occasions). Though intimate, it provokes and occupies a great deal of social activity, not only in the courtship and negotiations which will lead to conditions of proximity and intimacy, but also in the social divides between those who do or do not participate in various types of intimacy. Such negotiations will invariably involve the type of demarcation of gender, identity and social boundary with which we have been concerned so far, but with the complication that while sexual activity (within established narratives of love, desire and adultery) apparently confers on the participants some type of identity boundary in the form of gender, it simultaneously brings about all sorts of boundary-transgressions in terms of class.

The idea of sex as a communal activity in *La Regenta* emerges if we rewrite, as John Rutherford has done, in his *Critical Guide*, the "pure" story of *La Regenta*. His new account of the novel rightly emphasizes dynamics and tensions related to control, which he later replaces with his own account of the dynamics of the novel (Rutherford 1974: 55). An alternative version of the narrative which takes into account the thematic underscoring which food provides might run as follows: "Ana was sexually hungry and an affair with Mesía promised to satisfy that hunger. At the same time, members of Vetustan society, including Mesía, wanted her to participate in the consumption of sexual activity, which had its social manifestation in communal feasting. De Pas, meanwhile, sought to dissuade

Ana from the satisfaction of physical appetite. Torn between Mesía and De Pas, between the desire to 'eat' (sexually or otherwise) and the desire not to participate in communal consumption, Ana fell ill. After a brief illusory regaining of a happily-regulated appetite and re-integration of feeding processes within marriage, she succumbed to the charms of Mesía at a public *cena*. De Pas, who had tried to curb her appetite in parallel to his own, rejected her on discovering her over-indulgence at the sexual feast."

If we look at the narrative rewritten thus in terms of appetite, hunger, consumption and patterns of communal behaviour which are contingent upon those fundamental drives and processes, we can see that an important layer of the action of *La Regenta* is focused around the idea of joining in activity in common with others, and not just with a meeting of needs. Ana's decisions about whether to eat or not to eat come therefore to entail decisions about acting in common with others, or marking herself out as different. Since from the outset of her narrative she is marked as distinct, one could argue that there will be an urge to sameness, so that difference does not entail occupying the position of the scapegoat. So long as she remains perceptibly different from others, she is a living reproach to their activities. Her identity is then, in a sense, not in question: she is separated out from the rest. But survival requires an environment, and her problem is to discover an environment which will validate and recognize her without overpowering her and subsuming her into its predominant culture.

Communal activity needs to be explored first, then, as being the background against which the activity of eating (or anorexia and hysteria) will be played out, the two conversion maladies acting as the strained and distressed figure on a complex ground which throws them up, or out, as it were, rather than supporting them.

There are the public or communal spheres of *La Regenta* recognizable as distinct from one another by their spatial occupation: the Vegallana household, the Casino, the Church. The taking of meals in common illustrates either the idea of a reconciliation and a recognition (as with the meal to mark the welcome into the fold of the Casino of don Pompeyo), or a permitted mixing of spheres (as when clergy form part of the gathering at the Vegallana house to celebrate the name-day of Paco in Chapter 13). The key role in the novel of the communality of eating is evident from the importance of meals in its structure. The detailed account of the importance of cooking in the Vegallana household in Chapter 8, and in particular the eroticism which gives the edge to the cooking party of Visitación and Obdulia (I. 321-6), alerts us to the meaning which food and eating have for the Vetustans. A lengthy passage (I. 319-20) outlines for us the contents of the Vegallana kitchen. The ambiguous significance of food (it may give life, but it may also be associated with indigestion or death) is signalled by the description of the larder where the excessive quantities of food attest to the fact that in the Vegallana household all meals are banquets, that is, occasions that are both public and excessive. This information, provided early in the novel, gives special significant to what "eating at their table" might involve for Ana.

The amosphere of the Vegallana kitchen and larder is plainly erotic. The contents of the larder are an "ajuar" (I. 320), a term carrying the import of the intimacy of the table as bedchamber. The chef, Pedro, is a man who mirrors Álvaro in his leanings to *donjuanismo*: "Tenía cuarenta años muy bien cuidados; amaba mucho y se creía un lechuguino" (I. 321-22). Like Álvaro he is an expert, and presented as a gourmet both within his profession, and in his enjoyment of eroticism. When Obdulia flirts with him over the preparation of food, the suggestion is of sexual foreplay, not of cuisine: "un apretón de manos, al parecer casual, al remover una misma masa, al meter los dedos en el mismo recipiente... El cocinero estuvo a punto de caer de espaldas, de puro goce" (I. 323). That this context carries meaning for the affair between Ana and Álvaro is spelled out by Visitación who announces to the latter that Ana, like a fish, "ya tragó el anzuelo" (I. 332), and urges him at the end of the chapter, "¡Cómetela!" (I. 336). We are thus reminded, early on, that the process of eating entails an object, or a victim. While later we may view Ana as one who comes to consider that she may be subject in the act of eating and sexual participation, our perception of her participation will be overshadowed by the concept of her as object, as helpless morsel laid out ready for consumption by others.

The meal at the Vegallana's (Chapter 13) sets the main action of the novel moving. Here De Pas and Ana are moved from the private (though observed) intimacy of the confessional to the enveloping social sphere of the aristocratic household, with its permissive attitude to the breaking of conventional social boundaries. At the same time Ana and Álvaro are also brought into public proximity, so that the three-way tensions that will operate later through the novel are given their first acute expression. During this chapter the reader retains the memory of the erotic sexual/culinary foreplay that had occurred in the Vegallana kitchens, and the parallelism of sex and eating is clear to both men contending for Ana, even if initially the parallel between the two activities is dismissed by both. Thus Álvaro's thoughts: "No pensaba, Dios le librase, que el Magistral buscara en su nueva hija de penitencia la satisfacción de *groseros y vulgares apetitos*" (I. 494, emphasis mine) while Fermín de Pas too, uses the idiom, its origins in the confessional, when reassuring Ana that "los *placeres del mundo* pueden ser, para un alma firme y bien alimentada, pasatiempo inocente, hasta soso, insignificante" (I. 495, emphasis that of De Pas). The terms "groseros y vulgares apetitos" and "placeres del mundo" both emanate from the puritanical language and the condemnatory classification of the confessional. The former is used – with irony one assumes – by Álvaro in an attempt to make a mental put-down of the man who is already patently his rival, but it is also conceivable that there is some sort of self-imaging here which gives Álvaro part of his thrills as a Don Juan. By appropriating the language of the confessional – albeit to refer to the confessor and not to himself, Álvaro is able to indulge in the thrill of the erotic intensified by the prohibition laid on sexuality by the Church. What is evident also is that Álvaro is able to contemplate the more extreme form of terminology for sexual activity, while the bland and distanced "placeres del mundo" is used by Fermín.

Fermín's reassurances to Ana about the "placeres del mundo" run counter, of course, to the advice to young girls given by Claret in his *Remedios contra la impureza*, mentioned in Chapter 3, namely "1. Comer poco. 2. Comer vegetales, poca carne, y aun poco pescado. 3. No beber vino, cerveza, ni licores. 4. Cenar poco" (Claret 1862: 84). Furthermore, the reader at least has knowledge that eating at the Vegallana table, with the social and sexual connotations that are entailed, is far from a matter of simple and healthy nutrition. Besides the known habits of the household, in which entertainment and amusement ride on the edges of social acceptability and respectability, the practices of the Vegallana parental couple themselves convey in the code of food a message that is the reverse of a message of innocence in relation to eating. The Marqués has a habit of pre-prandial gorging, in Roman style, on sardines which he will vomit so as to have room for the main meal. The Marquesa has a habit of eating lettuce with everything, and dousing her food with pungent condiments. The latter suggests jaded experience which repetitively seeks titillation in eccentricity, while the former (given the presence of laudanum in lettuce, and the consequent domestic reputation of the lettuce as a soporific) pointing to a desire to damp all sensation down, in that urge to non-feeling, lack of sensation that constitutes one of the polar pulls of the narrative. The chapter closes with a final reminder of the meaning of the idiom of food as we are told of a new liaison between Obdulia and Joaquinito Orgaz "quien jamás hizo ascos a platos de segunda mesa en siendo suculentos" (I. 519). As in the first paragraph of the novel, left-overs, and their potential unsavoury nature, again come to the fore. It is not difficult to imagine how the process of eating could become distasteful.

Simple domestic communality of eating, and its attendant problems are then explored in the crucial and masterly Chapter 15, where we see the consequences of Fermín's failure to return home for a meal. When he comes back, his mother Doña Paula significantly declares herself unable to eat. We have seen Fermín in the previous chapter irked by this domestic tie, in which he feels himself treated like a child (I. 529-30). Chapter 15 now sets before us all the meaning of betrayal that is given by his mother to his eating out (thus foretelling the impact and import of Ana's later refusals to eat), and her accurate reading of his desire to be close to Ana (I. 544). Here Alas, through the motif of food, indicates levels of feeling, especially jealousy and betrayal, in the mother/son relationship that go beyond pure sociability or nutrition. We learn through Doña Paula's reaction that to eat at one table arouses jealousy, because it is the betrayal of the other table. Here we are immediately and significantly given the history of Doña Paula herself, in a manner that highlights in no uncertain terms the uncomfortable *parentesco* between appetites for food and for sex. Doña Paula's history contains her manipulation of the "apetito" of the priest (I. 550), and an account of how her running of the *taberna* involved her in a series of sexual compromises (I. 552-6) – between them sufficient to allow us to gauge the strength of her investment in having Fermín at her table, since for her tables are clearly not neutral territory. Furthermore, it is Fermín's mother who articulates for us most pointedly the meaning of meals as an act of communality and society: they cannot be enjoyed, or even had, in isolation, because of the idea that they express the fact of being in common with another: "¿Te has acordado de tu madre en todo el día? ¿No la has dejado comer sola, o, mejor dicho, no comer?" (I. 544).

Meals continue to provide the structure of the novel after this divisive (for Fermín and his mother) meal at the Vegallanas, and there is a further layer of meaning available at the level of the seasons. The Vegallana meal is in October, and the novel then passes through the damp and cold of winter, in which minor and private details about hunger and orality appear: Ana's perception of herself as resembling the half-consumed cigar left by Víctor (II. 10) (a symbol not only of his less than adequate virility, but more pointedly, of his inability to finish consuming anything, whether his wife, or the object he uses for substitute oral gratification); Visitación's jaded appetite, that in a pattern of addiction seeks further stimulation (II. 15); the notion that "comer poco" is a feature of "romanticismo" (II. 17). There is a further reminder of Ana as being the eaten rather than the eater ("Ana, que se dejaba devorar por los ojos grises del seductor" [II. 49]). In addition, a detail about a factor which adds to the pleasure of eating is introduced briefly, to be taken up and elaborated later. Ana is suddenly aroused from her "hastío" (yet another appetite image) and comes to the belief that she and Fermín have "gustos idénticos" (II. 25). The motif of *gusto* which belongs to both the alimentary and the sexual will later be explored at length in the form of *gozo* in Chapters 21 and 28. In this fantasy about *gusto* and *gozo* there is a type of pleasurable indeterminacy which betrays the possibility that the locus of pleasure is in fact known, but it is felt that it is indelicate to make reference to it. Hence in the illustration from *Punch* of 7 October 1871, reproduced by Helena Michie in *The Flesh Made Word*, in which a girl sits on her mother's lap, titled "Indigestion Delicately Described," the discomfort, and its locus, both certain and uncertain, related both by location and uncertainty of public designation to sex rather than indigestion, is described by the girl as being "O – just in that place where a doll's wax ends; and it goes all the way down to my legs!" (Michie 1989: 14). A further hint of what may be to come is given in connection with Víctor. He has seen the winter as some sort of uneasy "tregua" in which ultimately he may not be the winner, and confirmation of this comes in the culinary defeat of Chapter 18: "Hasta en el comedor se le había derrotado" (II. 85). He now has to eat according to the fantastic tastes of his wife, linked to a phase of mystic elevation she is engaged in with Fermín.

Chapter 20 begins the end of the lull in activity which has characterized the winter, with a discussion of women at a *cena* in the Casino (II. 172), and the dramatic scene in which Víctor, Álvaro and Fermín enter into conflict over Ana's failure (or perhaps it is actually her refusal?) to eat. This is the point at which the novel returns to the motif of "opting-in" by eating, preparing the ground for the crucial *cena* of Chapter 24 at which Ana reaches a state of crisis, at which her need to follow her appetite for Álvaro surfaces, or at which she finally opts for entry into this narrative of gender and desire. This opting in is, through the language of food and eating, made public. No longer can she refuse the invitation to "eat," and she joins in the activity. The result, her affair, is again articulated through the code of a meal: at the start of Chapter 29 Víctor invites Álvaro to a Christmas meal with himself and Ana (II. 443), although significantly one can only infer from the references in the invitation to Valdiñón and "mi tierra" that it is Víctor who makes it, suggesting that he is not the subject of hospitality and generosity that he imagines himself to be. In fact he enacts through his invitation the typical role of the gullible cuckold husband who now asks the lover to feast at the common conjugal table.

PRIVATE CONSUMPTION

If we turn to more private and intimate meanings given to eating, we can see that individual acts of participation in normal and necessary (and occasionally pleasurable) activity can be further coloured by the public and social meanings of the consumption of food. I shall concentrate on the way in which Ana and Fermín relate to food, although they are, of course, only two of the many consumers in the novel. As we look at them as individuals, we can see that they react not only in the context of the meaning of food which surrounds them in society, but also that their reactions are decisively affected by their personal histories. As with hysteria, we can see how the malady designated as properly that of Ana in the text comes to be one shared by Fermín, demonstrating among other things the degree to which there is a difficulty of establishing difference between them, a difference that would be crucial to the playing out of a narrative of sexual adventure. In the re-telling of the history of each of them, therefore, there is interest in perceiving the parallelism, rather than the separation, of their lives.

Ana, from the outset, is an outsider, an observer of the social context of Vetusta where sex and food are so frequently interchangeable and understood as currencies of negotiation, and where it is an unspoken rule that participation in the context of feasting and indulgence betokens membership and affiliation with a set of mores and beliefs. To this she takes her own historical context, her status of waif, of which we are reminded constantly in the novel, and which is allied to her function of being one who is to be eaten, rather than one who will eat. It is perhaps in her desire to avoid being "eaten" that she periodically tries to withdraw from the whole process of "eating," which necessarily entails her own "starvation": thus the identity can only be protected, or indeed boundaried, at a mortal cost, as with an anorexic.

The feeling that she should not be there at all, and which leads her to eat as little as possible in her early orphanhood, is outlined in Chapter 5. Her sudden and acute illness on her father's death, which converges with, or indeed provokes her coming to puberty, is in a period and situation where she is without rights, and she reacts accordingly by effacing herself: "hacía muy buena enferma. No pedía nada; tomaba todo lo que le daban..." (I. 214). This sudden bout of illness, identified by Simone Saillard as the "síndrome de fiebre histérica" defined by Legrand du Saulle (1988: 322-3), is one of extreme passivity. Her very compliance, now as later, makes it difficult to know what her nature is. This is a crucial issue, given that she has just reached sexual maturity, and thus might be thought to have realised it, but her lack of knowledge of her own nature is scarcely a surprise given the retreat from identity, and especially from sexual identity, that she was obliged to engage in so as to abstract herself from the oppressive and perverted triangle with Camila and Iriarte. It becomes evident to her, from overhearing her aunts' conversation, that her only way to escape from them and relieve them of the material burden she constitutes, is paradoxically to grow plumper, so that she might provoke the appetite of a man who will then taken her away. Even in the formulation of this underlying strategy, one which provides no escape for her, appetite (desire) belongs to another, not to herself. To engage in eating, therefore, is to engage in a type of self-imprisonment, a preparation of self for the table of others. Nonetheless, it appears to be the only option, and preferable to that of remaining, a burden and unwanted, in their household. Given, furthermore, the background of deprivation of the aunts (deprived financially in relation to Ana's father, deprived romantically through a series of failed, or never-consummated unions), there may be a curious satisfaction bordering on the sadistic in cramming the orphan with food she does not desire in order to give her to a fate she does not desire either. That is, in vengeful mode, they can be perceived as preparing her sadistically for a painful experience, the pleasurable version of which they had had denied to them. Ana feels that she is under an obligation to accept their feeding, which reverses her perception of her place in the household: "A no haber oído aquella conversación de las tías, la pobre huérfana no se hubiera atrevido a comer mucho, aunque tuviera apetito, por no aumentar el peso de aquella carga: ella" (I. 220). Ana puts her new realization of her position into the crudest of terms: eating for her will not be the meeting of her appetite, but a preparation for the cattle-market. If the narrative is read as Ana's words at this stage, it conveys considerable levels of anger and bitterness: "Pero ya sabía ya a qué atenerse. Querían engordarla como una vaca que ha de ir al mercado. Era preciso devorar, aunque costase un poco de llanto al principio el pasar los bocados" (I. 220). It is not just that effort involved in eating is highlighted (an effort that will precede the anorexic desisting from food), but that the linking of submission and eating is one which shows the possession of identity and the capacity for individual survival to be placed at risk.

Ana's perception of a connection between food and sex at this point is no figment of her imagination: it is clearly present in the mind of her aunt, Doña Agueda, whose expert hands prepare the food which is to fatten her up. Three chapters later, the image of the dabbling of fingers in food in the Vegallana kitchen will underscore the sensual investment in Agueda's activity, albeit with a sensuality that is dislocated and placed into Ana. Doña Agueda, talking to her sister, and overheard by Ana, signals the coincidence for her of sexuality and the gaining of flesh. She comments on her own progress into puberty: "así fui yo, y después que... empecé a engordar, a comer bien y me puse como un rollo de manteca" (I. 218). We learn that Ana's cheeks flame in the gap left by Agueda here. Given that the preceding part of the conversation has been about what did or did not happen in the episode with Germán, and in which the aunts consider "la verisimilitud del delito desde el punto de vista fisiológico" with all the expertise of "dos comadronas matriculadas," one wonders whether the content of the gap in Agueda's speech, the unmentionable detail, is indeed simply puberty, or perhaps some hidden scandal. Certainly one suspects that in fattening Ana up, Agueda is displacing onto her some of her own desires for fulfilment, not simply as it might have been in the fattened state, but perhaps with the function of mirroring her own displacement from sexual desire into appetite for food. Investment in fattening there evidently is: "Doña Agueda con unos ojos dulzones, inútilmente grandes, que nadie había querido para sí, miraba extasiada a la convaleciente que iba engordando a ojos vistas" (I. 223). That eating constitutes capitulation, a relinquishing of control over one's own fate and identity, and, enacted as submission, may also be a displacement of desire, is thus made clear not only through Ana, but also through Agueda who wants her to share the fate of object, the identity of having no persona but simply a sexual identity that is expected to attract.

The narrative eventually reveals that Ana then continues to have a stop/go policy on eating, or rather – put in less crude terms – a failure to eat adequately for health, and then a resumption of eating at the instigation of others. This disturbance occurs in the early years of her marriage, and there is an explicit correlation (made explicit also to Ana by herself) between the appetite for sex and the appetite for food. That is, she appears to have a level of insight in this area which is to be lacking in her understanding of the experience of hysterical attacks. In Chapter 10, in particular, we see her awareness of issues to do with appetite. This is a point at which she looks back on periods of frustration, sexual and otherwise, and she recalls how, with the changes of the seasons, her appetites have been awakened only to meet with frustration: "Pero llegaba la primavera, y ella misma, ella le buscaba los besos en la boca; le remordía la conciencia de no quererle como marido, de no desear sus caricias; y además tenía miedo a los sentidos excitados en vano" (I. 377). I shall discuss at a later point the degree to which the narrator of *La Regenta* appears to subscribe to some degree to that view of hysteria which links it to sexual frustration, or lack of sexual gratification through intercourse, but for now would simply indicate that there appears to be in the case of Ana's appetite also a relatively simple equation being made. While, as I shall argue, there are other aspects to Ana's fluctuating attitude to food, not least her desire to evade the control of others, and re-assert it over herself, there are nonetheless traces of the simpler contemporary construction that "C'est toujours la chose génitale!" The narrative at this point is remarkably discreet, and does not tell us whether the "sentidos" in question belong to Ana or to her aging husband (a man who, as we shall see later, suffers from timidity rather than from lack of inclination, an inclination which remains however without satisfaction, as evidenced in the ill-defined and needy relationship with Petra). That the "sentidos" may indeed belong to Ana is hinted at by the information that these desires in the past seem to have been associated with repeated states of crisis. Furthermore, we are told of her apparent solution to the crises: it is a type of substitution which goes on throughout the novel, notably in the case of Visitación, which consists in the feeding of one appetite in lieu of feeding another. Thus, in this same Chapter 10 which highlights her awareness of her own functioning, Ana remembers crises that occurred in Granada, Zaragoza and Valladolid (I. 377). Oddly enough, it is left to Víctor to point out the manifestation of her solution to the problem of unmet appetite. Typically he remains unaware of the strategy which underlies what he has observed: "¿Y en Valladolid? Recobraste la salud gracias a la fuerza de los alimentos" (I. 383). He has seen the crisis and the cure, but without, one assumes, understanding the sexual cause of the crisis, or what might have been involved, as a type of existential suicide, in the cure by food.

I have been discussing Ana's relationship with eating in terms of anorexia nervosa. Recognized as early as 1689 by Richard Morton, the phenomenon of refusing to eat to such a degree that severe weight loss is produced, eventually causing threat to life, and which is known as anorexia, was thought by some to have been originally a bout of slimming that had gone wrong. More recent work on the disorder has emphasized the view that it is much more likely to be a strategem, and an expression of a struggle for autonomy and the establishment of an identity free from the control of others. In this context, consumption of food is correlated by the anorexic with the acceptance of a regime, or of control by others, and thus the refusal to accept food is a desperate statement of independence and one which can prove to be mortal (Macleod 1981; Bruch 1978). Ana does not go so far, but if we look at the pattern of her crises, she does seem to be grappling with problems of identity and control, and this is in the context of her vacillation between eating poorly, and eating with a spirit of compliance or obedience (characteristically prime issues for the anorexic). Only rarely does she relate to food with straightforward appetite and enthusiasm, and this correlates with the rarity of her equilibrium in sexual and emotional matters.

For Ana, the act of eating is an act of "opting-in" to life, of agreeing to participate not just in its communality, but also in its continuation and its flow. To do so, in the sense in which continuation and flow are to do with boundary-less states, is an extremely risky venture. In this context, the flow includes the move towards that particularly female flow, menstruation. For the anorexic it is frequently the realization that puberty is a type of moving on that spurs the desires to starve, since moving on towards sexual maturation is a development that cannot be countenanced. The starvation actually brings about a type of desired result, because dropping below a particular weight threshold brings on amenorrhea, and effects a type of regression, in physical terms, to a pre-pubertal stage. Thus not eating is a tool for achieving or re-achieving a physical state where the problems of mature sexuality do not have to be dealt with, and it is a tool grasped in a state of anxiety. Ana Ozores does not reach such extremes. But an understanding of the mechanics and the motivations of starvation may indicate what lies below her behaviour, and is consistent with the general concern about the establishment of boundaries in the novel.

Ana, with her reluctance to eat, becomes the focus for a great deal of activity, and we can see how other characters in their reactions to her seem to have a subliminal understanding of the meaning of food. She also elicits a sharper, more precise response through her difficulties with food, than with the *ataques*. It is generally recognized that to survive one has to eat, but it is not clear which vital processes are laid at risk by the attacks suffered by the hysteric.

The response to Ana

The other characters respond, sometimes individually, sometimes competitively. Víctor, besides noticing some correlations between Ana's crises and her eating patterns, tries to cure the former with the latter. But at the same time, there is an indication that he realizes a social significance in what he is doing. In Chapter 19 we find him trying to get Ana to accept some broth, typical invalid food, and one which Ana has great difficulty in taking, perhaps not least because she cannot help but see the import of Víctor's message contained in the offer of food: "Sus mayores congojas eran al tomar el primer alimento: unos caldos insípidos, desabridos, que don Víctor enfriaba a soplos, soplando con fe y perseverancia, dando a entender su celo y su cariño en aquel modo de soplar" (II. 118).

The offering of broth holds underlying meaning. Not only is it the characteristic strengthening food for invalids (here, significantly "insípidos") recommended in domestic medical practice. In the light of the observations of Lévi-Strauss it is also offered in order to strengthen domestic bonds. For Lévi-Strauss the raw and the cooked signify the difference between the natural and the civilized (Labanyi 1986: 62). In addition, there is social significance in the different types of preparation of food. Thus, according to his studies, the preparation of boiled food is associated with family eating (endo-cuisine), whereas the grander and more extravagant process of roasting is associated with what is offered to guests (exo-cuisine). More than this, the manner of cooking of food can be used to consolidate or hasten certain social processes, so that for some societies boiled food is used for occasions where there is to be a tightening of familial or social ties, while roast food is prescribed where familial or social ties are to be loosened (Lévi-Strauss 1964, 1966; Labanyi 1988). In this light, we can see Víctor's offer of broth not just as the offer of typical and appropriate invalid food, but also as an attempt to strengthen their matrimonial bond. At the same time, according to the precepts of Monlau cited earlier, it will not be the food to awaken and strengthen Ana's sexual appetite – an occurrence which presumably Víctor would not wish to encourage. The broth also fits in with Víctor's own tastes, which tend to the domestic rather than to the exotic. He favours the plain and the substantial (shown in Chapter 18), and has already suffered some defeat in his preferences: "Amante, como buen aragonés, de la clásica abundancia, había ido cediendo poco a poco, sin conocerlo, y comía ya mucho menos, y pasaba por los manjares más fantásticos y suculentos que agradaban a su mujer" (II. 85). It would seem that his intake has been limited and his desires curtailed. His efforts to get his wife to take broth are partially an attempt to regain lost ground, even the upper hand, both in the affections and in the contents of the table. The offering, however, light and lacking in substance, timidly set forward, shows even this attempt at a bid for influence to be a feeble one.

Battle is engaged in a much more overt way in Chapter 20, where Ana is surrounded by the three men in her life, Víctor and Álvaro urging her to take food, and Fermín defending her right to refuse it. Alas sets it out simply and graphically: "Una tarde comía la Regenta en presencia de su esposo, don Álvaro y De Pas. Le costaba lágrimas cada bocado. El Magistral opinaba que a la fuerza no debía comer. Entonces Mesía tomó con mucho calor la defensa del alimento obligatorio" (II. 161). For Álvaro, the issue is a simple one: he needs Ana to eat so that she can become his sexual partner – if she is weak from under-nourishment, he does not stand a chance. His mechanistic concern is emphasized by Alas, who highlights the frustrated anger of the would-be lover: "Don Álvaro calculaba, furioso de impaciencia, cuánto tiempo tardaría aquella *naturaleza* en adquirir la fuerza necesaria para volver a sentir los impulsos sensuales, que eran la fe viva del señor Mesía y su esperanza" (II. 160). If Ana's refusal to eat is a stratagem to avoid the affair with Álvaro, and thus retain some control, not only over her destiny as others might fashion it, but also over the flux of her own desires, it is, for the moment, a successful one. Álvaro would even opt for the crudest, most direct form of alimentation; "yo aconsejaría carne cruda, mucha carne a la inglesa" (II. 161), as though he is following humoral theory in order to convert Ana into a lusting sanguine being. The idea that the meat be raw here signifies his desire to move Ana to a more natural, less civilized, and thus more sexual and sensual state, as though civilization were at odds with sexuality and sensuality.

Fermín seems to hold a different brief, and our interpretation of his attitude at this point may well depend on our view of him overall. Not to be excluded is the degree to which he identifies with Ana, and is even capable himself of abstaining as an evasion of control, as evidenced in Chapter 15 where, having been reproached by his mother for having failed to eat lunch with her, he refuses to eat supper with her (I. 542). In Chapter 20, it is not surprising therefore that he defends Ana's rights to refuse food. While it is possible that his position is one of a disinterested defense deriving from compassion, her refusal is thus arguably something he can recognize as something engaged in so as to preserve her identity. It is probable that there is also some fellow feeling. A more sceptical reading indicates Fermín's probable realization that the consumption of strengthening food would make Ana the less available to come under his influence, as so many other slender young women of Vetusta have done, and of course, eating little is in accord with Claret's recommendations for young ladies who wish to resist impurity. Fermín's outer role is that of compassion, his inner workings perhaps those of self-interest and identification. There is also ambiguity in one of the most loaded comments he makes at this point. He signals a conundrum which summarizes the confusion about eating in the novel: "comer no es lo mismo que alimentarse" (II. 161). We can see this comment in its restricted sense as coming from a man conscious of his role as spiritual mentor, contrasting with the materialist/sensual educator that Álvaro sets himself up to be, and with the well-meaning but inept Víctor, who would have Ana opt in to the table of marriage. The comment carries, however, more general significance in the narrative as a whole: the meeting of the needs of the appetite ("comer") is not necessarily going to achieve nourishment leading to growth ("alimentarse"). Mere eating is not the same as feeding.

Ana: Anxiety and Negotiation

As the narrative moves more deeply into the question of Ana and food, simultaneous with the movement towards the commission of adultery, the emphasis moves more firmly from the social and the communal towards the personal – including the prospect of personal pleasure, or benefit from the feeding (or the adultery), and also personal anxiety (within Ana) about the flow and flux that are involved in both food and sex. Thus, we begin by seeing Ana's periodic phases in which she eats less than is necessary for health as a retreat from becoming an object, and avoiding what she may perceive as social manipulation, as with her aunts. Then, increasingly, there is the impression that she is retreating from the more general, disturbing and intimate threat of sexuality. Ana herself appears to be less aware of this progression than the narrator is, and believes that her strategy for dealing with society will also deal with her own personal anxieties. This places the narrative in an intermediate no-man's-land or what we might call the "middle-period naiveté" of the novel (Chapters 21-28).

As in many other things, Ana in sex is apparently an innocent, despite her upbringing with Camila and Iriarte, the episode with Germán, the forced growth with her aunts, the dislocated sensual substitutes she finds in her bedsheets. She appears to believe that it is possible to draw boundaries between her activities in a way that can only strike us as naive. Thus, in Chapter 21, a chapter of relative recovery, she deludes herself that it is possible to establish an equilibrium between her marriage to Víctor and her relationship with Fermín, although to do so may deny her the degree of gender-definition that might be provided by opting for either one or the other. She longs to be part of both worlds, and thus in her belief that she can maintain boundaries in fact allows a great deal of blurring to go on. She believes that it is possible to enjoy a well-being resulting from the relationship with Fermín in which she insists on viewing expressions of affection as safely non-carnal, given the "spiritual" context Fermín appears to impose. In the same period, she tries to blur things on the domestic front, and tries to persuade Víctor to opt in to the spiritual feeding of communion (II. 217). The narrator makes it quite clear that he at least is not in the same state of confusion as his protagonist, and describes Ana's sensations at this stage with clarity. If Ana thinks the nature of her involvement with Fermín is non-sensual, the reader is not given the luxury of that illusion: "Sentía, medio dormida, a la hora de amanecer sobre todo, palpitaciones de las entrañas que eran agradable cosquilleo; otras veces, como si por sus venas corriese arroyo de leche y miel, se le figuraba que el sentido del gusto, de un gusto exquisito, intenso, se le había trasladado al pecho, más abajo, mejor, no sabía dónde, no era en el estómago, era claro, pero tampoco en el corazón, era en el medio" (II. 212). The meaning of this pleasure, the location of which is unsure (for Ana, but not for the reader), is deferred until Chapter 28 when Ana finally connects it to the sexual excitement she feels with Álvaro (II. 426).

There seems to be a curious equation by which the greater Ana's confusion, and her illusion about what she can achieve in the management of her relations with men, and her own satisfaction, so her capacity for pleasure is greater, perhaps the more so because of the uncertainty of its souce. This opens up a number of possibilities. If we pursue further the analogy between Ana and an anorexic, we can view some of her capacity for pleasure in the middle-period naivete of the novel as being related to the period of euphoria characteristically experienced by anorexics in the early phases of their control over eating, a euphoria which is not a simple light-headedness for lack of food, but which also derives from the belief that they have managed to control their existence (Bruch 1978: 73-4; Macleod 1981: 64-83). A more obvious explanation is the straightforward innocence of Ana, which allows her to be taken in so cruelly by both Álvaro and Fermín, and which nontheless is her passport to a freshness of experience and intensity that others are too jaded to enjoy. It is also possible that her imprecision about the source of pleasure may give it an added piquancy.

We find Ana in a state of particular confusion in Chapter 25, at the *cena* at the Casino which heralds the ultimate success of Álvaro, and the confusion leads to her loosening of controls. The dinner is preceded by coquetry with Fermín in the discussion of her dress for the evening (II. 292-3), and this arguably contributes as much to her heightened sensibility as does the presence of Álvaro in the Casino. Her appetites are stirred by the occasion, and as she sees Álvaro and touches his hand, she is overcome (an example, one is tempted to suggest, of fantasy on the part of the masculine narrator about the power of the virile seducer). The language at this point hints at invasion, with images which relate as much to the ingestion of food as to sex: "Debajo de la piel final del guante, la sensación fue más suave, más corrosiva. Ana la sintió llegar como una corriente fría y vibrante a sus entrañas, más abajo del pecho" (II. 305-6). As she lapses into dizziness, she is borne off by the others, and the reported question and answer denote both her helplessness, and the inexorable process that is now set in train: "¿Adónde la llevaban? A cenar" (II. 306). The narrative informs us not simply that dinner is served (although it is, as it were, at this stage only served, and not being eaten by Ana), but that the action has reached a decisive point. And even though we may see her as helpless and silly victim, she has an intense and primary quality of experience that contrives, partially, to redeem her as she relinquishes her control. She is not of the same category as Visitación and Obdulia: "El ruido, las luces, la algazara, la comida excitante, el vino, el café..., el ambiente, todo contribuía a embotar la voluntad, a despertar la pereza y los instintos de voluptuosidad... Encontraba a su pesar una delicia intensa en todos aquellos vulgares placeres, en aquella seducción de una cena de baile que para los demás era ya goce gastado. Todo le llegaba a las entrañas, todo era nuevo para ella" (II. 309). The "groseros y vulgares apetitos" and "los placeres del mundo" (I. 496) commented on earlier, have miraculously crossed all the boundaries and have been conflated. At this point in the novel, not only does the whole sense of pace increase, so that the narrative echoes the dervish-like whirling of the dance at the Casino *cena* which takes place, but also there is a sharper polarization into extremes of feast and famine. The extremes of excitement of the Casino meal are followed by an intensification of the relationship with Fermín (during Lent, a time of fasting). This in turn is terminated by Ana's catastrophic indulgence in the extremes of denial (a paradox that seems particularly typical of her) when she takes part in the Easter procession (Chapter 26). This is followed by another type of extreme – a highpoint of well-being and domestic peace when Ana retreats to the country with Víctor (Chapter 27). In this interlude we might be deceived into thinking that there was some momentary equilibrium if we did not notice the exchange about dinner. Here the invitation "¿Vamos a cenar?" is greeted unequivocally by Ana: "¡A cenar!" (II. 374). This is uncomfortably close in the novel to the last time it was said, in the Casino, and it is shouted by Ana, suggesting a too strident, too desperate opting-in to the communality of domestic life. The eating of Ana and Víctor is one of full enjoyment, but, exaggerated in its gestures, is revealed as a willed euphoric and unrealistic celebration of the delights of the domestic table: "Ana hablaba a veces con la boca llena, inclinándose hacia Quintanar, que sonreía, mascaba con fuerza, y mientras blandía un cuchillo aprobaba con la cabeza" (II. 374-5). In Ana's eyes she is at this point not in excess, even though the narrator reveals her as so being. She sees her eating as the sign of a well-balanced life, a view she makes briefly evident at the end of her letter to Fermín, written during her recuperation with Víctor. Eating is now, for her, the alternative to the fasting and soul-searching connected with her spiritual phase: "No *puedo ser más larga*. Me está prohibido – ¡otra vez! – . Acabo de cenar" (II. 379). And with that declaration that she is now not in the fasting camp, Ana signs off.

Álvaro's insistence in Chapter 20 that Ana eat more (so that, as the reader readily construes, she might become his lover), may have indicated that his theories about food and sex were, to say the least, a shade crude. The latter part of this novel, however, seems to vindicate his point of view, as we see that Ana's reunion with "material" pleasure and the consumption of food pays off. Thus the masculine narrator underwrites the masculine fantasy played out by Álvaro. The vague pleasures Ana had associated with the soul, located "en el medio," are now, we are told, recognized as "puramente material," and with their "proper" location found (II. 426), she enters with few restraints into a social milieu where seduction by Álvaro is inevitable and accepted. Thus the entry into the hysterical narrative of adultery is confirmed as the tactic of the novel as a whole.

Fermín: The Diversions of Appetite

What, however, of Fermín? In many ways he is the balancing factor in the novel, the foil to Álvaro, the natural mate for Ana, and also the most impossible one. If we look at him also in the context of eating, he comes to echo Ana's desperation with regard to the appetites in a way that is almost more tragic than hers (in a way not unlike the manner in which Freud's male patients, such as the Wolf-Man, seem endowed with greater heroic grandeur than Anna O. and Dora). We have seen how Fermín is associated with the pattern of not eating, not only because of the asceticism traditionally connected with spirituality (an association reinforced by the precepts of pastoral theology of the time), but also because of those young girls who are associated with him as spiritual daughters. Alas even seems to use the motif of thinness as denoting a closeness to Fermín. This closeness deriving from the state of *beata* is reserved for girls as they become adult, and there is a transition to be made which can be perceived in the catechism class in Chapter 21. This has as its prize figure a *rubia* in her teens, with a "torso de mujer" and "muslos poderosos, macizos, de curvas armoniosas, de seducción extraña" (II. 202). Her physical splendour (one which has a strong dose of masculinity about it, not unlike the attributes of Doña Paula, and Álvaro's conquest, Ramona), is combined, somewhat unnervingly, with a voice that is far from natural ("metálica") as are the fanatical words she speaks, indicating her destiny as *beata*. Others in the class are already "pequeñas, pálidas y recias, mujeres ya" (II. 201). A close link with Fermín is spelled out by the fact that Ana in her "spiritual" phases is thin, and has no "physical" appetite, reaching her culmination of affiliation in the Church's fasting period of Lent (Chapter 25). More equivocally, Teresina also seems to grow thin when closest to Fermín. When Alas says, almost coyly, of Teresina when she takes Ana's letter for De Pas, "la recibió... sonriente, más pálida y más delgada que meses atrás, pero más contenta" (II. 441), it is as though here he is using an indistinct code to indicate not just closeness, but also where, for the moment, Fermín is getting his physical satisfactions.

Much of Fermín's relationship to the meeting of his needs has perforce to be realized in ways that are more covert than otherwise. We could even view the fact that his confessional daughters are young women noted for their thinness as a sign of his own need to deny appetite which he transfers to others. Rosita Carraspique notably declines to an absolute degree. Her ailment, "tisis caseosa," is one which would traditionally also suggest the undercurrent which was thought to link tuberculosis with an overactive sexuality (Sontag 1983), and thus points to a mechanistic dynamic, by which the appetite, directed inward, causes consumption and wasting away. In Fermín's domestic circumstances with his mother there is a considerable air of constraint, and the frustration (presumably not only his sexual frustration, but the plain domestic frustration he and his mother have to live under because of the need to repress their sexuality – a *modus vivendi* of long standing) comes explosively to a head in the example mentioned earlier, when he fails to return home to eat, having been at the meal with the Vegallanas (Chapter 15). If we were following a line here based on the idea in Lévi-Strauss of associating the raw with nature, and the non-civilized, then we might pause with interest over the detail that on his return the food he refuses is salad (I. 542). Further, the one Francisco whose name-day is not celebrated by Fermín by eating with his mother, is his natural father.

Fermín himself does not starve. Although only thirty-six, a "panza" is beginning to become evident (I. 525), and information about the past with the Brigadiera (I. 546) and hints about the present with Teresina who is recorded as "más pálida y más delgada que meses atrás, pero más contenta" (II. 192), suggest that he does not starve sexually either. Most graphically of all, the shared *bizcocho* at the end of Chapter 21, a blasphemous parody of the giving of the communion host, conveys, again through the image of intimately shared food, a hidden closeness. The image remains, with its clear and titillating details, so that Fermín's earlier view of the life of the flesh as unholy, and to be condemned, being "el lodo de la carne" (I. 409) rings false. It is, moreover, a sexual communion, celebrated in the absence of Fermín's mother, who thus occupies the place of prohibition, and the assumed masculine strength taken on by the phallic mother.

There is one cluster of the text, centring on Chapter 21 (that is, just after the conflict over whether Ana should be forced to eat), where Fermín's desperate hunger and need to devour is explored. The motif around which the exploration hangs is a rose – traditional symbol of love and mysticism, but also of sensuality, now subjected in the text to the most bizarre of treatments, and where we find Alas rivalling Buñuel in his ability to explore the vagaries of sensuality. Among other things, the rose combines associations of the sacred and the secular, the rose of courtly love, of ephemerality and vulnerability also being the symbol of the Virgin Mary (Warner 1976: 307-09). Between Ana and Fermín the rose is apparently a safe symbol of their spiritual love, and as such Ana feels able to give him "una rosa de Alejandría," believing, with him, that there is not extra-spiritual meaning to the gesture: "Estaban solos. Tácitamente habían convenido en que aquellas expansiones de la amistad eran inocentes. Ellos eran dos ángeles puros que no tenían cuerpo" (I. 224). It is clear, however, that Ana's gesture with the rose is that of a lover, even an accomplished one: "metiéndole una rosa de Alejandría, muy grande, muy olorosa, por la boca y por los ojos," as it is also clear that Fermín's response is in the same vein: "Y el Magistral sonrió como un ángel, mientras aspiraba con delicia el perfume de la rosa de Alejandría, que Ana sin resistencia había dejado en manos del clérigo" (II. 225). In the languor, the succumbing to gesture, the sheer leisureliness and luxury of this whole section we have a foretaste – ironic and dislocated – of the slow and delicious prolongation Alas gives to the account of Ana's final fall, as though slow motion is introduced to extend the pleasure, giving the reader subtleties of postponement and anticipation. As with the acting out of perversion, ritual, performance and postponement are of the essence.

Earlier passages of the novel ensure that we will see the episode of the rose in no uncertain terms as relating to Fermín's desires. In a sense, the rose is shared between him and Ana as the food they do *not* have to deny themselves, the one that is safe for their anorectic selves seeking to avoid control. But the rose is fully laden with sensual meaning. In an earlier passage, Alas indicates Fermín's guilt, desire, limitless urges, as he observes him plucking a rosebud: "El Magistral arrancó un botón de rosa, con miedo de ser visto; sintió placer de niño con el contacto fresco del rocío que cubría aquel *huevecillo* de rosal; como no olía a nada más que a juventud y frescura, los sentidos no aplacaban sus deseos, que eran *ansias de morder*, de gozar con el *gusto*, aquellas capas de raso" (II. 197-8, emphasis mine). The violence of the desire here echoes the extremes recounted by Álvaro, in Chapter 20, the preceding chapter, when telling of his battle with Ramona (II. 176), with distinct textual echoes of the action of biting as connected with sexual pleasure. It is a desire which is acted on by Fermín in concrete and surprising fashion, as he bites into the rose, and shows himself as oral in his inclinations as is Álvaro: "mordió con apetito extraño, con una voluptuosidad refinada de que él no se daba cuenta" (II. 198). Lest the carnal meaning of the rose escape us, Alas elaborates it again two pages later as Fermín gazes at the young girls of the catechism class, with a rose-petal, evidence of his folly, still on his lips: "Mirando estos capullos de mujer, don Fermín recordaba el botón de rosa que acababa de mascar, del que un fragmento arrugado se le asomaba a los labios todavía" (II. 210). And should the precise meaning of the rose still escape us, we are reminded of it four pages later, in the description of Ana's return to health (and simultaneously to the possibility of sensuality): "ella en cuanto sintió aquella bienhechora fortaleza de los músculos, que es como el amor propio del cuerpo, gozóse en distender los miembros, que volvían a cubrirse de rosas pálidas, otra vez repletos de vida circulante" (II. 214). In the light of this build-up, the play with the "rosa de Alejandría" (II. 224-5) is heavily charged with intention.

As noted at the outset of this discussion, food is an absolute necessity for life, sex a more relative one (absolute only in the community's need to continue its existence). By drawing close parallels throughout the novel between the two sorts of appetite, Alas suggests strongly, and insidiously, that it is urgent to meet both needs. He also uses the clearer, less enigmatic code of food as sex, its acceptance and refusal as signs of sexual acceptance and refusal, as a highlighted motif which will throw a light on the possible meanings of the more elusive manifestations of disorder in hysteria, which are signs without a ready decoding. The narratives of food and sex are intertwined through the novel until Chapter 28 where, after a leisurely account of Ana's succumbing (II. 423-7), the adultery is finally achieved. The narrative is not so crude as to produce flagrant images of food, feasting or devouring at this stage, nor is it necessary. Curiously, at this point sex appears to become intimate, and hence removed from the page. By this point in the novel, the reader has been educated to pick up and recognize the references that complete the cycle.

UNFINISHED CONSUMPTION

A final, end-of-season meal is held for the Vegallana coterie, Obdulia, Visitación, Álvaro, Ana and Víctor all being a part of it. By now there is an atmosphere of a somewhat untidy ending, of tiredness, but still with some appetite in the participants. Everything is terribly *passé*, and not very pleasant: "Todo era allí ausencia de honestidad; los muebles sin orden, en posturas inusitadas, parecían amotinados, amenazando contar a los sordos lo que sabían y callaban tantos años hacía" (II. 440). After the meal, Álvaro and Víctor find themselves alone, Álvaro now at the mercy of his appetites, which demand to be met instantly, while Víctor is also unsatisfied, but in a different key, re-telling another attempt at extra-marital dabbling in which once again he has lacked the necessary decisiveness at the last minute: "Lo de siempre, me faltó la constancia, la decisión, el entusiasmo..., y me quedé a media miel..." (II. 441). All of this whets, or at least irritates Álvaro's already aroused appetite. And in the fact that Ana is not part of this post-meal digestion, there is the indication also that she – now abandoning her strategy of abstention – is unsatisfied, and waiting for the eating to begin: "volvieron a la mesa, donde reinaba la dulce fraternidad de las buenas digestiones después de las cenas grandiosas. No estaba allí Anita" (II. 441). Typically it is Ana who is singled out here, despite the fact that neither Víctor, nor Álvaro, have – in the sexual sense – eaten. Nor is the reader allowed to "eat" the experience of reading the account of the accomplishment of the adultery, since the narrative leaves us to imagine what happens when the task of the satisfaction of appetites is finally undertaken (in the gap between Chapters 28 and 29).

It is on Ana that Alas concentrates his final and his most disturbing observations, to do with the failure to digest, rather than excesses of feeding or its denial, as noted in Chapter 1. The novel ends forcibly with the news that in a sense perhaps the anorexic Ana was right. The final images tell not of satisfaction, nor even retribution or repentance, but the terrible consequences of bloated *hastío* and indigestion with which the novel opened. Meanwhile, on the plane of the secondary characters the most disturbing suggestions about food and sex are articulated. Denial of satisfaction – Ana's strategy for most of the narrative – can be literally devastating, as shown by the death of Santos Barinaga in Chapter 21. That consumption is, with horrible irony, no proof of desire, is exemplified in the final kiss of Celedonio, a kiss of perverse and detached curiosity that relegates Ana finally to the world of objects, and the status of being no more than the agent for the desires of others.

Chapter 5

HYSTERIA

> The womb is an animal which longs to generate children. When it remains barren too long after puberty, it is distressed and sorely disturbed, and straying about in the body and cutting off the passages of the breath, it impedes respiration and brings the sufferer into the extremest anguish and provokes all manner of diseases besides. (Plato, *Timaeus*)

> So, then, if hysteria – as it manifests itself – appears like a lie or a pretence, it is because its functional disturbances are not "really" symptomatic of a lesion, which is known to be connected in simple and direct relationship with such disorders... What we are left with is that they are *sine materia*... an illness without a lesion, a bodily illness in which the body's only role is that of a keyboard for expression. (Henri Ey, 1964)

THE HYSTERIC'S STORY: ATTACK AS A FORM OF DEFENSE

I have perhaps given the impression so far that hysteria is a disorder which has a definition, or a definition that can be used, and have implied that it can be used both in relation to Ana, and to the narrative of *La Regenta* as a whole. I have argued that what the characters enter into in order to achieve some form of self-definition and gender-definition is a hysterical narrative of adultery. In so doing, I have had in mind particularly the understanding of hysteria as offered by Lacan. For him, the question posed by the hysteric, is "Who am I? a man or a woman?" (Lacan 1993: 171). Yet while, as we shall see, traditional and medical understanding of the hysteric's disorder is one in which sexuality clearly appears to play a part (both in aetiology, and in the gender-relationship of power that ensues between the hysteric and the medical practitioner) the nature of the hysteric's fantasy is that somehow, through the manifestation and the traumas of hysteric attacks, the reality of sexual life, sexual intercourse, and reproduction are avoided. It is analogous to having one's cake and eating it, a disorder in which the hysteric might be said to have sex and deny it. And given the complexities of roles and role-exchanges in situations of hysteria, what may result, as Kahane observes in relation to Dora's case, is that the narrative of the case reveals the terms "masculine" and "feminine" to be "unmoored in the psychic life of hysterics" (Kahane 1985: 23).

The nature of hysteria is far from clear cut. It is known as the illness which imitates others, which conceivably has no known set of symptoms. For many, it is above all a syndrome, which can with some difficulty be identified, and yet what is striking is the degree to which it continues to be characterized in similar ways across the centuries. This elusive consistency arguably opens the way to allowing a discussion of it in relation to *La Regenta* which is not limited strictly to the historical and geographical confines of the text. Let me illustrate the consistency.

Slater, in a paper on the "Diagnosis of 'Hysteria'" (1965) (the inverted commas around hysteria conveying a wealth of attitude), talks of the difficulty of *knowing* when one is confronted with this disorder. His list of factors that might lead to the diagnosis of hysteria is telling in its confusion, its negative or puzzling demarcations, and a characterization that seems as typical of the nineteenth-century hysteric as it might of a modern sufferer. He refers to an absence of relevant physical finds, the presence of a multitude of symptoms, some evidence of psychogenesis, and some suspect (conversion) symptom such as aphonia or amnesia, that is, something that can be brought to the attention, or indeed arrests the attention. This is the sign that the hysteric adopts, her (or his) conversion into a physical form of a trauma (according to the early theories of Freud and Breuer) which cannot be spoken. Slater's following comments present a vignette which carries all the social weight of the hysteric as experienced in the last century, consonant with the characteristics of hysteria outlined in Showalter's *The Female Malady*:

> Strong motivations for the diagnosis of "hysteria" are provided by the signs of certain personality traits. These may be shown in any tendency on the part of the patient to seek more attention than he is thought to deserve; any tendency to play up or to exaggerate symptoms; extraverted manners and lively phraseology; self-pity and self-concern; dependence and immaturity; any tendency either to over-react emotionally or to show what is thought to be *belle indifférence*. All these phenomena seem to be entirely irrelevant to the formulation of a trustworthy diagnosis. People with, say, a histrionic temperament naturally lend the stamp of their personality to their symptoms, whether they are suffering from an organic or a neurotic disorder. All that one can say is that these modes of behaviour seem to constitute part of a stimulus-response system between patient and doctor. Unwittingly, inevitably, from his very nature, the patient applies the hystero-diagnostic stimulus; unwittingly, inevitably, from the long process of conditioned training through which he has gone the doctor reacts with the hystero-diagnostic response. (Slater 1965: 1395)

The focus here on the distress and irritation caused to others by the hysteric, the high profile given to the possibility that the illness is a piece of theatre, the maddeningly self-enclosed nature of the hysteric, combined with a relentless demand for attention (features which would today be considered classic of the narcissist), highlight features of Ana's malady, temperament and behaviour which will be displayed in the tracing of her various elusive disorders, before she acts out the final social disorder of adultery, opting at the finish for the disorder that, in a sense, society (or perhaps just the narrator) thrusts upon her.

Similarly, E. James Anthony, writing on hysteria in childhood (1982), produces a checklist of symptoms which not only are not confined to this century, but which, when placed against the characterization given to Ana by Alas, also have remarkably strong points of similarity. He lists: conflict around triadic relationships (Ana is involved in numerous confusing triangles); an ambivalent dependency on the mother (Ana longs for union with an idealized mother figure, yet desperately needs to escape from the non-definition that is characteristic of the early infant/mother relationship); an overall constriction of content affecting the screening, blurring, or blotting out of internal and external stimuli, particularly with sexually provocative material (Ana cannot remember what occurred with Germán, blots out troubling experiences, particularly when account of them is to be rendered in the confessional); an inner conflict between passive, dependent, and asexual relationships and phallic-sexual ones (Ana figures herself as the former, "'Ni madre ni hijos'" [I. 165], yet shows capacity for the latter in her frustration with Víctor and her affair with Álvaro); a father image that is very strong as well as very weak (as discussed in Chapter 4); a body that is seen as beautiful and valued by the parents but at the same time dirty and open to injury from them and a body shown as active, energetic, and excited, and simultaneously as a prison; immobile and passive (see the discussion in the earlier part of this chapter); projective stories that have a fairytale, Pollyannaish quality about them where the helpless, childish, useless, innocent individual is being rescued by powerful individuals (from the outset Ana is portrayed as "representing" herself, to herself, in the form of trite, popular, romantic stories, the only mirroring that is possible for her, just as the only hopes of salvation have to be garnered from melodramatic literature).

Compare these modern accounts of the disorder with that of Dr Joaquín Martínez y Valverde, writing his diagnostic guide to mental illness in 1900:

> En edad temprana ya demuestran las histéricas lo que han de ser, presentando la emotividad tan propia de ellas, por lo que tan pronto ríen como lloran, por cualquier pretexto que impresione: precoces, coquetas, procurando llamar hacia sí la atención, dadas a la mentira, sujetas a pesadillas, a palpitaciones y a la anemia. La movibilidad más exagerada es el principal distintivo intelectual; susceptibles de una instrucción extensa y brillante, les es imposible dedicarse a nada serio y constante. Son el espíritu de contradicción, dadas a la controversia, fantásticas, y con las mayores rarezas de carácter, su sensibilidad es exagerada y las variaciones de sus sentimientos no guardan proporción con la causa que las motiva; cambian a cada instante de pensamientos y afectos; tienen una afición innata al engaño, a la calumnia y a los chismes, inventando, para justificar cualquier cosa, una bien urdida novela... se les nota además una debilidad marcada de voluntad y de inteligencia. (Valverde 1900: 242-3, quoted in Aldaraca 1989: 409)

There is much about Ana's career of hysteric that should, and will be contextualized into her own time and place. But my point in bringing forward modern psychiatric concepts of hysteria is to emphasize the idea of a phenomenon which continues to puzzle, is always changing, and yet fundamentally always recognizably the same as illustrated by the last quotation. The modern texts temper, slightly, their irritation with the hysteric, but there is a fundamentally similar attitude shown to the hysteric.

One of the main mechanisms that hysteria throws us into, as those who surround the hysteric, or who are the readers of the hysteric, is a search for meaning. But it needs to be above all not a meaning traced merely back to origins, in which a mechanical cause and effect is a line traced to link the hysterical conversion symptom with some early trauma, but one where the message may be divined. As Porter reminds us, "hysteria pertains not to a Cartesian ontology but to a semiotics, being communication by *complaints*. Since the hysteric is engaged in social performances that follow certain expectations so as to defy others, the pertinent questions are not about the origins, but the conventions, of hysteria" (Porter 1993: 234). In *La Regenta*, as was characteristic of the medicine of the time (including those who specialised in the "treatment" of hysterics), what is notable is first the apparent lack of interest in the aetiology of Ana's hysteria, let alone the possible meaning, and yet at the same time, the narrative is replete with detail which hints heavily about *both* aetiology and meaning. All that happens to Ana is that she is "treated," in a manner consistent with the materialist trends in psychiatry in the latter part of the nineteenth century, but also with general practice of "hygienic medicine," treated simply in ways that will calm, or alleviate her condition. There is no tracing back to a trauma in the manner which will be proposed later by Freud and Breuer.

Tradition has it that Hippocrates identified hysteria, and although this is a tradition based on misreadings and misinterpretations (King 1993), the Hippocratic corpus does have observations of some interest and relevance. Much emphasis was laid on menstrual regularity, the need for *flow* if health was to be maintained. Women were thought of as being "wetter" than men, and the womb particularly susceptible to "dryness" which might result from lack of intercourse (King 1993: 17-18). This essentially humoral theory was in no way distant from the medical theories in sway in nineteenth-century Spain, where the medical course of

Boerhaave still had influence, and where, at the root of the theories of Felipe Monlau, the doctor and hygienist whose work had central influence on domestic understanding of medicine in the second half of the century, an urge to balance humours and tendencies can still be seen. The emphasis on the desirability of menstrual regularity, and indeed the question of how to ensure that young girls would begin to menstruate on time, is a topic on which Monlau, in his *Higiene del matrimonio*, writes with some energy (Monlau 1853). In the light of the discussion of mud and nausea in Chapter 1, furthermore, the idea of flow in *La Regenta* can be seen as associated with all that is uncertain and threatening, whether it be eroticism or death. But standing in tension with the belief that *flow* was necessary to health and life, was an other tradition which saw the desire to seek out moisture as an urge which threatened the natural stability of things, and which simultaneously linked the feminine with all that was uncertain and destabilizing. This link between the nature of the feminine and wetness and flow is spelled out in ancient theory of hysteria where, as noted, women are frequently figured as "wetter" than men. Given that this was seen as their essential nature, any tendency towards dryness was problematic, particularly if the dryness was experienced by the womb. Such dryness was a notable risk for the childless woman, particularly if she did not have the "moistening" activity of sexual intercourse. In these circumstances, it was believed that the womb would go wandering in search of moisture, and hysteria would set in, with a variety of unpleasant physical symptoms of blocking, choking, aphonia and so forth (King 1993: 18-19).

If lack of sexual intercourse was the cause for hysteria (aggravated by childlessness), small wonder that marriage was recommended as a cure, quite consistently. Whereas Hippocratic theory viewed the necessity of intercourse on a basis that was physical and pharmacological (King 1993: 24), in later centuries the recommendation of marriage as a cure for the condition of hysteria would carry the social import of containing woman in the patriarchal system. Rousseau, in his survey of hysteria between 1500 and 1800, notes that in the seventeenth century "intercourse through marriage as a prescription to avoid hysteria" was increasingly recommended by (male) physicians (Rousseau 1993: 134).

What was it, however, that marriage (or sexual intercourse) was expected to satisfy in the hysterical woman? As we move into the nineteenth century, an interesting shift of emphasis occurs in the traditional womb theory, in that the ovary comes to take the place of the womb (Micale 1990: 369). The significance of highlighting the ovaries rather than the womb of the woman as the cause of disorder is one of social function, in that the ovaries were thought to relate to woman's sexuality, while her womb was concerned with reproductive activity (and hence presumably "safer" in sexual and social terms). This theory was expounded by Robert and Fancourt Barnes among others: "the active dominant organ of the sexual system is the ovary. The reign of this organ is expressed by menstruation, the part taken by the uterus being secondary, or in obedience to the impulse of the ovary. The ovary reigns supreme until conception takes place; then the uterus succeeds, and rules until the child leaves it. Then it is deposed, and yields its place to the breast. The breast rules until it is more or less supplanted by the ovary which is ever struggling for supremacy, and cannot long be kept in subjection" (Barnes and Barnes 1884: I. 202-3). Ornella Moscucci, who quotes this passage, comments: "while the uterus and breast symbolized woman's maternal role, the ovaries were woman's tie with a subterranean world of drives and automatic behavioural responses over which she had no control" (Moscucci 1991: 189). What this might mean, if applied to the case of Ana, is that while there is a "plausible" and "socially acceptable" cause of her distress, in that she is childless, there is a much more credible cause, which the narrative encourages us to see, namely that she is sexually frustrated in her marriage, as is made explicit (I. 377), and as is heavily suggested in the pages leading to her preparation for general confession in Chapter 3.

The background traditions on hysteria which pre-date the work of Freud and Breuer, with their *Studies on Hysteria* (1893-5) trace a cause and effect for hysteria, even though we might regard as farfetched the notion of cause in a schema of unsatisfied ovaries and dried wombs. Maudsley, cited *de paso* in Chapter 27 by Ana, who writes to Benítez while under his care (II. 377), adduced the possibility that hysterical attacks in the form of quasi-ecstatic or cataleptic states were "the effect of some condition of the reproductive organs on the brain," and thought that hysterical instability, like nymphomania, followed from "the irritation of the ovaries or uterus" (Porter 1993: 254; Maudsley 1886: 464, 1873: 79-80). The new insights of Freud and Breuer, however, were in a sense similarly mechanistic, and also pointed to cause and effect, in that it was concluded that early trauma, characterized initially as either seduction by or abuse by the father or other male relative, gave rise to the later physically inexplicable symptoms of paralysis, choking, aphonia, dizziness, and so forth. It was believed that if the trauma could be made explicit, could be *named*, or, if one likes, boundaried but also simultaneously declared in language, then the converted symptom of the trauma would disappear. While hysteria as a disorder was known long before the writing of *La Regenta*, the talking cure as such was not. The extensive work of Charcot, at La Salpêtrière, was of careful observation and detailed record-keeping, rather than therapy, of mapping rather than cure (see Micale 1990, 1991).

Ana, hysteric

What I would like to consider, therefore, is the treatment of Ana as hysteric, and the understanding of her as hysteric. It will be seen that, despite the fact that her hysteria can be construed as a strategy simultaneously of escape and of self definition, it is a strategy that is doomed by social and historical circumstance. In both the presentation of the disorder through the narrative, and in the "treatment" accorded her, she falls either into a mold that is traditional and popular, and thus restraining, or into one that is modern and medical, and equally restraining. The talking cure is not yet with us, save through the confessional, and, as we have no direct access to it (Valis 1994: 107) the "cure" in that form, for the reader, never moves beyond Ana's examination of conscience before the confession. If results, and Ana's abandonment of Fermín are anything to go by, we learn that if Ana is the recipient of some model of the talking cure in the confessional, it is a failed therapy.

Even the strictly medical treatment is one which we learn of through second-hand and through intimation. What emerges, however, is an initial sense of difference between what is offered in the confessional, and what is offered by the family doctor. Ana's treatment in medical hands is resoundingly traditional. Though modern in its outlook (at least when she sees two younger doctors at moments of crisis) (Saillard 1986: 320-22), a close examination of the practice of the doctors and the confessor in the novel, and the interrelation between medical and confessional treatises of the time, shows the two approaches, the two discourses, to be closely woven together. The result is that Ana, trying to escape into a narrative of her own construction, in which she can figure both her fate and her gender-identity to be what she will, is caught – just as she will be caught literally by the hunting-traps of Víctor, and caught, imprisoned in the narrative, in the web of innuendo and power-discourse which is used to describe and define her.

Ana is not, of course, defined outright by Alas as a hysteric in the main body of the narrative. After the death of Víctor, and her slow and painful convalescence, we see her now converted fully into the obedient patient of Benítez, using the terminology she has heard used of herself to explain, if possible, her final visit to the Cathedral to seek confession. She realizes that she still harbours feelings about the lost relationship with Fermín: "Volver a aquella amistad ¿era un sueño? El impulso que la había arrojado dentro de la capilla ¿era voz de lo alto o capricho del histerismo, de aquella maldita enfermedad que a veces era lo más íntimo de su deseo y de su pensamiento, ella misma?" (II. 533-4). The fact that throughout the whole text she has behaved and has been perceived as a hysteric has, however, been identified by critics including Labanyi (1991), Valis (1992) and Sobejano (1981). Her career as hysteric is outlined directly to the reader, and internally between characters. But there is no systematic telling. The whole narrative, as observed by Labanyi (1991: 43-4), who aptly relates it to Steven Marcus's comments on Freud's presentation of the case of Dora (Marcus 1985), is typical of the hysteric's tale. There are loops, there are fissures, there is backtracking, there are gaps, changes in the information.

How to conjure Ana, the hysteric? In a sense she is already there, in Chapter 1, in the displaced but none the less disturbing sensations of nausea. When she is first glimpsed, she is introduced firmly in the third person, someone whose arrival at the Cathedral and whose dismissal is related by others. Moreover, she is, as it were, at the point of being "referred," handed on from one confessor to another, just as later she will be referred on by Somoza to Benítez. The medical analogy is continued, in that the reason of Cayetano for handing her over to Fermín de Pas is similar to that of the doctor who refers to a specialist. She has gone beyond his competence (I. 398). But even in this first handover, there is ambiguity. Cayetano adds, "¡Lo mejor será que ustedes se entiendan!," an encouragement to precisely the type of liaison that will hover above their confessional relationship, carrying with it the widespread belief, perhaps, that Charcot was right in his comment, "C'est toujours la chose génitale!" This word of referral, teasingly placed out of order in the narrative, carries a clear weight of *double entendre* given that meanwhile Ana has been shown in Chapter 3, preparing in her bedroom for general confession and in Chapter 5 as the subject or rather victim of a hysterical attack. Meanwhile, the referral from Somoza to Benítez is not simply a sign that Somoza has reached the limits of his competence, but is more troubling in its implications. Already at the moment when Rosita Carraspique languishes in her fetid cell, we learn that Somoza's habit is not to stay with patients whose death he foresees: " 'El no servía para ver morir a una persona querida' " (I. 427), so that his reported reason for handing over to Benítez is troubling: "creía llegado el caso de inhibirse; ya se sabía, él no podía asistir a las personas muy queridas cuando llegaban a cierto estado..." (II. 118).

Both scenes characterize Ana as a hysteric in classical lines, resonant with the images of the hysteric produced from La Salpêtrière. The preparation for confession is an arresting intimate view of the woman who is presented as enjoying the public reputation of the town beauty and the town paragon of virtue. While the depiction of Ana in Chapter 3 confirms the former, it simultaneously undermines the latter. The swift passage from the life of the spirit to the life of the flesh moves almost at the pace of a hysterical conversion. Thus Ana, so aloof in her virtue that she does not participate in local religious bodies such as *cofradías* (I. 161), remembers Fermín's eyelids, "cargados de carne blanca" (I. 162), thinks of her response to the confessional question "*Si comió carne..*". (I. 162), and then undresses, slowly, sensually, as she thinks of general confession. Lou Charnon-Deutsch (1989a) has aptly characterized this scene in terms of pornography, noting the blank look on Ana's face which calls to mind the characteristically blank look on the face of the female victim in works of pornography. At the same time, Ana's posture is one of curved sensuality: "quedó sobre la piel de tigre, hundiendo los pies desnudos, pequeños y rollizos en la espesura de las manchas pardas. Un brazo desnudo se apoyaba en la cabeza algo inclinada, y el otro pendía a lo largo del cuerpo, siguiendo la curva graciosa de la robusta cadera" (I. 165). As she strokes the sheet with her cheek, there is the first hint of the auto-eroticism which might be the suggested but undeclared cause of her hysteria to come. While her posture is not yet the full *arc-en-cercle* thought by Charcot's circle to be characteristic of the hysteric during a seizure of "grand hysteria" (Gilman 1993: 345), it prefigures the curve of her fainting body in the dance at the Casino, where it will be observed that "A la Regenta le había dado el ataque," and conjures up at an early stage that forgetfulness, the unconsciousness of herself, that will be the sign of Ana at the points where she engages in her hysterical narrative.

Unstated in the text, but evident to the reading public of the time is the enormous gap between the mode of preparation of Ana for her confession and what was recommended. Valis (1994) has traced the ways in which Ana's preparation for confession follows an accepted confessional framework. And yet, the circumstances of the preparation are extraordinary. General confession was recommended to be used with discretion. In the *Directorio de la confesión general* by the B. Leonardo de Porto-Mauricio (1859), it is stated that while the practice of general confession should be of sparing occurrence, perhaps once a year, there were circumstances in which it was recommended. It is presented as a tool finely tuned to discover what has been left concealed, and thus needed for those who "por rubor o por otro motivo han callado maliciosamente algún pecado mortal al confesor; o que verdaderamente creían, o a lo menos dudaban que fuese mortal, y en todas las confesiones han proseguido en callarlo por malicia," for those who "se han confesado sin hacer examen de conciencia, aunque agravada de pecados mortales, o a lo menos han usado de notable negligencia en examinarse, poniéndose en peligro de faltar a la debida integridad de la confesión," and those who divide their confession between two, "diciendo parte de los pecados mortales a un confesor y parte a otro, por no hacer sabedor de todo a uno solo" (Porto-Mauricio 1859: 95-6). On the side of the penitent, austerity is in general recommended, and, given the importance of general confession, we may infer that austerity is also to be observed in relation to preparation for it. The contrast between Ana examining her conscience in a state of *déshabille*, which, it is implied, is in fact nudity, and the suggestion of Claret in his *Remedios contra la impureza* that in addition to a frugal diet, young women should have a "cama dura, o a lo más un colchón, no de lana, sino de clin, o jergón de paja de maiz, si puede ser, y evitando en cuanto pueda el calor de la cama por la noche," and his view that on going to bed the young woman should "echarse del lado derecho, nunca de espaldas ni boca abajo" and "Si durmiendo se toca, se pondrá una camisola de mangas cerradas y atadas al cuello..." (Claret 1862: 84-5) is striking.

Ana as penitent is thus aberrant, when considered within the context of pastoral confessional theology. Her image as hysteric is similarly one which suggests the aberrant, and is significantly filtered through the eyes of others. Hence the importance of the fact that she will be portrayed in her *ataque* by Visitación for the consumption of Álvaro, Visitación engaging in an example of that verbal *lascivia* which is linked to the female characters in the novel (see Chapter 2). There is also the combination of the attractions of her body, as observed by Obdulia (who in the Easter procession will look at Ana and long to be a man), alongside the fundamental statement of sex and no-sex of the hysteric. Obdulia notes the gap between the vulgar "cama de matrimonio," and her perception that in the bedroom as a whole "no hay sexo" (I. 164). Visitación's description in Chapter 8 combines the hint of sham in the reference to Ana as a *bacante* as portrayed in the *opera bufa* of Arderíus (she affirms Ana must be better than the theatrical model), with a description that could have come from one of Charcot's Tuesday lectures. This includes the connection made, as ever, between hysteria and sexual longing or deprivation: "Eso parece cuando se retuerce. ¡Cómo se ríe cuando está en el ataque! Tiene los ojos llenos de lágrimas, y en la boca unos pliegues tentadores, y dentro de la remonísima garganta suenan unos ruidos, unos ayes, unas quejas subterráneas; parece que allá dentro se lamenta el amor siempre callado y en prisiones ¡qué sé yo! ¡Suspira de un modo, da unos abrazos a las almohadas! ¡Y se encoge con una pereza! Cualquiera diría que en los ataques tiene pesadillas, y que rabia de celos o se muere de amor..." (I. 331).

Chapters follow in which what Ana suffers are *ataques de nervios* (a common term for hysterical attacks that holds back from the marginalizing label of the hysteric). But in Chapter 18, Álvaro, who has been educated by Visitación into the nature of Ana's attacks, characterizes her to Paco as "una mujer rara... histérica... hay que estudiarla bien" (II. 98). The implications of "estudiarla," aligning Ana with Charcot's patients in their condition of objects to be observed, rather than beings who might speak, are to rank Ana with all those other collectable objects in the novel which will be accumulated by male characters – whether by Víctor, Álvaro, Frígilis or Fermín.

Conversion and Aetiology

Ana lacks effective language, and turns thus to the discourses of others, engages in a complex and unsatisfactory relation with them (Urey 1990; Sieburth 1990; Mandrell 1990). That is as far as language goes. But the characteristic of the hysteric is to convert that which cannot be said into a symptom. At the onset of puberty, Ana is victim of a disorder described as a "fiebre nerviosa" (I. 211). This "attack," and that suffered in Chapter 19, have been identified by Saillard as examples of "síndrome de fiebre histérica" as described by Legrand du Saulle (Saillard 1988). In both cases, a sharp feverish onset is followed by prostration. The severity of the first attack includes a quasi-paralytic state: "Un día, tres o cuatro después de enterrado su padre, Ana quiso levantarse y no pudo. El lecho la sujetaba con brazos invisibles" (I. 213). The coincidence of hysteria with puberty is unsurprising, given that its occurrence was habitually between puberty and menopause (Porter 1993: 251-3). But while the ordering of events in the narrative suggests that this is simply a crisis of Ana's age, coupled with the death of her father, there are hints that this may be an attack that denotes a rebellion against the onset of womanhood. The preceding chapter, Chapter 4, has outlined the degree to which Ana is subject to the unwanted attentions of Iriarte, and obliged to be spectator to the relationship of the latter with Camila (see Chapter 3). By the age of puberty, there is every reason to see Ana as muddled, to say the least, about her sexual identity. Her upbringing by her father has been inconsistent and patchy at best, and frequently confusing, his attitude toward her resulting in an "educación neutra" (I. 200). She has not been *told* what or who she is in terms of gender. Furthermore her age is uncertain. The attentions of Iriarte have given every reason for her to wish to draw back, like the anorexic, from the attainment of sexual maturity, because of the risks foreseen. Nonetheless the flow of life continues. Thus her arrival at womanhood is unsought, repressed and denied: "Aunque Ana llegaba a la edad en que la niña ya puede gustar como mujer, no llamaba la atención; nadie se había enamorado de ella. Entre doña Camila y don Carlos habían ajado las rosas de su rostro; aquella turgencia y expansión de formas que al amante del aya le arrancaban chispas de los ojos, habían contenido su crecimiento; Anita iba a transformarse en mujer cuando parecía muy lejos aún de esta crisis; estaba delgada, pálida, débil; sus quince años eran ingratos, a los diez tenía las apariencias de los trece, y a los quince representaba dos menos" (I. 201).

Signs of paralysis continue, and indeed are evident to Ana's consciousness. In her convalescence, and after the point at which she has realized her "duty" is to submit, to eat, and be fattened for the sexual market, it is as though her very awareness needs to move away from the locations of digestion and/or sexuality: "Se le figuraba que toda la vida se le había subido a la cabeza; que el estómago era una máquina parada, y el cerebro un horno en que ardía todo lo que ella era por dentro" (I. 221).

No doubt an analysis on the Freud/Breuer model would have paid attention to the confusions arising from the Germán episode, and the combined perverse sexual tutelage of Camila, parody of the Freudian nurse image who is the first guide to sexuality, and Iriarte, parody of the masculine model of difference and sexuality. All this is speculation. But if disorder here results from an apparent need to turn away from sexuality, there is an explicit reference to hysteria as a conversion of the urge to rebellion. Consider Ana's associations to the impoverished children whose tongues press against the windows of the *confitería* where they can see "golosinas que no eran para ellos" (I. 353). No sooner does she feel "una ola de rebeldía" in her identification with the children and their state of deprivation, than it is converted: "Temía otra vez el ataque" (I. 357).

There is a distinction to be made between what the narrative tells us about Ana's hysterical attacks, and what medical discourse has to say, even though there may be some indistinct coincidence. The word used most consistently for Ana's hysterical crisis is *ataque*. It is a word adopted, almost fondly, by Ana. She knows about this type of *ataque*, is an expert on it, she will explain its nature to Fermín and how she knows whether it comes or not (II. 289). Thus, the example above, where she fears its coming, as though she recognizes the faint but inevitable stimulus. But it is, as observed by Showalter, conceivably a useful disorder: it brings attention (1985: 133). In Chapter 3 the course of her associative memories brings her to thoughts of Álvaro. She converts this rapidly into thoughts of having a child (convenient substitute). Álvaro, all evident masculinity, reappears in an interesting pose where she is the dominator, he the submissive one: "al saludar humillaba los ojos, cargados de amor, ante los de ella imperiosos, imponentes" (I.

174). The image of Álvaro gives way to the presumably more permissible one of her husband, and "la casualidad" at this point announces with convenience the apparent imminence of an *ataque*: Ana hastens to *reassure* herself that this is so, a gesture which confirms the attention-seeking of the hysteric, and the clarity of meaning that should be attributed to it. A hysterical attack replaces the sexual attack (in which, it should be stressed again, she is seen as instigator – a prefiguration of what will be her sexually demanding role once the affair is under way): "Se tomó el pulso, se miró las manos; no veía bien los dedos, el pulso latía con violencia; en los párpados le estallaban estrellitas, como chispas de fuegos artificiales, sí, sí, estaba mala, iba a darle el ataque; había que llamar; cogió el cordón de la campanilla, llamó" (I. 174).

The meaning of *ataque* is clear from the observations of these associations with it. But lest it escape us, it is emphasized elsewhere. It is Álvaro's code for the "attack" on Ana's virtue, and is made absolutely explicit in Chapter 16, when Álvaro contemplates his campaign: "el día que yo me atreva, por tener ya preparado el terreno, a intentar un ataque franco, *personal* – era la palabra técnica en su arte de conquistador –, no ha de ser en el campo" (II. 17). Thus, when Ana faints in Álvaro's arms at the dance in the Casino, the narrative supplies us first with her sensations: "no veía, no oía, no hacía más que sentir un placer que parecía fuego; aquel gozo intenso, irresistible, la espantaba; se dejaba llevar como cuerpo muerto, como en una catástrofe; se le figuraba que dentro de ella se había roto algo, la virtud, la fe, la vergüenza; estaba perdida, pensaba vagamente..." (II. 312). Then public opinion labels clearly the meaning of her sensations: she has had an attack: "A la Regenta le había dado el ataque" (II. 313), the superficial meaning being the socially acceptable one of a hysterical attack in public, with a less acceptable one in which the implied subject of the verb is Álvaro, source of the sexual attack. And in Chapter 17, in a minor key, falling between these two examples in the narrative, there is a vignette of Víctor. In a gesture that underlines symbolically his "between men" competitiveness about masculinity with Frígilis (an unlikely exemplum of sexual potency, and indeed an example of sexual deferral), Víctor sits down to see whether he can load his gun faster than his friend. The verb? Crucially, it refers us back to the scenario of hysterical narratives of sexual intercourse, hysterical attacks, and myths of phallic power in their Don Juanesque speed and repetition: "don Víctor se puso a atacar con rapidez cartuchos y más cartuchos" (II. 74).

An alternative version of Ana's hysteria runs alongside that of sexual *attack* whose source is another. The hysteric, today regarded as a subset within the disorder of narcissism, shares with the narcissist the capacity to do without others. She lives in an enclosed world, where pleasure is dislocated or deferred, and where there is no need for real encounter with the Other. She can enter into fantasies about sexual activity without taking on board the facts and the tribulations of sexual difference. This modern conceptualization of the hysteric is strikingly resonant with one of the theories pertaining to hysteria in the nineteenth century, namely, that hysteria resulted not simply from deprivation of sexual intercourse, but that the alternative method of gratification, auto-eroticism, or masturbation, was frequently the cause of the disorder.

Aldaraca has pointed out that one of the terms for female disorders in the nineteenth century, "irritación nerviosa," was in fact a code for female sexuality (Aldaraca 1989: 405). Micale, expert reader of the historiography of hysteria, observes that the "hysterical attack," the cause of which had been thought to lie in the womb or the ovary (as noted earlier), was seen "as a sort of bodily symbolism for childbirth, the female orgasm, and feminine nature in general" (Micale 1991: 212). Interspersed in the medical literature of the nineteenth century, however, we find a further theory that is yet more particularized, namely that hysteria was the result of masturbation, or self-abuse. What is of particular import is the fact that it was on this area of medicine that confessors' manuals drew in their advice.

Belief was widespread in the nineteenth century that masturbation was the cause of madness (Porter 1987: 203). Tissot, major theoriser of the ills of masturbation, produces a description of self-abusing women that is remarkably close to the picture of the hysteric: "Their stages are very irregular, their symptoms capricious, and their periods incertain; which after much difficulty the disorder is surmounted, the patient still remains rather in a languishing state, than on the mending hand" (Tissot 1766, quoted in Porter 1987: 204). Tissot's work appeared in Spain in 1807 in a clandestine publication (Dr Enrique Perdiguero: private communication). That it reappeared later in the century, more officially, is evidenced by the fact that Tissot is one of the many medical authorities cited by

Claret (1865), along with Debreyne, in support of his warnings against the ills of masturbation, defined by him as a particularly female tendency.

It is then in the field of masturbation that pastoral theology and nineteenth-century psychiatry join hands. Reading works of pastoral theology, one has the impression that confessors were entrusted not simply with the souls of their parishioners, but with keeping their bodies from the disorders caused by excessive venery. And it is here, in the overlap, that we find the source, and the significance, of Benítez's apparently puzzling comment in Chapter 27 on the cause of Ana Ozores's ills.

Benítez, the younger doctor, supposedly more modern than Somoza, comments on the sudden well-being of Ana in Chapter 27: "Sí señor; es un aforismo médico: *ubi irritatio ibi fluxus*" (II. 405). Benítez tells no lie. It is indeed a medical aphorism, but from the Dutch medical authority of the eighteenth century, Boerhaave, whose principal works, the *Institutiones Medicae* were published in Spain as a course in medicine between 1796 and 1797. Moreover, as aphorisms go, it is well-known, and is cited in Fumagalli's 1911 *Ape Latina* in almost identical form, "*ubi stimulus, ibi fluxus.*" Given that this is so, it is perhaps not surprising to find it on the lips of Benítez. In its "cause and effect" emphasis, however, it links Benítez back to earlier traditions in Spanish medicine, indeed to the idea that if there is an illness there must be a lesion. As Boerhaave sets out early in *Aphorisms*, 7, "Morbus, quum corpori inhaereat, erit effectus corporeus singularis determinatae causae" (A Disease when present in a Body must needs be the bodily effect of a Particular Cause directed to that Body) (Boerhaave 1728).

Let us consider the context in which Benítez cites this aphorism. It is in conversation with Víctor, overheard by Fermín, and is cited in an attempt to clarify what Benítez has been saying about strong stimuli causing Ana's ills, and equally strong stimuli being needed to cure them. Víctor is happy to name the first source of stimulus as the Church, or more precisely Fermín. But what of the new source of a changed state, namely Ana's well-being? We hear Víctor's fumbling attempts to follow Benítez, and indeed his effort not to be thought stupid: "¡Perfectamente! *Ubi irritatio...* justo, *ibi... fluxus!* ¡Convencido! Pero aquí el nuevo influjo, ¿dónde está? Veo el otro, el clero, el jesuitismo... pero, ¿y éste? ¿quién representa esta nueva influencia... esta nueva *irritatio* que pudiéramos decir...?"

(II. 405). What is not clear is whether Benítez believes the reply he gives: "Pues es bien claro. Nosotros. El nuevo régimen, la higiene, el Vivero... usted... yo... los alimentos sanos... la leche... el aire... el heno... el tufillo del establo... la brisa de la mañana..., etc., etc.;" (II. 405), the ellipses and pauses suggesting not a simple list, but rather a list that can be offered to this particular hearer. It may be that Benítez believes what he says, but as we shall see presently, it is unclear whether any medical opinion offered in the novel is really modern. Furthermore, in Benítez's manner of replying, what is noticeable is the hesitation, the overelaboration, and the generally unconvincing nature of the explanation.

The whole of this is within earshot of Fermín, "que fingiendo leer un periódico y a ratos atender a Ripamilán, se esforzaba en no perder ni una palabra del diálogo del balcón" (II. 405). Given that Ana is at this point, by dint of her illness following the Easter procession, in a period of being distanced from Fermín, and thus will undoubtedly now be open to influence by Álvaro, it is easy to construe Fermín's concern as jealousy. That his words have their effect is evidenced by the fact that he repeats the aphorism to himself in the mad excursion through the woods with Víctor to find Ana in the storm (II. 411). Here his apparent double concern is with the aphorism, construed as an "alternative stimulus", that is, Álvaro (one infers), and with the fact that *they* are likely to be in the woodcutter's hut, scene of Fermín's own recent encounter with Petra. The simple reading is that he thinks of her sexual transgression, and of his own. But the likelihood is that these particular words uttered by Benítez will also strike other uncomfortable chords in him, unspoken in the novel, but suggested in the emphasis in the narrative on the apprehensions related to flow, and on Ana's self-absorbed state.

We know little about Fermín's reading in pastoral theology, but we do know some of the writers he recommends to others. Hence an authority he uses with Ana is Alfonso Maria di Liguori, cited as San Alfonso Ligorio (II. 22). Víctor is clearly under the discomfort of Liguori's prohibitions (as well as Kempis's writings on death), in Chapter 21 (II. 216). One of the most widely read writers of pastoral theology of the mid-century, however, is Claret, already cited, and who has frequent recourse to Liguori in his various theological tracts. In Claret's *Llave de oro* (1862), he organizes his advice around the Commandments (within the traditions in Spain at this time being eight in number). Like other theological writers of his time and persuasion, he pays particular attention to the sixth commandment, "No fornicar," a commandment deemed to include the full range of possible acts of "impureza." He gives precise advice on how to confess children, beginning with boys. Girls, he says, are different: "Solamente se ha de advertir, como me lo ha enseñado la práctica y experiencia, que las niñas son más fáciles en cometer impurezas que los niños, mientras son pequeñitas; pero cuando son mayores va enteramente al revés, pues más son los mozos y hombres lascivos que las muchachas y mujeres." But, he observes, girls often play at mummies and daddies, including at times playing at giving birth, and it is this that gives rise to a tendency to masturbation:

> De aquí es, que si hay alguna de perversa, las enseña lo que deberían ignorar, y como en la naturaleza *ubi est stimulus ibi est fluxus*, luego corresponde, y en las niñas más antes que en los niños. Por esto despertada la naturaleza, fácilmente se habitúa a este brutal deleite con gravísimo perjuicio de su salud, pues enseña la experiencia que llega a enfermar y aun a matar los niños, sin poderse a veces atinar la causa que produce tan fatales efectos. A veces las niñas se hallan habituadas a este maldito vicio por sus mismas amas de leche o criadas niñeras, que para acallarlas cuando lloran, les hacen acciones indecentísimas para excitarlas al deleite, y este deleite hace olvidar la causa de su llanto, y se callan al momento. Cuando son mayores, el rubor, natural a su sexo, las impide entregarse a estos excesos. (Claret 1862: 139)

Claret then proceeds to give extremely detailed information, in Latin, on the ways in which little girls masturbate, but does not supply such information in relation to boys. He cites, among his authorities, Descuret, Devans, Siniscalqui, Parcheppe, Debreyne, Doussin-Dubreuil, Deslandes, Tissot, Gottlieb-Wogel, Franck Areteo, Boerhaave, Hoffman, Ludwig, Kloekhof, Campe, Bossuet. Whether or not those in medicine read what was written beyond the Pyrenees, it seems that priests at least did so. The same aphorism, "*ubi stimulus, ibi fluxus,*" appears in a work by Descuret, *La médécine des passions, ou les Passions considérées dans leurs rapports avec les maladies, les lois et la religion* (1841). Descuret, again offering advice to confessors, is particularly emphatic about the need to know the effects of masturbation. What he refers to as "pollutions" are sufficient to change "le caractère des personnes, y impriment un cachet de tristesse, de mélancolie et d'hypocondrie, à tel point que les malades, car c'est une vraie et fâcheuse maladie, perdent non seulement la santé par l'abolition totale des fonctions digestives et par le marasme, mais encore poursuivis qu'ils sont par une immense et inexorable ennui ou dégoût de la vie, ils peuvent se livrer au désespoir et terminer leur triste vie par un affreux suicide" (Taxil 1883: 321). Suicide apart, Ana Ozores is arguably recognizable within this vignette. In his discussion of female masturbation, he draws attention to the fact that it may cause a discharge. "Stimulation" acquires a quite precise significance, but the idea of stimulus and discharge, or flux, occurs again in the context of our aphorism: "C'est donc ici évidemment la stimulation ou la perturbation nerveuse seule qu'il faut accuser comme cause de tous les désordres. Si, dans les jeunes sujets, il y a parfois quelque légère évacuation elle est l'effet de la stimulation locale portée à l'excès, d'après ce principe physiologique; *ubi stimulus ibi fluxus*, (partout où est le stimulant partout est l'écoulement)" (Descuret 1841: 59).

My suggestion is not that we have any textual basis for considering that Ana masturbates (though an extension of her rubbing against the sheets in that early preparation for general confession could easily be construed in that light), but rather that the action of the narrative takes place against a shared preoccupation in medicine and in pastoral theology about the tendency or indeed the likelihood that women might masturbate, and that this would be the cause of a multitude of disorders, including hysteria. This conviction was not, of course, to escape Freud (1905a: 110-19). At this point in the text, it seems unlikely that the phrase would have been without an underlying, unnameable import for Fermín, just as the nameable import of adultery is barely one that can be contemplated. A case ripe for hysteric conversion, and just one more example of how the idea of flow, flux and change, coupled with the representation of the individual who defies society by living as an isolate are central to the novel.

The Well-Tempered Patient

Henri Ey's suggestion in the epigraph at the start to this section, that the hysteric's body becomes a keyboard for expression, has a number of implications which are not teased out in his paper. A keyboard is played on by another. That is, it is responsive to the stimuli that another will make in relation to it. It can, as it were, only play the melodies which it is asked to play – a conclusion which is reached by Slater in the quotation given earlier. Furthermore, a keyboard is habitually tuned, so that the notes stand at the correct pitch in relation to one another, and again this tuning is performed by an outside agent. I would like to suggest that Ey's evocative figuring of the hysteric's body as keyboard is therefore apt not only for the idea of the hysteric as one who cannot speak, save through the bodily manifestations she experiences, and *shows*, but also for the relationship between the hysteric and her physician, in which she will respond to the treatment and relationship offered, and further, will in all likelihood become finely "tuned" to the expectations of that doctor/patient relationship, so that the nature of the keyboard comes to be such that it can be played upon effectively by the doctor so as to produce a melody that *to him* sounds as if it is in tune.

There is an explicit split between medical authorities in *La Regenta*: Somoza, the traditional family doctor, a practical man, is set against the picture of his opposite, the image of the "mediquillo moderno de los que se morían de hambre en Vetusta" (I. 427). Somoza goes with the motions of the day, passing from one style of diagnosis to another: "Años atrás, para él todo era flato; ahora todo era *cuestión de nervios*" (II. 427). When he appears in Chapter 12, it is to speak on the imminent death of Rosita Carraspique, his comments revealing him not just as a *médico higienista*, but also *ambientalista*, both firmly in the tradition of Monlau. For him, Rosita's surroundings, the *cloaca* of her cell, are sufficient to produce the fatal nature of her illness. In a sense, the philosophy behind the medicine of Monlau is that one can hope to alleviate illness by a change in the *medio*, a change in the circumstances or atmosphere. Hence his concept of the *primavera médica* referred to at the start of Chapter 19, in which climate is defined as the cause of ills. It is the aim of alleviation, rather than the diagnosis of cause, that sets him aside from the alternative, "modern" style of medicine which was to become concerned with diagnosis, nomenclature, and the identification of the cause of a disorder, rather than with the manner in which that disorder might be cured.

Somoza presents himself as a simple man, one of good sense, but who has in fact a habit of avoiding clarity. That is, it would be a wonder if he were able to "play upon the keyboard" of a hysteric, since he himself draws back from the use of precise language, much in the same way as he draws back from death. We are told that it is his way to remove himself from the scene of a death (II. 118), and indeed we see that not only is he unwilling to accompany his patients to the moment of death, but also that he is unwilling to put into words with them the certainty of their death. Hence his typical phrase would be "–¿Conque se nos quiere usted morir, señor Fulano? Pues vive Dios, que lo hemos de ver..., etcétera" (I. 427). He is reported as being unwilling to use "muchos términos técnicos, porque, según él, a los profanos no se les ha de asustar con griego y latín" though he is willing to invoke "Science" as his ultimate authority if necessary: " 'La ciencia manda esto; la ciencia manda lo otro' " (I. 427) in a way that again absolves him from personal responsibility in the transaction. Yet we find him in a stand-off with Foja as they discuss the likely fatal nature of Barinaga's acutely alcoholic condition in Chapter 22. He throws names and technicalities at Foja, referring to Todd, Campbell and Chevrière, and cuts Foja out of the right to engage in discussion because of his ignorance of "la palabra":

> – (...) ¿Conoce usted a Todd?
> – ¿A quién?
> – A Todd.
> – No señor.
> – Pues no hable usted. ¿Sabe usted lo que es el poder hipotérmico del alcohol? Tampoco; pues cállese usted. ¿Sabe usted con qué se come el poder diaforético del citado alcohol? Tampoco; pues sonsoniche. ¿Niega usted la acción hemostática del alcohol reconocida por Campbell y Chevrière? Hará usted mal en negarla; se entiende, si se trata del uso interno. De modo que *no sabe usted una palabra...* (II. 234-5, emphasis mine)

Somoza's references are, predictably, not to contemporary authorities, but to those who would have been authorities at the time of his *formación*. Similarly, when questioned by Víctor about Ana, Somoza mixes an apparent desire to be friendly and helpful with a distinct inability to speak clearly, and an ultimate recourse to defense in the *difference*, indeed, the unassailability, of the doctor's position: "Hombre, los nervios siempre andan en el ajo... y la primavera... la sangre. La savia nueva... es claro... todo influye... pero usted no puede entender esto..." (II. 117).

Saillard (1988: 320, 322) highlights the fact that on the two occasions of acute crisis suffered by Ana, the doctor who is brought to see her is a young substitute. It is implied by her that it is in the figure of the young doctor that Alas, albeit in covert manner, displays his knowledge of contemporary medical and psychological advances. But what matters is arguably not what Benítez knows (in comparison with Somoza), but rather what he is assumed to know, given his apparent modernity. It is as though he is placed by Alas in the position outlined by Lacan as "the Subject who is Supposed to Know" (Lacan 1979: 130-8), and thus plays out for us the drama of the supposed authority when meeting requests for authority.

Saillard also talks of the way in which Benítez is reluctant to reveal to Ana the pathology of her condition (a bedside reticence which, Saillard implies, is shared by Alas). Indeed, when he does speak, it is in a way which shows him closely related to Somoza, that is, he uses technical language as a barrage, and to signal his place in the medical priesthood. Thus, at the transfer in Chapter 19, he is described as "different": "No le gustaba usar los nombres vulgares y poco exactos de las enfermedades, y empleaba los técnicos si le apuraban, no por ridícula pedantería, sino por salir con su gusto de no enterar a los profanos de lo que no importa que sepan" (II. 118).

And if language is power, so too is silence, and the silence of Ana's doctors with her is arguably the silence of many doctors of the time with their hysterics. Most typically in the novel, she is a patient *about* whom, not *to* whom doctors talk, so that she is forever objectified, relegated to the third person singular. Hence the consultations referred to already are with Víctor, not with her, much as Freud, even while engaging in the talking cure with Dora, actually engaged in a set of *between men* exchanges with her father and Herr K (Lacan 1985: 100). More than that, at the close of Chapter 9, Víctor, having found the chaos caused when Ana is caught in one of his hunting traps, thinks that he must "consultar seriamente *lo* de su mujer" (I. 387), so that there is a separation between his wife and her disorder – all to be consulted at a distance.

Ana is well-versed in the art of being a patient, from the early days when she learned to conform with the model expected of her by her aunts: "hacía muy buena enferma. No pedía nada; tomaba todo lo que le daban" (I. 214). This is not the demanding hysteric who irritates those about her, nor even the obliquely "demanding" person that Ana will become as victim of her hysterical attacks, demanding attention to herself. Here it is as though her aim is to deflect attention. And yet, in this description, a central feature of the hysteric as characterized in the period stands out: she is capable of enactment. If she is compliant, it is a compliance that not only is the *conversion* of rebellion (as suggested earlier), but is the action which through evasion makes rebellion unnecessary, since the object that is dangerous or threatening is quite simply evaded by the assumption of a state less than that needed for normal social contact. That is, Ana performs, she does what is expected or convenient, but the ability by which "hacía muy buena enferma" will become later in the novel that tendency to have *jaquecas* when convenient. Thus she plans one in Chapter 9 (I. 346) as a way of solving the problem of taking communion or not the following day; it is her excuse to Fermín in Chapter 16 (II. 57), to avoid going to confession (an untruth that it is uncomfortable to sustain when Fermín asks her about it [II. 58]), and it is perceived as nothing less than an affront by Fermín (II. 61), because of the evident fiction; she thinks of feigning illness in order to avoid greeting Álvaro (II. 302). All of this is illness in the pursuit of avoidance, so that illness becomes, as it were, the safe place. In the light of this, her crises of *nervios* can be seen as the longer-term strategy of the hysteric who, whether known to herself, or unknown to herself, abstracts herself from normal social intercourse because evasion of that intercourse is absolutely essential. Nor is Ana the only one to feign. Víctor's retirement was, by his own admission to himself, "fundada en una enfermedad que no tenía" (II. 217), so that there is, as it were, a possible recognition and identification between the two, encapsulated in that example cited earlier where in her convalescence what he offers her is invalid's broth (II. 118), the suitable diet for remaining still "in-valid," and out of the requirement that she act, contrasting with Álvaro's desire that she eat meat to engage with the world and with sexual life.

Feigning we can regard as a diversion from being a good patient, even though it is the means to bring about that impression. But there are perhaps other gains for Ana in the position of patient, beyond that of avoiding the requirement to participate in life, and it is above all in the relationship with Fermín, as "spiritual doctor" that this is made evident. A curiosity of the text of *La Regenta* is in its omissions. Just as there is an omission of direct reportage of the proceedings of the confessional (Valis 1994: 107), so too there is a notable lack of direct reportage of the exchanges between Ana and her medical attendants. There is reflection on what she is told, there are her references to her treatment in her letters in Chapter 27, but more than this is kept secret from the narrative. The secrets of the sick-room become similar to the secrets of the confessional.

What we are told about more directly is Ana's relationship with Fermín in so far as it is cast in the doctor/patient mold. This exposition of the medical model of relationship in the confessional domain could simply be construed as a placing of this type of power-relationship in an area of the plot where it is of most interest: the main concern of the surface narrative of *La Regenta* is, after all, around the fate and interests of Ana Ozores, and not with the niceties of medical etiquette of the time. But a different construction is to argue that once again, we have placed within the text concerning Fermín other foci of interest, because he can be considered as suitable. It is not just that (as in this case) the model fits, but that he can be used as the vehicle of criticism, and the exposure of power relationships. He is thus not neutral territory, but fair game. And in the transposition to confessional mode of the relationship with Benítez we can perceive Ana as the now well-trained hysteric, the hysteric's aptitude for training being proven time and again by the patients exhibited at Charcot's Tuesday lectures.

Fermín claims for himself the role of doctor, and one of the tradition of Somoza: he is "médico higienista." Not only this, but, in this passage where he is explaining to Ana the features of their future confessional relationship, he is designating their respective roles of health and illness. She must obey: "el confesor es médico higienista; pero así como el enfermo que no toma la medicina o que oculta su enfermedad, y el sano que no sigue el régimen que se le indica para conservar la salud, a sí mismos se hacen daño, a sí propios se engañan" (I. 343). In his imagery, Fermín is doing no more and no less than present the model of illness which was prevalent in contemporary pastoral theology. The irony is that while religion presented a belief in the separation between body and soul, literature of the confessional seems to have difficulty in believing in such a separation. The body is to be subjugated: it cannot simply be ignored. Ana responds with ease to the suggestion that she is the patient, and is increasingly apt at responding with the signals required of the patient's position. Thus when Fermín speaks to her as "médico del alma" (II. 66), she comes back with the suggestion that "acaso estaba loca" (II. 69), and indeed pathologizes herself: "¿no serían tampoco más que nervios? ¿Serían indicios peligrosos de un espíritu aventurero, exaltado, torcido desde la infancia?" (II. 70). Fermín speaks to her with severity, and though his words are couched in theological and pastoral terms, what she is portrayed as feeling grateful for is his assumption of control, a control which Benítez will later exercise in Chapter 27. Her increased submission to Fermín in Chapter 18 is couched again in terms of the patient – one who is presented as a hysteric, without foundation, firmness or boundary: "Yo estoy enferma... sé, señor, a pesar de estos colores y esta carne, como dice don Robustiano, estoy enferma; a veces se me figura que soy por dentro un montón de arena que se desmorona... No sé cómo explicarlo... siento grietas en la vida... me divido dentro de mí... me achico, me anulo... Si usted me viera por dentro me tendría lástima" (II. 107). By the time she reaches Benítez after the Semana Santa disaster, she is fully trained into obedience and servitude, such that she appears to take pleasure in it. Benítez, though apparently modern, is singularly non-interventionist in his practice, confining his recommendations to rest, strict measurement of bodily functions (a sign that he intends to work with the functioning of the body only, in contrast with Fermín), and a prohibition on language in the form of reading and writing. The recommendation of the quiet life, repose, startlingly like the "rest-cure" of the period which was so potent a weapon of control (Showalter 1985: 138-44) is obeyed and enacted with pleasure by Ana in Chapter 27. She writes her diary (Benítez permits it), cites to Benítez those (medical) authors she feels strong enough to read, submits joyously to his control: "estoy como un reloj, que es la expresión que usted prefiere. El régimen respetado con religiosa escrupulosidad. El miedo guarda la viña, seré esclava de la higiene." Out of obedience, she gives up introspection (or says that she does), there being in this an implied reversal of the relationship with the confessor that requires introspection, while at the same time, the austerity of the action denotes the austerity and self-denial required by the confessional: "Continúo mi diario, en el cual no me permito el lujo de perderme en *psicologías* ya que usted lo prohibe también" (II. 377).

The Hysterical Narrative and the Hysterical Narrator

Bernheimer notes that Freud, in calling Dora's case "a continuation of the dream book" seems to indicate that we should read the case "as a symptomatic continuation of his ongoing self-analysis, as a fragment of the analysis of his case of hysteria." That is, Bernheimer points to Freud as the hysteric, who, as it were, dislocates his hysteria into the patient whose case he describes. What is the implication of applying this to Alas and his character Ana? Bernheimer suggests that we can see Freud as "involved in a powerfully ambivalent counter transference," and that "Resisting not only his desire for Dora but also... his identification with her, Freud rejects as other and aberrant the feminine side of himself that he had embraced in the transferential relation with Fliess. He can accept his femininity, it seems, as a 'passive' response (his term) to fantasized male superiority but not as an identification with a woman whose sexuality is pluralized through multiple bisexual impulses" (1985: 17). If we consider Alas from the point of view articulated by Lou Charnon-Deutsch (1990), then his writing is both a defensive separation of himself from the feminine, and yet, there is apparently a fascination with the feminine. The reasons for which Freud characterized Dora as "passive," as a type of hysteria which he can regard as separate from himself, are arguably the same reasons for which Alas so decisively separates himself from his female protagonist at the very point at which she acts out the hysteric's needs, and sets herself beyond the social pale. Not only this, but while he allows Ana to walk out on Fermín, as Dora did with Freud, he follows this with retribution: he makes her return, and she is rejected.

STRATEGIES II: PERVERSE RITUALS

The absence of parental figures has been a constant in the discussion so far. Thus in the question of triangular family configurations, fathers were absent, mothers robbed of their reputation, and substituted for by unnameable unsatisfactory figures. The absence of fathers figured in Chapter 3 as the most immediately identifiable causes of the absence of desire, at least as construed in terms of oedipal theory. In the two following chapters, in which the strategic retreats into illness of Ana Ozores were discussed, a constant in the backdrop was her awareness of her condition, both motherless and childless. In both of these chapters, Ana's strategies were identified as consisting in evasion of desire, and evasion of control, and both were perforce strategies passive in their nature and in the form of their acting out. In both the disorder of anorexia, and that of hysteria, there is an indication of the crucial nature of coming to puberty: both disorders traditionally have their onset around the age of puberty, and cease before the menopause. They are, then, disorders concerned with the resistance not of sexual identity, but of the confirmation of adult possession, and acknowledgement of that sexual identity.

Because of the emphasis on the oedipal background to these chapters, the weight has fallen on a traditional Freudian interpretation of desire, with its implied triangular configuration. In the triangles discussed there has been a noted absence of the father to indicate the route to desire, or to act as a model for identification. The absence of the father is displayed as injurious equally to men and women, but it has not been so openly lamented (by Ana, the main character concerned) as has been the absence of a mother who would have provided everything, it is imagined, that is found to be lacking. Some discussion of paternal absence in the novel has been undertaken by Nimetz (1971), in a manner that is in part consonant with what has been argued here but with two main caveats. First, Nimetz idealizes the potential role of a father: "Only the advent of a father will rout the sexual nightmare of impotence, homosexuality, and lesbianism on the one hand, and the institutional nightmare of Church and State on the other" (252). The characters of *La Regenta* do not, perhaps, ask quite so much. Second, he takes no account of the awful presence of the mother. It is this which proves to be crucial, for if the absence of fathers signs the absence of effective and executive desire (a conclusion that emerges from the discussion of Chapter 3), then the presence not of mothers in general, but of a single, all-dominant one, is sufficient to set in motion not the surface text of the socially allowable adultery, but the illegitimate subtext of Fermín's desperate ritual in order to overcome his mother, and which drives the adultery narrative to its ill-fated conclusion.

In the last two chapters, then, we shall find that fathers are still absent as ever, but the family constellation that concerns us shifts, in that in the discussion of masculine strategies to define identity, and to provide demarcations around the self, what comes to be of prime importance is an active resistance to, and need to overcome, a mother who is far from absent. The struggle with a mother whose life and presence constitute a problem could be viewed against the arguments put forward by Elisabeth Bronfen in *Over Her Dead Body* (1992). But whereas Bronfen considers the deaths of beautiful women in works of art, *La Regenta* is one where death of women occurs only discreetly, off-stage. The two central women, Ana and Doña Paula, haunt us simply because they fail to die, or they fail to be allowed to die.

Chapters 6 and 7 concentrate on the Fermín/Paula dyad. Here it is seen that the dyad without the third point (of the father) is not simply problematic in the question of desire, but that it leads to situations that are ever inward-turning. Since desire and freedom are blocked (for Fermín), his only options are to replicate the dyadic relationship that he knows, or to try to overcome the intolerable situation of his relationship with Paula, the woman of the first dyad by using Ana as his perverse object in a self-created, non-oedipal triangle.

Chapter 6

THE FORCE OF PARENTAL PRESENCE

The absent mother

Protagonists of novels are well-known for their facility for losing parents, particularly mothers, *en route* to the opening pages of chapter one. Ana Ozores is no exception to this, but *La Regenta* as a novel is exceptional in the degree to which it counterpoises against the traditional image of the absent (because dead and lost) mother, that of a present and intolerable one. This is made the more dramatic because the intolerable presence is not that of the protagonist's stepmother (beloved hate-image of fairy tales), but that of a real mother, attached to the man who appears to promise spiritual deliverance to the protagonist: namely Fermín's mother, Paula de Pas. Thus the reader (not to mention the protagonist) is deprived of the let-out provided by a step-mother (she is not really ours, there is no fundamental connection between us and her, other than the simply legal one). Paula poses for us the drama that we cannot avoid, that of a close relationship that suffocates and yet cannot be rejected. She is inescapably there, physically and mentally, throughout the novel: ever-present for Fermín, and ever-present for the reader as a reminder that the mothering Ana desires might not be the idyllic experience she appears to long for, were she able to achieve it. Paula is also at the root of Fermín's relationship with Ana, affecting the reasons for which he is drawn to Ana and the manner of his separation from her. My intention in this chapter is to examine two central features of Doña Paula's presence in *La Regenta*: her influence on Fermín's style of masculinity, and her effect on the nature of the relationship between Fermín and Ana. I shall argue that throughout the text, Fermín and his mother remain locked in an infantile, essentially pre-oedipal relationship, never resolved and unchallenged by an appropriate father-figure. At the same time I shall highlight the gender-associated resonances of the Fermín/Paula dyad when understood in the context of the honor/shame cultures typical of the Mediterranean.

Ana's absent, or lost, mother is the cause of considerable idealization of the maternal state, and her absence has been adduced by some (notably Urey 1987) as the root cause of Ana's problems, a diagnosis with which Ana would presumably concur, since it fits her representation to herself of her orphaned state. Mothering is imagined rather than experienced, and in Ana's case, longed for rather than rejected. Awareness of the piteous state of Ana Ozores as a motherless child, indeed as eventual orphan, permeates the narrative, not least in that of Ana herself to herself. Thus her initial recounting of her life undertaken in preparation for the general confession with Fermín de Pas in Chapter 3 verges on a rehearsal or performance to herself of her perceived role in which she appears in a state of solitude that has all the appearance of abandonment. The sense of solitude evoked here is akin to the desolation of loneliness which for Klein was the characteristic of the first sense of the experience of separation from the mother. It contrasts with Winnicott's understanding of solitude as an experience which need not be desolate providing that the child has come to experience solitude within the presence of the mother (Klein 1963; Winnicott 1985). Her vision of motherhood, or rather of the mothering of which the child is object, is, despite its literary self-consciousness, simple and unequivocally positive, in that it presents a traditional, idealistic vision of the mother's role, nature and function. It is an ideal formulated in the absence of the "reality" of Ana's mother, who is never presented directly in the text, and whose shifting nature is encapsulated in the way her occupation changes from dressmaking to dancer in the mouth of Vetusta's gossips.

Other images of mothers in the text are less than positive, ranging from Visitación, who neglects her family for the social excitement of the Vegallana circle, to the pious and ineffectual Doña Lucía Carraspique. These mothers, however, pale in significance, when compared with the all-too-present, terrible mother of the text, Paula, whose appearance is delayed until a third of the way through the novel, and the dramatic re-telling of her shared history with Fermín occurs significantly in Chapter 15, the mid-point of the narrative.

The Present Mother

La Regenta is concerned as much with the excesses of the material world as with the insecurity and inadequacy of human fantasy. Paula's first appearance portrays her as an immovable physical obstacle, and signals the symbolic and emotional connotations she has in the dynamic of the text. Her appearance in Chapter 11 is sudden, her physical bulk dominating Fermín's field of vision:

> Cuando Petra iba a atravesar el umbral, ocupó la puerta por completo una mujer tan alta casi como el Magistral y que parecía más ancha de hombros; tenía la figura cortada a hachazos, vestía como una percha. Era doña Paula, la madre del Provisor. (I. 412-13)

Her second appearance, at the opening of Chapter 15, is equally dramatic:

> En lo alto de la escalera, en el descanso del primer piso, doña Paula, con una palmatoria en una mano y el cordel de la puerta de la calle en la otra, veía silenciosa, inmóvil, a su hijo subir lentamente con la cabeza inclinada, oculto el rostro por el sombrero de anchas alas.
> Le había abierto ella misma, sin preguntar quién era, segura de que tenía que ser él. Ni una palabra al verle. (I. 541)

The two delineations of Paula, looming, huge, an icon of power, are of a figure that is larger than life. She blocks the doorway, and bars the way up the stairs. In each case it is as though she is perceived from the perspective of the child, towering above him, so that Fermín's perception of her is presented not as that of a man in his mid-thirties, and of considerable local importance, but as that of the child under the control of an omnipotent mother. On these two occasions, moreover, she appears just as a misdeed of some sort has been committed. In the first instance, her arrival clashes with Fermín's preceding thoughts on his lost "otro yo" (I. 410), and those aroused by Petra's visit with a letter from Ana. In the second instance, Fermín has failed not only to return home to lunch, but to inform his mother of his absence. The two instances thus are overlaid with the sense of guilt and powerlessness a small child might feel in an relationship with his mother unmediated.

Paula is presented not only as terrible and omnipotent, but as a symbol of death. Significantly, however, this is conveyed through her portrayal as an "amortajada," an image which draws on a tradition linking women to the transitions of life, from the threshhold of birth to that of death. She is all that Jung alludes to in his comments on the negative aspects of the mother archetype, which may "connote anything secret, hidden, dark; the abyss, the world of the dead, anything that devours, seduces, and poisons, that is terrifying and inescapable like fate" (Jung 1938: 110). Paula qualifies on all scores as the negative archetype, not least in the sense of representing an inescapable fate. Unusually, however, Paula is not so much the death-bringer as the one who has herself been victim. She is already dead, her appearance tells us, and her physical image evokes the mortality that awaits the living. It is, in a sense, the physical, material form of the fate of death that is present throughout the novel, in a form of *cuerpo presente*. Her appearance also prefigures in graphic form the reproach she will consistently make to Fermín that he is bringing death (failure) to their joint enterprise of social elevation, and, on an emotional level, that by his neglect of her he is causing her death. There is about her presence a strange combination of physical indeterminacy (she appears younger than her age, she appears similar to Fermín, her gender is ambiguous), and yet an awful clarity:

> Tenía sesenta años, que parecían poco más de cincuenta. Debajo de un pañuelo de seda negro que cubría su cabeza, atado a la barba, asomaban trenzas fuertes de un gris sucio y lustroso; la frente era estrecha y huesuda, pálida, como todo el rostro; los ojos de un azul muy claro, no tenían más expresión que la semejanza de un contacto frío, eran ojos mudos; por ellos nadie sabría nada de aquella mujer. La nariz, la boca y la barba se parecían mucho a las del Magistral. Un mantón negro de merino ceñido con fuerza a la espalda angulosa, caía sin gracia sobre el hábito, negro también, de estameña con ribetes blancos. Parecía doña Paula, por traje y rostro, una amortajada. (I. 413)

The uncertainty of Paula's age echoes, in terrible parody, the lack of clarity about Ana's age, and reveals, by the echo, the fate that may await Ana, the death's head that she may become. Ana is to occupy Paula's place in the dyad. On her re-appearance on the landing as Fermín mounts the stairs Paula has become a solid object, blocking his way, but with the aspect of a ghost:

> El hijo subía y la madre no se movía, parecía dispuesta a estorbarle el paso, allí en medio, tiesa, como un fantasma negro, largo y anguloso. (I. 541)

In both cases, Paula stands at an entrance and bars the way by filling its space. In the first case, the doorway connects Fermín's part of the house to her own. He is in the seclusion of his part of the house, but has no freedom to move beyond that seclusion. Her presence there at that point signals the way in which she will block his attempted move out of the seclusion of the priesthood in which she has placed him and his move into an alternative relationship with Ana. In the second case, the doorway leads from the outside world (traditionally the domain of the male) to their shared residence. Her presence this time at the top of the stairs signals not only the heights to which she has elevated the two of them, but the power-relationship between them in which she is the dominant, he the subjugated partner. The "palmatoria" in her hand, here understood in its first meaning of "candlestick," but also carrying the meaning of the ferule traditionally associated with the schoolteacher in the schoolroom, reinforces the image of the mother who is in control and the mother who will punish, at the same time signalling her "magisterial" position, the emotional reality of which is set against the publicly imaged relationship in which he is the magisterial one, the Magistral, and she the subordinate female keeper of the house.

Paula's story, placed before us in full in Chapter 15, is violent, entangled, a struggle for social betterment via the route of sexual compromise and astute manipulation of the weakness and susceptibility to public opinion of others, particularly priests. Her experience is such as to render her hypersensitive to Fermín's vulnerability to gossip. Valis has indicated the link between Paula, the earth, the activity of the miners, and the symbolic status contained in her surname Raíces (Valis 1981: 43). These are archetypal associations, and the link between mining and the activity of creation has been explored by Mircea Eliade in *The Forge and the Crucible* (1971). Paula, however, embodies these associations in travestied form. Within the social setting where she grows up, poverty reigns; the earth may render riches but rather than natural ones, they take the form of money (for the miners). Moreover, as a girl Paula is disempowered, prevented from participating in the riches: all she can do is to *carry* earth (I. 548), not profit from its contents. Her way of desiring money is not initially in the form of ambition, but as something which will fill a void: it is desire rooted in lack , on a clear material level but with all the resonances of lack of power in a patriarchal society. She learns of the worth of money "por la gran pena con que los suyos lo lloraban ausente" (I. 548), but she can only fulfil ambition vicariously through her son. Vicarious and dislocated action and feeling are hallmarks of the novel, not least in this mother-figure who dominates emotionally precisely because she is disempowered.

An example of this dislocation is found in Paula's sexuality. She exudes a strong sense of the sexual, but is portrayed as being ambiguous of gender. It is as if her experience of sexuality is a tool employed merely to achieve social betterment and material comfort. Her strong, ungainly form arouses the appetites of the miners (not to mention the priest to whom she becomes housekeeper), but she is as detached and calculating about her use of her capacity for attraction as might be any pimp for his prostitute. The image of sex as brutal and energetic is not, of course, restricted to the evocation of Paula's battles, whether with Francisco de Pas, the priest, or the miners who sup at her tavern. Significantly it is reiterated in the description given by Álvaro in Chapter 20 of his battles with Ramona, conducted, as are the struggles of Paula with Francisco, in a *panera*. This building, being a "casa de madera sostenida por cuatro pies de piedra, como las habitaciones palúdicas sustentadas por troncos, y las de algunos pueblos salvajes" (II. 175-6), suggests a fragile, intermediate dwelling place, the temporary and transitional connotations of which relate to the habitual use of intermediate zones for adultery in the novel which has been signalled by Labanyi (1986). The struggles are silent, conducted with kicks and punches, and in Ramona's case, aggressively oral (the association of orality/sexuality will recur in the cigar motif discussed below). Indeed the textual resonances between the story of Paula and that of Ramona are such as to arouse within the reader the question of whether the secret history of *La Regenta* might conceivably contain an encounter, however incongruous, between Álvaro and Paula.

Paula's history contains those elements which will underlie her relationship with her son: men have access to riches and power, but men are foolish, men can be tyrannized. If they are prey to primitive passion, desire for the earth, riches characterized as *lodo*, then women's route to power is by their connection with earth and *lodo*: if men have appetite, that is, if they suffer hunger and thirst, then women's power lies in their ability to assuage that appetite. The hunger and thirst of the miners is real and physical enough (I. 554), but is also symbolic of the physical longing and appetite of man. Women, at least to Paula's mind (and arguably more generally in this patriarchal novel [Mandrell 1990]), do not enjoy an analagous appetite, simply the power to exploit male appetite for their own comfort and freedom from poverty. Not for nothing is Paula aware of the dangers Fermín ran in his relationship with the Brigadiera. Men are also characterized in the narrative as wild beasts, as "fieras," which it is the woman's role to tame or civilize. Thus woman, somewhat surprisingly, falls on the side of "Culture" rather than "Nature."

By contrast, Fermín is portrayed either as unaware of his own sexuality, or conveniently denying it, or satisfying its needs in a place distant even from the text, so private a function is it. As a result, his sexuality is not dislocated but ambiguous, intimately linked with the struggle between himself and his mother for the possession of power and the burden of shame.

Honor and Shame

In Paula's role in society, in her relationship with men and in her resulting relationship with Fermín, there is the characteristic splitting of gender attributes that is to be found in Mediterranean honor/shame cultures. At the same time the habitual distribution of such attributes is periodically redistributed in a way that accounts for, and is explained by, the sexual ambiguity of the two characters. Within honor/shame cultures, honor is that positive quality which can be possessed by men, whereas women are associated with shame, or loss of honor. Although there are ways other than sexual misdemeanour in which loss of honor can occur, the real or suspected sexual transgressions of a woman are prime reasons for a man's loss of honor. As a result, such cultures produce a vigorous splitting off by men of the attributes of sensuality, flexibility, emotion, and the physical life which are are deemed to pertain to women, carrying the major risk of honor-loss (Caro Baroja 1965; Pitt-Rivers 1965).

Fermín and Paula do not constitute the husband/wife pair basic to an honor culture, or even the father/daughter dyad in which honor is traditionally held or won by the former and lost by the latter, but are son and mother. In the first instance, Fermín, being the child, is the dependant, and then the object used by his mother for social advancement. Thus, in a sense, where Paula moves into the masculine domain of controlling money and entering into transactions, Fermín occupies the position of the woman whose usefulness and status is that of an object to be used in social barter and gain. He is "possessed" by his mother as a useful object, rather than being himself a subject with its own volition. In the way that Paula casts the relationship, Fermín has the female part, the shame. Uppermost in her mind is the awareness that he is the instrument through which honor for the two is liable to be lost, and that this will be through his sexual indiscretion. The case of the Brigadiera has been ample proof of this (I. 419). Paula's suspiciousness about Fermín's potential indiscretion with Ana is conveyed in graphic, physical form at the close of Chapter 11 as she examines his room, seeming to "olfatear con los ojos" (I. 424), the sense of smell being connected, as noted in Chapter 3 with a salacious detection of illicit sexual activity. (Underlying this situation of honor, shame and marketability, there is the parallel with Ana, also an object, mercilessly subjected to the sexual market by her aunts, her value placed in question by the incident with Germán, as Fermín's value is placed in question by the Brigadiera.)

There is effectively a struggle, even competition, between Fermín and Paula over the question of which of them is to be associated with feminine shame, filth, and lack of purity. Initially the two of them occupy traditional places in the honor/shame dyad: Paula associated with secret filth, the physical life, the dubious traffic with the miners; Fermín kept distanced by his mother from all of this. The way he is viewed publicly as an adult, however, suggests a sexual ambiguity rooted in his unclear place in the honor/shame dyad.

The opening pages in which he excites the interest and envy of Bismarck and Celedonio on account of a mixture of attributes declare an uncertainty of gender, or of publicly recognized gender. Hence the prurient interest of Celedonio in Fermín's reputed use of make-up (I. 96), and Bismarck's admiration for his "señorío," or "lordliness," which consists in his feminine attribute of spotlessness: "¡Aquello era señorío! ¡Ni una mancha! Los pies parecían los de una dama..." (I. 101).

Bismarck's comment about Fermín's lack of any "mancha" alludes to the success of his public separation from shame, while the attribute of having a woman's foot (a motif which will acquire its full measure of shame when Vetusta in its entirety turns out to glimpse Ana's naked feet) places him firmly within the feminine realm, as does the narrative's outlining of the high colour in his cheeks, a denotation relating to love and shame (I. 102).

In their shared past, Paula is shown as regarding herself as the one who is stained by contact while her son is to remain pure, her activity justified by the fact that in her contact with filth she will accumulate wealth (*lodo* here having become associated with *tierra*): "Allí estaba ella para barrer hacia la calle aquel lodo que entraba todos los días por la puerta de la taberna; a ella la manchaba, pero a él no; él allá dentro con Dios y los santos, bebiendo en los libros la ciencia que le había de hacer señor; y su madre allí fuera, manejando inmundicia entre la que iba recogiendo ochavo a ochavo el porvenir de su hijo" (I. 556). But insofar as she takes a masculine part in the dyad, she assumes responsibility for ensuring that he, like a woman, remains pure, and does not cause the pair of them to lose honor and status.

Fermín is thus placed in the straitjacket of purity, and more than that, of social respectability. His role as priest, with its requirement of celibacy, prevents him from expressing his masculine sexuality, making him subject to internal splitting. There is a private self, aware of this unrealised masculinity, and a public self invested in the role of purity foisted on him by his mother's ambition and activity, which is inclined to make her the repository of all shame, as a way of disowning his physical appetites.

Though kept separate from the history of his mother's traffic with the miners, Fermín is clearly aware of it (I. 555-6). The combination of commercial enterprise and sexual barter leads to his association of his mother with money, and hence filth. The association between money and filth is not of course exclusive to Alas. In a paper outlining a psychoanalytic explanation for the connection between the two, Ferenczi emphasizes the fact that the filth concerned is one's own, that is, excreta (Ferenczi 1914), a link that we might bear in mind when considering Fermín's attitude to the filth accumulated (or swept away) by his mother, and his consignment of Rosa Carraspique to a convent cell that is considered to be a *cloaca*. Fermín projects onto Paula all the shame-associated financial activity. Thus at the end of the fateful day in which he has eaten with the Vegallanas, failed to return home to eat with his mother, and has projected his own guilt over sexual indiscretion on to the priest from Contracayes (I. 460-4), the prospect of going downstairs to be present for the accounts inspires nothing less than "asco": "imaginaba que abajo había un gran foco de podredumbre, aguas estancadas" (I. 564).

Situating the concerns of money in the lower part of the house is symbolic of the way both Paula and Fermín push financial dealings below a surface that is apparently pure to public eye. Within the space occupied by them for living, Fermín's apartments are kept strictly separate from those of his mother, and the residence and their entire way of life is marked by austerity, orderliness and astringent cleanliness. This emphasis on the cleanliness as the domain of woman who is associated with shame is characteristic of honor/shame cultures, and demonstrates how the private domain of woman must always remain irreprochably unstained to potential public view (Sánchez Pérez 1990: 89-91).

Despite their sharply demarcated separate realms in the house, Fermín is nonetheless locked into an uncomfortably close dyad with his mother. For him, her history associated with filth is liable to drag them down, whereas for her it is his potential future action which could have this undesired effect. We can see him struggle to separate from what she represents, taking on as he does so the "honor" part of the honor/shame relationship. If he has had contact with filth, it is all his mother's fault: " 'Era su madre la que atesoraba; por ella, a quien lo debía todo, había él llegado a manosear y mascar el lodo de aquella sordidez poco escrupulosa' " (I. 423). Thus, whereas his mother's thoughts on filth (at the time when she acknowledges her contact with it) are that she is there to sweep filth from the house, Fermín's attention is taken by the fact that his mother's accumulation of filth in the form of money is one that has obliged him to have contact with it. He tries to separate himself. He envisages himself as a conqueror (Valis 1981: 43), possessed of his own nobility, and "ambición de dominar," separate from his mother's sins and "aquellos a que le había arrastrado la codicia de su madre" (I. 423). In taking on the guise of conqueror he is also reacting defensively against his own experience of being conquered or dominated by his mother, just as he resorts to her technique of the icy, silent, stare in order to subjugate others to his power. Reminiscent of the surveillance of the panopticon, it is a maneuver of compensation. It is no surprise that the theological issue we find Fermín contemplating in Chapter 11 is the doctrine of infallibility, a doctrine described as a desperate and heroic act like that of the Christians thrown to the lions, the images used to describe it reiterating the view of the miners at his mother's tavern as beasts to be tamed, yet also retaining a keen sense that the opposition with which he might meet is one of mockery, and dismissal: "un desafío formidable de la fe, rodeada por la incredulidad de un siglo que se ríe. Era como estar en el Circo entre fieras" (I. 402). Yet when it comes to his own sexual needs, he splits for his own convenience and accepts those provisions for his sexual satisfaction made by his mother (and insinuated to the reader), rationalizing his actions on the grounds that Ana is unconcerned with anything other than his spiritual side: "¿qué le importa a mi doña Ana que mi corpachón de cazador montañés viva como quiera cuando me aparto de ella?" (II. 244).

THE ABSENT FATHER

As outlined in Chapter 3, the Paula/Fermín dyad is spectacularly lacking a father, despite Fermín's possession in the past of a real father, Francisco de Pas, and the effective second father found for him by Paula in the person of Camoirán, the Bishop (I. 559). The two offer elusive and contrasting possibilities for identification. Francisco, the natural father, represents qualities of strength, sexuality and aggression, proven by his physical conquest of Paula (I. 550-2). He is a wastrel, a man of fantasy, who escapes the control even of Paula. This very detail suggests that the necessary reaction to Paula may be evasion rather than opposition. Fermín passes over any awareness of the lightweight side of his natural father, and instead calls him to mind in the stereotypically masculine guise of the "cazador." This image is present when Fermín looks at himself in the mirror and sees a strong body capable of physical exertion (to be exercised in the contained and potentially ridiculous episode of the swing in Chapter 13). Conveniently his gaze takes in what he wants it to take in, and he fails to notice the incipient paunch which will be brought to the attention of the reader in the following chapter, and of which, it would seem he is not unmindful, at least when walking out in public: "Llevaba el manteo terciado sobre la panza, que comenzaba a indicarse" (I. 525). He forgets Francisco's less admirable qualities in a desperate need for a model for identification, his desperation later being conveyed by his lack of judgment when in the last visit to El Vivero he appeals dramatically and ridiculously to Víctor as a fellow huntsman: "Vamos, Quintanar, usted que es cazador... y yo que también lo soy... ¡al monte! ¡al monte!" (II. 407). Connections with Francisco will be negative throughout. The occasion of what is to be the fateful meal at the Vegallanas in Chapter 13 is his father's saint's day: he visits all the Franciscos of Vetusta society, unmindful of the Francisco most closely related to him.

The bishop Camoirán, weaker, effeminate, emotional, represents the emasculated form of masculine power open to Fermín within the Church. His example is of failed rather than achieved masculinity, and he and Fermín engage in avoidance of one another. While Camoirán refuses to submit to the influence of Fermín in the capricious, frivolous femininity of his salon (I. 439), Fermín differentiates himself by his style of preaching. Camoirán is all effusion and feeling, but Fermín bases his preaching on dogma, closely argued texts, offering an austerity of presentation, a definitiveness of message that reflects the austerity of his life-style, and an attempt at a masculine demarcation within the feminine boundaries of the Church. The essential asexuality of his public figure and mode of activity is the nearest he comes to establishing masculine gender, forming part of the tradition by which science comes to be associated with a mode of being labelled as masculine, but actually de-sexualized in nature (Keller 1985: 91).

Nimetz (1971: 247) argues that Fermín in the course of the novel undergoes a second adolescence. Even adolescence, however, is disowned, lodged in Camoirán who on being found by Fermín in the company of Visitación and Olvido "se ruborizó, como un estudiante de latín sorprendido por sus mayores con la primera tagarnina" (I. 454-5). The association of active masculine sexuality and smoking, a set piece in European novels of adultery, appears in *La Regenta* in details ranging from Ana's exasperated contemplation of her husband's unfinished cigar (II. 10), to Álvaro's leisured smoking while others in the Casino talk of their sexual conquests (II. 172) and Paula's indication of her phallic masculine tendency in her rolling of a cigarette (I. 414). If Fermín shows his adolescence, it is in his exasperation here with an inadequate parental figure, with whom identification is impossible. It could equally be argued that Fermín is locked into the earlier pre-oedipal phase, given the markedly infantile manner of his relationship to his mother, which is transferred onto the relationship with Ana.

THE MATERNAL LEGACY

This primary relationship is powerful and dramatic. Chapter 15 reveals the primitive way that Paula uses silence, the enormous "parches untados con sebo" on her temples being the visible signs of her anger. The power of the non-verbal anger, familiar to Fermín, is no less powerful for its familiarity. When the accusations come (I. 544) they are pitched at his absence. His offence is ingratitude, abandon of his mother: "¡Si no hay madre que valga! ¿te has acordado de tu madre en todo el día? ¿No la has dejado comer sola, o mejor dicho, no comer? ¿te importó nada que tu madre se asustara, como era natural?" (I. 544). What is produced here is the rage and fear of the child when the mother is absent, the terror of separation before a sense of time has developed. Here Paula reverses roles and the mother adopts the position of the child: it is she who has been left and is defenseless, and she who can now throw a temper-tantrum in response. But she also subjects Fermín to a catechism inviting submission, to which he responds with Pavlovian promptitude:

> Fermo, ¿te fue bien toda la vida dejándote guiar por tu madre...?
> – ¡Sí, madre mía, sí!
> – ¿Te saqué yo o no de la pobreza?
> – ¡Sí, madre del alma! (I. 546)

Later, a simple state of union (or is the narrator's tongue in his cheek?) results from this emotional bullying. There is calm after the storm, and, what is noted with most favour is that difference of opinion is still possible. The account is idealized: "La tempestad se había deshecho en lluvia de palabras y consejos. Ya no se reñía, se discutía con calor, pero sin ira. Los recuerdos evocados, sin intención patética, por doña Paula, habían enternecido a Fermo. Ya había allí un hijo y una madre, y no había miedo de que las palabras fuesen rayos" (I. 547). The restoration of the mother's power is signalled by her familiar use of "Fermo," the familiar name that fixes her son in his position of submission in the dyad (Gullón 1990).

Early emotional habits resurface in the relationship between Fermín and Ana. Fermín's desire for an ideal mother is partly a rejection of Paula, partly a desire for early non-differentiation, for an escape from the alternatives of solitude and conflict. His desire for a perfect, non-conflictive mother comes, unsurprisingly, at the end of the dramas of Chapter 15 when, in his solitude, he resembles Ana in her consciously motherless state. He engages in a mood of self-lamentation: "Su madre le quería mucho, a ella se lo debía todo, ya se sabe... no sabía ella sentir con suavidad, no entendía de afectos finos, sublimes... había que perdonarla. Sí, pero él necesitaba amor más blando que el de doña Paula... más íntimo, de más fácil comunión por razón de la edad, de la educación, de los gustos..." (I. 561). Ana responds in Chapter 22 to his "palidez interesante" and other Romantically accentuated signs of tiredness, speaks to him "con voz de madre cariñosa" (II. 243), and in Chapter 23 shows her responsiveness to his declared motherless state (II. 288).

Exposed to the turmoil of his feelings for Ana, Fermín displays a variety of features of the paranoid-schizoid position, Klein's term for the infant state in which all feelings of discomfort are projected out, thus rendering the external world more hostile and terrifying (Sinclair 1993: 6-8). Characteristic of this are Fermín's violent mood swings, within which Ana is given the attributes of the bad mother. Betrayal, which we might equate with absence or a foreshadowing of the oedipal crisis, is Ana's crime, one he does not impute to his mother. When Fermín hears of Ana's faint in the arms of Álvaro, he thinks not of her, but of his mother: "su madre no le había hecho nunca traición, su madre era suya, era la misma carne." Ana's fundamental fault, it would appear, consists in not belonging to that original dyad, and thus being alien, an indisputable Other: "Ana, la otra, una desconocida, un cuerpo extraño que se le había atravesado en el corazón..." (II. 314).

Fermín also places on Ana that same label of ingratitude Paula had given him. After the interpolation of Paula's story in Chapter 15 (I. 547-60), there is a doubly-oriented passage where Paula's version of her struggles and his ingratitude is presented as a version of reality: "Ella le había hecho hombre..." (I. 559-60), and within which the restricted masculinity imposed on Fermín by his mother is expressed with disarming and repeated naiveté: "ella le había hecho niño mimado de un Obispo, ella le había empujado para llegar adonde había subido, y ella ganaba lo que ganaba, podía lo que podía... ¡y él era un ingrato!" (I. 560). The full impact of what Paula has done, and irony in the presentation of her understanding of it, is conveyed by the following passage in which Fermín articulates as if it were his own what is in fact her version of affairs, and concludes, after the emotional bludgeoning which has occurred, that he is an ingrate. He apparently has no desire to defend against being dominated by his mother's version of events, but it is significant that when he encounters what he sees as Ana's betrayal of him, he adopts his mother's role in that newly-formed dyad, and, disowning or forgetting his own "ingratitude" to his mother, accuses Ana of it with consummate ease in his reproaches to her in Chapter 19, at the same time as he sees himself, or presents himself, or is perceived by Ana as some ethereal and spiritual being. Through his eloquence in the confession "ella comprendió que estaba siendo una ingrata, no sólo con Dios, sino con su apóstol, aquel apóstol todo fuego, razón luminosa, lengua de oro, de oro líquido" (II. 138). Fermín, full of reproach and apparent self-abasement, demonstrates how completely he has taken over his mother's capacity for emotional manipulation: "yo esperaba que usted fuese lo que aquella historia que llorando me contaba, prometía... lo que usted me prometió cien veces después... Pero no, usted desconfía de mí, no me cree digno de su dirección espiritual, y para satisfacer esas ansias de amor ideal que siente, tal vez ya busca en el mundo quien la comprenda y pueda ser su confidente" (II. 139). Accusations of ingratitude are infectious, so that Ana competes with Fermín in the matter of who is to bear the crown of being the victim of ingratitude. Thus in Chapter 23, where Ana will fall under Fermín's power, she reproaches him for failing to recognize her motherless state and for his ingratitude, while at the same time asserting her own claim to what now appears to be almost the virtue of suffering ingratitude: "No me ha comprendido usted... Yo soy la que está sola... usted es el ingrato... Su madre le querrá más que yo... pero no le debe tanto como yo... Yo he jurado a Dios morir por usted si hacía falta... El mundo entero le calumnia, le persigue... y yo aborrezco al mundo entero y me arrojo a los pies de usted a contarle mis secretos más hondos... No sabía qué sacrificio podría hacer por usted... Ahora ya lo sé" (II. 290). In dyads where ingratitude and betrayal are the key emotions, competitiveness about guilt or need for pity abounds, and extremes of reaction and counter-proof ensue. But more than this, Ana has found what type of acting out of self-sacrifice is open to her. Speaking figuratively to him at this point, she in fact outlines what will become material in Chapter 26: "Quiero que las piedras que le hieran a usted me hieran a mí... yo he de estar a sus pies hasta la muerte... ¡Ya sé para qué sirvo yo! ¡Ya sé para qué nací yo! Para esto... Para estar a los pies del mártir que matan a calumnias..." (II. 290).

The major irony of this is that it will eventually spur Ana on to the public submission to Fermín in the Easter procession, an event which will compound his effective betrayal of his mother in that it adds to those actions which compromise their public position. Contrasting with Paula's effective caricature of the Virgin (Simon 1989), Ana's dramatic adoption of the role of the Virgin in the form of the Dolorosa is a final response to his private dramatization of himself as child in Chapter 25. It also confirms the closeness of her association with Paula, the original self-sacrificing mother. Ana's appearance in the procession – "parece de escayola" as Obdulia says (II. 368) – echoes the earlier appearance of Paula as an "amortajada" and also the initial description of Fermín in which his skin had "reflejos del estuco" (I. 102). The procession will also draw the narrative full-circle in that Ana's abasement of herself is the acting out of the early fantasy of Fermín who in Chapter 11 imagines himself declaring his unworthiness to her (I. 422).

With Ana, Fermín passes through the gamut of possible formulations of the mother/son situation (II. 316): from betrayal, to the feeling that Ana is other, to that sense of timelessness as if confronted by death that the maternal betrayal evokes, and which will be repeated with each subsequent loss (Klein 1963). When, after a final outburst of emotion, he leaves Ana, his action is strongly reminiscent of the child who storms off, expecting fully that its mother will follow him to engage in pity and/or reconciliation: "Creyó que Ana le seguiría, le llamaría, lloraría... Pero pronto se sintió abandonado" (II. 321).

Ana does not immediately engage in her promise to join in the penitential Easter procession. Curiously, in this novel of absent and inadequate fathers, her reaction on realizing that Fermín's passion for her is human rather spiritual, is to think of her father, in a travesty of deference to the paternal veto over forbidden relationships: "había que dar la razón en muchas cosas a don Carlos, al que después de todo era su padre" (II. 331). Later her decision to play Mater Dolorosa to the publicly vilified and shamed Fermín (II. 336) is experienced as a gesture of suicide, an entry into a zone of feeling which will have no demarcations, no boundaries, no sense of judgement, merely passion: "quería matar dentro de ella la duda, la pena, la frialdad, la influencia del mundo necio, circunspecto, *mirado...* quería volver al fuego de la pasión, que era su ambiente" (II. 337). Here Ana arguably wants to return to a pre-oedipal warmth, or even state of imagined union between mother and child, before the impingement of alienating experience. Again, just as she fantasizes perfect mothering, so her idea of a return to an original warmth is phantasy. So, also, she can be viewed as taking on willingly the role Fermín gives her in the dyad: she phantasizes on his behalf the return to a maternal container.

The following chapter opens out further the discussion of the dynamic of the Fermín/Ana dyad. The impression given from the discussion so far is of an impasse, since Fermín's repetition with Ana of the infant/mother dyad leaves him as immobilized in his sexual ambiguity as is Ana in her social ambiguity. His lack of public possession of masculinity is brought to painful climax in the closing scenes where he endeavors to make Víctor the instrument of his revenge, unable to play the part he feels is his right (Sinclair 1993: 212-17). The final gesture in the Cathedral, in which he towers above Ana, replicates for the reader those powerful initial moments in which Paula appears, just as the impotence of the hand raised to strike, and which does not strike, resumes Fermín's imprisonment in the mold cast for him by his mother.

CHAPTER 7

PERVERSE RITUALS

> Using a fantasy about mothers – about the beginning – to foreclose the transference turns psychoanalysis into perversion, perversion in the only meaningful sense of the term: knowing too exactly what one wants, the disavowal of contingency, omniscience as the cheating of time; the mother who, because she knows what's best for us, has nothing to offer. (Adam Phillips, *On Kissing, Tickling and Being Bored*)

In *La Regenta,* I have argued, desire is characteristically dislocated, frustrated and perverted, and the adultery narrative is entered into as a hysterical diversion from the sense of an impending fate of dissolution, annihilation, nothingness. As outlined in the previous chapter, there is counterpoised against this diversionary portrayal of desire a balancing narrative of conflict within a dyad, conflict with an identified Other. This dyadic conflict, between Fermín, the man who dare not avow even to himself his love for Ana, and his mother, Doña Paula, is a relationship arguably more impressive than that between any two of the four principals in the adulterous drama. This chapter continues the discussion of Chapter 6 which demonstrated the way in which this dyadic, infantile relationship is fraught with issues of gender definition and separation, and traces how Fermín resorts to perverse mechanisms as a result of his relationship with a phallic and dominating mother. Ana becomes the object of these mechanisms, and is obliged to play out a ritualized and public submission to Fermín as the response to his lifelong experience of domination by his mother. At the same time,

Ana is also the public object of the collective perverse longings and voyeurism of the people of Vetusta, and simultaneously enacts for them their desire for a sexual exhibitionism which in its turn is a defense against the absence of desire.

LOVERS OFFICIAL, UNOFFICIAL AND SCAPEGOATED

The role of Fermín de Pas in *La Regenta* is central. Though not the official "lover" in the material sense, he provides us with the most detailed articulation of the desire, or of the possible form of the desire of the lover. The form of desire in Fermín is, however, demonstrably perverse, and one issue that it raises is whether this is exceptional as a form of transgressive masculine desire in the novel, or whether, more disturbingly, it might be typical. As background to this discussion we need to take into account the points made earlier in the book about the nature of desire in the novel, namely the degree to which it is characteristically elusive and dislocated, with envy the most frequently presented form of desire, occurring most frequently in relation to women and priests, and in same-gender relationships. Consequently there is considerable gender-investment in the style of desire experienced by and attributed to the various characters of the novel. In particular we may note the gender-investment in the attempts of Fermín to dissociate himself from his mother, attempts which will lead to his "perversion."

Unusual as it may initially seem, it is not exceptional to see little of official lovers in novels of adultery, and in a number of novels, *La Regenta* among them, the official lover is trivialised, demonstrated as unworthy and shallow (suggesting, among other things, that the heroine is even more to blame, since the object of her desire – if such he be – is such a patently unworthy person). In those cases (Rodolphe in *Madame Bovary,* Mesías in *La Regenta*) where the characterization of the lover is as a womaniser, there is a hint of possible pathology, as indeed there is in the whole of the Don Juan tradition, of repetition compulsion. This raises distantly the issue of whether these men are women-lovers, women-haters, simply men out to prove their masculinity, or, as Roustang (1988) suggests, driven by a combination of fear of women, and desire to identify with them. It is not clear why the official lover should be trivialised in narratives of adultery, but where this occurs, the result is that the framework of the novel effectively presents the lovers as less of a threat to the stability of society, in which husbands, while frequently presented as ridiculous and/or inadequate, are nonetheless not actually overthrown by the lover. In this context, the foregrounding of the priest as potential lover further diverts attention from the official lover in that the former provides a socially acceptable scapegoat, a form of masculinity that it is permissible to attack, perhaps for the very reason that it is presented as pathological, non-normal. Thus the attack on masculinity in the figure of the husband who is deceived, and the trivialization of masculinity in the figure of the official lover, is counterbalanced and attenuated by the ferocious attack on what is presented as the distorted and perverse form of the masculinity of the clerical alternative lover.

The selection of the priest in *La Regenta* for the extremely full articulation of the lover is then perhaps a strategy of safety in the patriarchal novel where it might be difficult ultimately, for a man to be trivialised, or made the butt of criticism. We might remember the observation of Lou Charnon-Deutsch (1990: 36-7), made in connection with the male protagonists of novels by Juan Valera, namely that "a male reader on the lookout for lessons would surely be relieved to learn that even the most mediocre of men can inspire passion in nearly every woman he meets." A man in clerical dress, by dint of that dress, can be imagined as not a man, a convenience for the masculine reader.

Jo Labanyi (1986) has pointed out that in *La Regenta* nothing is what it seems, and nothing is in the right place. Using the ideas of contract and transgression of Tanner, she presents *La Regenta* as a novel of flow and uncertainty. Noël Valis (1981: 39) had earlier indicated the sado-masochistic view Fermín has of himself and the universe, relating his cruelty to others to his domination by his mother. My intention here is to comment on the structure and nature of the perversity she indicates, combining it with an extension of Labanyi's view, and arguing that since nothing is what it seems, and that nothing is in the right place, *La Regenta* can be understood in terms of perverse rituals, communal and private fetishes, carrying within them messages about the thwarted and diverted nature of masculine desire.

Gender and Desire

A distinction between masculine and feminine desire in *La Regenta* is made by James Mandrell, in his Lacanian essay on the novel (1990). Here he observes that "all desire in this novel is masculine. In this way, the feminine cannot help but be subsumed by the masculine" (1990: 21-2) and he distinguishes between the "articulation of the mediation of desire itself, between the masculine, phallic desire found in *Don Juan Tenorio* and the feminine, non-phallic *jouissance* of Santa Teresa" (1990: 20). It is true that we are given the impression that masculine desire is clearer, more accessible in the novel, that masculine desire can have an object, and that the attainment of that object is something which will, or may, lead to satisfaction. By contrast there is a consistent presentation of the lack of clarity, frustration and thwarting of the desire of woman, particularly but not exclusively in the character of Ana Ozores. Furthermore Mandrell's argument is correctly one in which public is set against private and is declared to triumph. More crucial, however, is what he touches on briefly, namely the issue of tainting, particularly important in the context of Fermín and his mother. It is only in this dyadic relationship that the reader is permitted to see the wholly problematic nature of gender and desire in the novel. Thus although the comment that all desire in the novel is masculine is, in a sense, true, there are two difficulties. The example of Fermín demonstrates just how far masculine desire is beset with difficulties and unclear in origin and motivation, and secondly, it is an example set in a context which places in question the nature of the desire of any of the characters, whether they be masculine or feminine.

A question consistently posed about the nature of masculine desire in *La Regenta* is whether that desire relates to women as objects, or whether it has a greater fascination with other masculine subjects. In another context (1993: 199-217) I have explored the degree to which masculine desire in *La Regenta* can be understood in terms of Girard's triangles of desire. While it is not clear at all that either Álvaro or Fermín can be perceived as "desiring" Víctor, there is no shortage of material to show that there is a highly developed system of *between men* comparison of possession of masculinity, hiding beneath the apparently more acceptable social text of competitiveness about the possession of, or capture of, a woman, in this case Ana. This type of relationship is accompanied by the acute interest of the husband, Víctor, in the apparent possession of masculinity by Álvaro, the obvious lover, and local Don Juan, and this interest in the lover's masculinity is of the type shown by Charles Bovary in his meeting with Rodolphe after the death of Emma, and in which he muses that "he would have liked to be that man" (Flaubert 1857: 359).

A naive approach to a novel of adultery might foreground desire: there might be the belief, the illusion that the lover desires the wife; perhaps even that the wife desires the lover. European novels of adultery posit examples both likely and unlikely. In the realm of the unlikely, in *Effi Briest* (1895) one could question whether anyone desires anyone else to any significant degree, with the exception of Effi's mother. Frau Briest provides us with one of the clear-cut examples of dislocation in the novel of adultery: she denies herself the marriage to Innstetten, accepts the more established Briest, the man more clearly of the material world, and finally has an oblique union with Innstetten through her daughter Effi. When Effi's adultery with Crampas comes to light, it is Frau Briest who effects the family punishment of ostracism of her daughter, a punishment of the woman she has allowed to be her substitute in pleasure. As for what Crampas desires, that seems to be all too elusive, unless one places it under the heading of quiet diversion.

Similarly in *Madame Bovary*, masculine desire, whether in Charles Bovary or in Emma's lovers, seems to border on the verge of being an irrelevant concept. Certainly in the case of Charles there is a high degree of enchantment, of a delight and idealism that could be perceived as matching those of Emma were it not for the distraction for both her and for the reader of his clumsy, bovine, blundering nature. There is evidence, however, in the meeting between Charles and Rodolphe after Emma's death, that there is a desire in Charles to know of, to possess the masculinity that is apparently the quality of Rodolphe, since it is this that had attracted his wife. What remains unclear is whether Rodolphe ever desired Emma, any more than Crampas desired Effi. As for Léon, he is an object to embody the romantic idealisation of Emma: whether he actively desires her is elusive as a concept.

By contrast, Tolstoy manages, both with Vronsky of *Anna Karenina* (1874-6) and Trukhachevsky of *The Kreutzer Sonata* (1890), to create personae of lovers whose attractiveness to the wife in question is plausible, and who in the case of Trukhachevsky at least, can be seen as embodying and enacting the disowned physical desire and potential for sexual and emotional excitement of the husband. But at the same time in *The Kreutzer Sonata* we find articulated more clearly than in the other novels so far mentioned the possibility of perversely dislocated masculine desire: a dislocation, or channelling of desire, is found in the activity of violin-playing, itself a symbol of expressiveness, and, in the co-operative work of the violin and piano duo, symbolic of intercourse.

In *La Regenta,* virtually all examples of desire are perverted, dislocated, frustrated, whether in the reversion to oral gratification by Visitación, or in the incitement through rustling silk by which Obdulia tantalizes Saturnino as he shows the works of art in the Cathedral to her country cousins. Saturnino's acceptance of the excitement is a further example of diverted desire, since he lacks the nerve to declare himself to anyone, and his preferred object is not Obdulia but Ana (I. 123), to whom he has expressed himself verbally and lengthily, but obliquely, "con ciertas parábolas y alegorías que tomaba de la Biblia y otros libros orientales" (I. 123), the "libros orientales," with their suggestion of exoticism and mystery being presumably the closest he gets to an articulation of desire.

Saturnino, an emblem of sexual and social ambiguity (classed by Alas as being not *clérigo* but *anfibio*) in his turn stands for Fermín, in so far as he embodies in more highly caricatured form a man imprisoned in the uniform of a soutane, and shows all the transgression of boundaries (he mixes periods and styles) characteristic, for Tanner (1979) and Labanyi (1986), of novels of adultery. In Saturnino's case, it is not a soutane that is his by profession, but one which, as Rogers (1984: 88) observes, his clothing, willy-nilly, evokes in the eyes of the onlooker. Saturnino is not just an embodiment in the novel of what we cannot be told about Fermín, but in response to Obdulia acts out in advance what will be Fermín's final hysterical choking, here presented as ridiculous, undignified, a piece of social untidiness: "Una noche en la tertulia de Visitación Olías de Cuervo, Obdulia le había tocado con una rodilla en una pierna. Él no había retirado la pierna ni ella la rodilla; él había tocado con el suyo el pie de la hermosa y ella no lo había retirado... Una cucharada de sopa se le atragantó" (I. 128).

Obdulia and Saturnino present an initial surface view for the reader of the perverse fears and desires that will eventually be acted on in the later stages of the novel. It is perhaps significant that these two characters are of uncertain, unfinalized sexual orientation. Do what he may, Saturnino cannot escape from falling into the image of a *clérigo*, however much attention he pays to his clothing. In his case the problem is not that he fails to be avowedly masculine, as that he becomes visually indeterminate, his outer form fixing him in a class of person prohibited from amorous dealings: "Lo de parecer clérigo no era sino muy a su pesar. Él se encargaba unas levitas de tricot como las de un lechuguino, pero el sastre veía con asombro que vestir la prenda don Saturno y quedar convertida en sotana era todo uno" (I. 122-3). Meanwhile, Obdulia, who by her excessively flirtatious manner, her way of flaunting her sexuality so as to tease, is notable for taking Saturnino as one of her prime targets, as though the particular perverse pleasure is in exciting one who is not going to be able to respond, except in passive, if excited, silence. This is arguably consistent with her later desire, on seeing Ana in the Easter procession, to be a man. The two details together signal a woman who in her outrageous occupation of the role of the *femme fatale* is arguably engaging simply in masquerade to cover the uncertainty of gender identity that she shares with the rest of the characters.

It is within the context of the undeclared drama of arousal and titillation of Obdulia and Saturnino that we are presented with a crucial visual image early in the novel. As Chapter 1 moves between background information and slow-moving description of action, a detail glimpsed in the half-light encapsulates the dislocated sexuality which will come to permeate the novel. Fermín, after his telescopic survey of Vetusta from the tower, studiously ignores the activity of El Palomo clearing away the mess left by a cat, and approaches the group of Obdulia, Saturnino and the country cousins. The canvas they are looking at is dark: all that can be seen is "el frontal de una calavera y el tarso de un pie desnudo y descarnado" (I. 121), these images being prefigurations and distortions of what will be the icon of Fermín (the skull, indicating his self-presentation as the man of intellect and not physique in the church) and that of Ana (the foot that will draw the attention of all when she is in the self-adopted role as Dolorosa, the Virgin of Sorrow) in the Easter Procession of Chapter 26, at the other extreme of the novel.

The skull and the foot, as emblems of desire in *La Regenta*, belong to the unrecognized, because unpermitted, desire between

Fermín and Ana. The skull relates to those dead qualities of Fermín and his mother suggested in physical descriptions of them that draw on images of plaster, of shrouds, and the foot relates to the fetish that Ana comes to embody. The surface text of the novel will go on to weave this desire, this sketched out and unresolved affair, into a more everyday tale of adultery, the habitual social norm of the old husband, young wife, and apparent sexual virtuoso of a lover. Then, in the narrative of what appears to be the desire of Fermín for Ana, there will emerge a further subtext, that of perverse ritual, which relegates Ana to being not object, but mere adjunct to a performance with its roots in the history of Fermín and his mother, which echo, through all the honor/shame connotations, the history of cultural and social relations between the sexes which forms the backcloth to the novel. The clue to this underlying and fundamental subtext is contained in the prefigurative images of foot and skull, and resumed in the closing pages where Fermín's rejection of Ana occurs.

The tale of adultery is Ana's main preoccupation at the opening of the novel, and will be the main motive in her change of confessor. Her final position as ostracized wife is that of Effi Briest. We assume that Ana too will die of neglect, sooner rather than later. The fact that she does not die in the course of the novel, however, allows her to continue to be the rejected, because hated and spurned, object of Fermín's desire, and this spurning by the priest replaces rejection by either her husband or by the man who is her physical lover. The possibility of a confrontation between Ana and her husband is neatly excised from the text. Between her ghost-like appearance after Víctor has been visited by Fermín, and the eventual sighting of her, in the text, two months after Víctor's death, there is nothing. In a sense she has been rejected by Álvaro in that he has escaped the Vetustan scene in short order after the duel with Víctor. But the essential irrelevance of Álvaro to the narrative is contained in his absence from the final, dramatic confrontation. What the reader is left with is an image of the perverted nature of desire in Fermín as an emblematic and explicit example of the perverted nature of desire found more widely in the novel.

Ana, perverse object of Fermín's desire

The spuring and shaming of Ana in the Cathedral at the close of Chapter 30 is the final episode in a perverse ritual engaged in by Fermín, with which she co-operates and colludes, in a manner consistent with the theory of the willingness of the accomplice in perversion as argued by Masud Khan (1979: 18-30). This ritual is partly a private expression of Fermín's personal and psychic needs, partly an expression of a communual perverse experience in a society where sexual ambiguity rules and ambivalence of desire reigns, and partly the solution within a patriarchal novel of the difficulty in presenting a strong heroine. What is gripping about *La Regenta* and its denouement is not only Fermín's inability to reach a satisfactory resolution with Ana, being limited to rejecting her with Nimetz's "womanly expression of wrath"(1971: 248), but the spectacular absence of resolution in his relationship with his mother. He has brought his perverse performance to an end, but it has brought no release, no reassurance.

The definition of perversion which I shall work from is largely derived from that of Louise Kaplan in her book *Female Perversions*, and which is based on a Freudian model. The work of Freud is posterior to the writing of *La Regenta,* but as in the case of hysteria, he can be argued to be a man who comes, directly, scientifically and philosophically, from his century. His conceptualizations of these disorders, indeed his identification of hysteria and perversion as strategies entered into because they provide responses to, or defenses against, trauma, are appropriate to an understanding of the dynamics of hysteria and perversion in the text. I shall not therefore enter into a discussion of Dollimore's return (1991) to Freud's idea of the polymorphous perverse in children (by which "straight" heterosexual orientation and activity is the result of repression at the oedipal crisis), although one could engage in a re-reading of the novel which emphasizes yet more than I have done the narrative of heterosexuality, which in this case is a narrative into which characters take flight, rather than being one which they struggle against having imposed upon them.

Freud's papers which touch on the subject are perversion are in particular the first of the three 1905 essays on the theory of sexuality, "The Sexual Aberrations," "Character and Anal Erotism"

(1908b), "A Special Type of Choice of Object Made by Men" (1910) and "Fetishism" (1927). I shall concentrate, however, on the model extrapolated by Kaplan since the account she offers of perversion bears a strikingly close relationship to the nature of perversion in *La Regenta*. If Kaplan's account of perversion seems bounded, limited, and is inflected with a sense of required forms of sexuality, it is for those very reasons appropriate to the discussion in this chapter. It incorporates strongly the notion of the rejection and punishment of a feminine side in men, and, given the strongly patriarchal nature of the novel in question, where characters and narrative express ultimately – for all their aberrations and perversity – a sense of the sexual "norm" which is nineteenth-century in its parameters, Kaplan's is thus a particularly useful model.

What does derive directly from Freud's theory in my discussion, however, is the particular understanding of the term "object" outlined by Freud in his 1915 paper, "The Instincts and Their Vicissitudes." Here Freud distinguishes between the instinct's aim and its satisfaction. Thus, while the aim of an instinct is normally satisfaction (in relation to pressure, or *drang*), the object of an instinct is the "thing in regard to which or through which the instinct is able to achieve its aim" (Freud 1915: 118-19). What I shall argue is that Fermín's aim derives from the pressures of his relationship with his mother, and Ana is thus the object, or, as it were, the tool that he employs in order to satisfy that aim. What she is clearly not is a person, or object, that is directly desired by him.

La Regenta is neatly split in its distribution of sexual disorders. Fermín is the paradigm in the novel of perverse feeling and acting-out, and Ana is characteristically the typical nineteenth-century hysteric as outlined by Labanyi (1991). This novel is thus characteristic of its time and curiously close to the theories of Freud, for whom women will be typically neurotic and hysteric, and men more likely to tend to perversion. Thus, as Brennan reminds us (1992: 144), quoting from Freud's *Studies on Hysteria*, "A male in the family will be more likely to be a positive pervert, meaning he will act on his perversion, while the females, true to the tendency of their sex to repression, are negative perverts, that is, hysterics." It is true that Fermín, as has been observed earlier, participates from time to time in Ana's hysteria, takes it over from her, and indeed also echoes in his own resistance to food at the family table her expression of her identity through her refusal to eat. And it is true that Ana's substitute activities of gratification, outlined in Chapter 3, and echoed in Visitación's substitution of *golosinas* for sexual pleasures, is a type of perverse object-usage. But in the larger-scale lines of the narrative, gender attribution of both hysteria and perversion follow the pattern of the hysterical female adoption of the passive response on the one hand, and the perverse masculine enactment of ritual on the other.

Kaplan's account of perversion (1991) is based on motivation not manifestation. That is, she rejects definitions which are based on the expression of perversion, on the form that the perversion takes, or as she puts it, "the 'kinky sex' of bondages and leather boots," and foregrounds the understanding of perversion as a psychological strategy, something that is adopted not with the simple aim of pleasure, but because the subject of the perversion is driven by need. The quality of perversion is of "desperation and fixity," and its purpose "to help the person to survive, moreover to survive with a sense of triumph over the traumas of his or her childhood" (Kaplan 1991: 9-10). Kaplan emphasizes the importance within perversion of performance, leading to complex rituals that must be repeated, scenarios to be enacted, and the feeling of risk and excitement that attend the performance. She highlights the repeated drama of the perverse act or performance and argues that it is related to childhood traumas, and specifically that it is designed to overcome, to master those traumatic events which could not be mastered in childhood. A further central element to Kaplan's understanding of perversion is that it involves a rejection within or by the pervert of those qualities, tendencies and desires, which are associated with the other sex. Hence a man's perverse enactments will entail a subjugation of his own feared feminine tendencies of passivity, for example, his "secret wishes to be a passive, submissive, denigrated woman humiliated and demeaned by a 'phallic' dominator of either sex" (Kaplan 1991: 13) while a woman's perverse enactments are designed to divert attention away from those of her wishes which society would construe as masculine, "to possess, to be instrumental, to dominate, to penetrate, to take over, to will, to succeed, to win" (Kaplan 1991: 197-8). Whether or not it is felt that this cross-gender rejection or avoidance of attributes is essential to all forms of perversion, there is good evidence for believing that it applies in the case of Fermín and Ana.

In the previous chapter I examined in detail the complex and essentially infantile relationship between Fermín and Doña Paula, his mother, in which the bullying, childish sulking, silences, stares, can be construed as strategies of behaviour learned in childhood by Fermín and then transferred to his relationship with Ana. A central element of both the initial and the transferential relationship is the possession or not of particular gender-attributes and connotations. There is also a cultural dimension to add to the psychological one in that Fermín and Paula can be seen as embodying the tensions of a Mediterranean honor/shame culture, where man is habitually the one who wins honor, and woman the instrument through which honor is liable to be lost. In their case, however, there is competition about which of the two is to be "branded" as being the possessor of female shame.

First let us look at the concept delineated by Kaplan: that the male pervert typically wishes to "be a passive, submissive, denigrated woman humiliated and demeaned by a 'phallic' dominator of either sex" (Kaplan 1991: 13) and will enact a performance that allows him to fulfil this fantasy. The performance may not take the form of the humiliation of the pervert, but can take the reverse form of being a defensive move against the attractions of the humiliated feminine aspect. The pervert thus may appear himself to be the phallic dominator. Initially this seems to be the appropriate pattern to suggest for the general activity of Fermín in relation to Vetusta, and to his female parishioners. There is little difficulty in identifying the representation of Fermín as phallic, from his extending telescope to his fondness for the tower of the Cathedral from which he surveys his city (though it should be noted that while Nimetz [1971: 247] identifies the tower as simply phallic, the description of it in the opening page of the novel suggests both masculine and feminine features). The phallic type is, however, a complex type, which engages in strategies and behaviour related to gender affirmation and rejection.

Fermín can usefully be defined not simply as "phallic" but as "phallic-narcissistic," one of the psychological types described by Wilhelm Reich. A brief survey of the main features of this type as defined by Reich shows some striking resemblances with the nature and behaviour of Fermín. The initial identifying features of "self-assured, sometimes arrogant, elastic, energetic, often impressive" accord well with the first view of Fermín. Reich's view of the likely facial features of the type is that they would combine hard and sharp masculine lines with feminine, girlish features. While this particular combination as such is not in evidence in Fermín, the mixture of feminine and masculine features certainly is. The imagery used in relation to his complextion either suggests that his high colour derives from make-up, or alternatively highlights the likeness between his face and the death-like mask to be seen on his mother in Chapter 11. The heavy flesh of eyelids and nose suggests a "feminine" lack of form, while the over-heavy nose itself a ready suggestion of a phallic symbol, is declared the "obra muerta" (I. 102) of the face. The patterns of subordination and domination of Fermín's life are also part of the type. According to Reich, phallic-narcissistic types tend to achieve leading positions, and when in hierarchical organizations (which the Catholic Church in Spain can be perceived as being) "compensate for the necessity of having to subordinate themselves by dominating those beneath them." Reich highlights the degree to which this type will tend to be influenced by irrational motives, a feature clearly that of Fermín, and one of the main sources of drama in the novel. The aggression of the type was conceived of as being in itself a defense and its aim that of "wreaking revenge on the woman." Finally, in consideration of the genesis of this type, Reich signals the frequency with which there has been a "severe disappointment in love with heterosexual objects," that is, for boys with the mother, and adds that in the case of male members of this type, "the mother is very often the stricter parent, or the father died at an early age or was not married to the mother and was never present." Later he comments that "again and again such men seek unconsciously to prove to women how potent they are." In addition, some gender confusion will doubtless arise from Reich's further observation that "along with the mother's frustration of phallic exhibition and masturbation, there is an identification with her" (Reich 1973: 217-22).

Kaplan (1991: 12) emphasizes the ways in which the habitual male perversions bring out "a defensive, phallic-narcissistic exaggeration of masculinity" in which the man will conform to a particular social stereotype of masculinity. This strategy becomes particularly pointed when employed by Fermín whose enforced celibacy and priestly, womanly skirts appear to cut him off even from prevailing social norms of masculinity in his society. Significantly, as noted in Chapter 6, the dress in which he imagines himself as possessed of masculinity is that of the *cazador* (huntsman), the occupation of his natural father Francisco, a costume he re-assumes in Chapter 30, in a brief fantasy of possible action about Ana's infidelity (II. 498-9).

The production of phallic-narcissistic masculine behaviour as a defense against suspected or feared or rejected femininity is readily exemplified in the degree to which Fermín's ambiguity of gender results from his role as priest. This type of exaggerated male response as a response to the role of passive femininity which has resulted from a relationship with a phallic woman, most characteristically a controlling mother, is also clearly evident in his situation.

Paula, in turn, fulfils with ease the specifications of the phallic woman. Her bulk equal to that of her son, her strength great enough to fight off all but one of the men who besiege her when she runs the tavern, her assumption of authority in relation to her son, her inscrutability and refusal to buckle to the gaze of the curious public: all these are features which endow her with a type of borrowed, or indeed robbed, masculinity. It is significant that there is considerable mirroring between the awkward physical presence, and clumsy limbs of Paula, features that perversely attract the men about her, and that of Ramona, the woman of Álvaro's narrative of conquest in the Casino. Thus Paula, we are told, draws the attention of the priest she first keeps house for on account of attractions that are masculine rather than feminine: "reparando al cenar que Paula era mal formada, angulosa, sintió una lascivia de salvaje, irresistible, ciega, excitada por aquellos ángulos de carne y hueso, por aquellas caderas desairadas, por aquellas piernas largas, fuertes, que debían de ser como las de un hombre" (I. 551). Ramona, meanwhile, is presented, perhaps even created through Álvaro's words, as his partner in a drama that lasts three nights, and he comments on "la protesta muda, pero enérgica, brutal de la moza, que se defendía a puñadas, a patadas, con los dientes, despertando en él, decía don Álvaro, una lascivia montaraz, desconocida, fuerte, invencible" (II. 176).

Paula and Ramona appear to be sisters under the skin when taken on the basis of their brute physicality, their union with the life of the earth (Ramona is conquered finally on the uncertain surface of a pile of grain), the strength of their resistance to sexual attack. The outstanding difference between them, however, is that if Paula experiences any pleasure in her (unresolved) sexual encounters, she bears no witness to it. By contrast, it would appear that Ramona does. But of course we should note that it is Álvaro who relates that "conocía yo que Ramona gozaba, gozaba como una loca en la refriega" and further that "callaba, forcejeaba, mordía con deleite, magullaba con voluptuosidad bárbara, y encontraba placer de salvaje en el martirio de mis sentidos, que tocaban su presa, y se sentían dominados por ella" (II. 176). Álvaro is being, as it were, allowed by his author to participate in one of the convenient fantasies of a patriarchal text and patriarchal society, namely that women enjoy violent sex, and is being permitted to offer it, as a type of aural pornography, for the pleasure of his male listeners, and for their consequent validation of his masculinity.

What is the connection between Fermín's relationship with his phallic mother, and Ana? Firstly, as I have suggested in Chapter 6, there is a repetition with Ana of the infantile relationship between Paula and Fermín, prompted in part by a search for an ideal mother to replace the terrible one. Secondly – and this relates to the first point –, it relates to the terrible physicality that Fermín cannot fail to separate from his image of his mother. The text gives all too graphic an account of the adolescent Fermín having to close his ears, or, rather, being unable to do so, to the sounds from the tavern. His mother prevents him from intervening in brawls, sending him back to his books (studying for the seminary is the adopted shared ambition of the two for him). Fermín obeys: "por respeto y por asco obedecía, y cuando el estrépito era horrísono, tapaba los oídos y procuraba enfrascarse en el trabajo hasta olvidar lo que pasaba detrás de aquellas tablas en la taberna" (I. 555). More than brawls take place within his earshot, and though the text refers to Paula hiding more than brawls from him, it goes on to detail the sounds of struggle between her and the occasional drunk late at night, while continuing to affirm that Fermín believed the sound still to be only of miners' fights.

Ana presents in the first instance the opportunity for Fermín to find the alternative to Paula, the phallic mother. But there is no simple adoption of an alternative object. In the first place the relationship between mother and son, intense and introverted, is strong, but contains fear, guilt and resentment as much as it contains love. In relation to the physical world Ana allows him to move into a strong reaction against the connotations of the messier aspects of the feminine that he finds within his mother, and against which he wants to defend. Kaplan (1991: 44) observes that a recurrent idea within male patterns of perversion is a sense of horror in the minds of the men concerned in relation to the vagina, which is associated with "the stigmata of humiliation, degradation, mutilation, and death." In reaction to this, what may be sought out is a non-physical form of the woman, and the worship of the madonna type. With Ana's voluntary early identification with the Virgin, there is no difficulty in seeing her presentation as madonna, in her own mind and in that of Fermín. More significant, however, is the issue of the emotional investment in the idea of the madonna who manages to exist in an environment of filth. Various examples in the text point to the over-invested association for Fermín of purity with the stench of the *cloaca*, as though there is a repeated need to hold on to a phantasy of purity that can remain in the *cloaca*, thus validating the phantasy imposed on him by his mother that her feminine purity was maintained in the moral *cloaca* of the *taberna*. Hence Rosa Carraspique, the girl enclosed in her nun's cell in an atmosphere of the latrine, a situation of which Fermín is made clearly aware, and yet in which he appears unable, and certainly unwilling, to intervene. Rosa, an example of purity, is relegated to the filth of the convent, her symbolic connection with the world of sexual desire designated by her adopted name of Sor Teresa (Mandrell 1990: 22). She is punished for the filth she signifies, while standing idealistically for the mirage that purity can survive intact and immaculate in surroundings of dirt.

Fermín is clearly disturbed by his relationship with Ana, even in the early phase, when disturbance takes the form of excitement. At the point at which he feels that betrayal has really occurred (on receiving the gossip that Ana has fainted in the arms of Álvaro at the dance at the Casino), his first thought is that his mother would not have betrayed him, and his reaction to Ana on seeing her is full of the bullying and manipulation he has himself experienced in the past at the hands of his mother.

It is Ana who, apparently, has the idea of becoming a martyred Dolorosa to Fermín, at the end of Chapter 25 (I. 336-7), standing in contrast with the earlier identification she had had with the Virgin, albeit without child (I. 282-3). Fermín develops this characterization of Ana as the Virgin to fit his psychological needs so that she is not just sorrowing, but the handmaid, even the servant. Thus when he goes to visit Don Pompeyo with Ana's impending participation in the Easter procession in mind, he thinks of her as his slave, and indeed wants there to be a public perception of how "La Regenta era sierva de su confesor" (II. 347). The use here not just of Ana's formal, functional name, but also of his functional title, in a context imagining the public view of the relationship, demonstrates the degree to which he now envisages not only his domination of her, her bondage to him, but perhaps even her humiliation to him.

The reference to the public connotations of Ana's participation in a ritual of bondage summarizes a chain of other female entities that have been subjugated by Fermín. An initial alternative female form to that of his mother had been that of nature: thus in his youth, and freed briefly from the intense pressure of his mother, he had enjoyed the surroundings of the open countryside. The pleasure was that of being in the open air, and quite distinct from the other, less open aspect of nature with which his mother is associated, that is, the depths, chasms and swamps which are also a part of the natural world, and which relates, arguably, to the horror of the vagina alluded to by Kaplan (Turner 1990: 70-1). It is nature that is able to excite his appetite, and although Chapter 1 describes his pleasure in surveying Vetusta from the tower, it is insufficient: "En Vetusta no podía saciar esta pasión; tenía que contentarse con subir algunas veces a la torre de la catedral" (I. 104). Valis has noted (1981: 59) his mother's role in taming men, a phenomenon counter to traditional gender norms, by which men tame nature. Fermín, both in his expressed love of nature, and in his intellectual activities developed as priest (setting him apart from the other clergy) articulates a re-conquest of the traditional masculine domain of power over nature, and a reversal of what might be construed as his mother's "perversity."

Fermín has a further array of subjugated female figures, serving as substitute conquered objects for the mother he cannot conquer, and simultaneously for his own feared femininity. The status of women as objects in the novel is general, "used, shared, and discarded" (Nimetz 1971: 243), but his dominion over his confessional daughters an explicit example of his perversity. The catechism pupils, on the edge of puberty, place before him a possible further range of "pure" objects, but as Benigno Sánchez-Eppler has pointed out (1987: 213), his visit to them is after his voluptuous feeding on a rosebud, itself a dislocated object of desire he partakes of after reading Ana's letter in the park.

When Ana takes part in the Easter procession, the eyes of the onlookers are not on her dress, nor her face, but the naked foot peeping beneath the specially designed robe. This re-appearance of the foot, glimpsed in the shadowy picture by the group in the Cathedral, more aware of what they feel than of what they see, fixes Ana as the object of Fermín's perverted desire. It resumes the concentration within the novel upon "los bajos." Everyone appears to spend their time peeping, or trying to peep, up one another's skirts. In his essay on "Fetishism," Freud (1927: 354) noted that the foot or shoe were preferred fetishes. For him, the fetish represented the child's disappointment at the discovery that the woman did not possess a penis, and relates the oddity of the foot for the representation of the absent female phallus to the circumstances of the discovery, namely that the "inquisitive boy peered at the woman's genitals from below, from her legs up; fur and velvet – as has long been suspected – are a fixation of the sight of the pubic hair, which should have been followed by the longed-for sight of the female member." Whether or not we now feel totally persuaded by Freud's conviction that all children must assume not only that all adults have penises, but that there might be something severely wrong in not having one, the foot as a sexual object is not restricted to *La Regenta,* the most notorious examples being from the Victorian era in this country, when excesses of sexual modesty required the clothing even of the legs of the piano. Certainly Freud seems to be accurate in his perception that looking at the foot is part way to looking up skirts, with a view to discovering secrets, and the link with the curiosity of the boy about the mother appears to be borne out by the fascinating comment of prostitutes reported by Kaplan (1991: 65) that in the late 1960s their clients required them to wear not the lingerie of the time, but "the kind of 'kinky' underwear worn by women a generation earlier, from the time when the men were little boys. 'It's like they want us to dress up like their mothers.' " Hence the fascination for Celedonio and Bismarck of Fermín's genteel, beautifully shod foot, the awareness of the rustling petticoats of Obdulia, and the grubby ones of Visitación, the horror of Fermín as he realizes that even Ana is involved in the joking about "bajos," if only to affirm "si no se ha visto nada... si estaba yo más abajo y no vi nada..." (I. 477).

In the Easter procession, what happens is that ownership of the foot has been transferred. The feminine foot of Fermín, sign of his sexual ambiguity, is now unclothed, having become the foot of Ana, there for all the world to see, the foot of his "sierva," whose public shaming he has brought about. Thus his own femininity can for once be owned and scorned, become a symbol of his power rather than of his weakness. The terror Kaplan refers to (1991: 27) as the pervert's experience, "of carrying out the full measure of the destructiveness aroused by the female body or any body that presents to a pervert the weaknesses and femininity he despises and fears in himself" is here contained in the ritual that signals Fermín as Christ figure (therefore both powerful and debased), and Ana as his Dolorosa, shamed in her appearance to the Vetustans, and yet contained within the pure role of the Virgin. Above all, Ana, as Fermín's fetish, and representative of his femininity, represents for him, in dislocated form, his own submission to the feminine institution of the Church, itself a repetition of his shameful submission to the power of his mother.

THE SKULL AND THE FOOT

As the Vetustans gaze fascinated, looking for the showing of Ana's foot, a variety of fixed and death-like faces re-trace the original highlighting of skull and foot in the painting in the Cathedral. They combine the motif of suffering with a disowning of the world of the flesh (in the form of Ana's foot) that arouses such vitality of curious observation, and with a desire to escape the world of feeling altogether. Don Vinagre, Ana's unwelcome and unexpected companion in the procession, shares with her the voluntary adoption of mortification, the text now making explicit the curious vicissitudes of sadism, highlighting above all the *pleasure* that this re-directed, self-directed suffering entails: "en su afán de mortificar a cuantas generaciones pasaban por su mano, se gozaba en lastimar a la suya, en su propia persona" (II. 362). Vinagre's head is crowned with thorns. His pain can be divined by external signals, and we read how the thorns "le pinchaban efectivamente, como se conocía por el movimiento de las cejas y la expresión dolorosa de las arrugas de la frente." But instantly, by the dehumanizing gaze of the schoolchildren who watch him, Vinagre's suffering face is converted to a skull: "Deseaban los muchachos cordialmente que aquellas espinas le atravesasen el cráneo" (II. 362). His suffering humanity lost, his twisted motivation emerges, with its mixture of ingenuity, vanity and perversion: "no sólo el prurito de darse tormento como a cada hijo de vecino, le había inspirado aquella diablura de coronarse de espinas y dar un gustazo a los recentales de su rebaño pedagógico, sino que era gran parte en aquella exhibición anual la pícara vanidad" (II. 362). Ana's face, meanwhile, alongside that of Vinagre both in the text and in the procession, is notable for its lack of expression, even its lack of identity, becoming invisible to the reader other than in its pallor which shades into a blush of shame. We go beneath Ana's face, to her inability to perceive, as though her face, her individuality has been erased: "Ana iba como ciega, no oía ni entendía tampoco" (II. 362). Devoid of flesh or expression, it becomes a type of textual skull. Not only does Ana's face become pale and/or blank, but so too do the faces of those who watch her. Even the face of Álvaro, watching from the balcony, is virtually disembodied by appearing pale above the black frockcoat fastened to the throat (II. 363). The procession becomes a series of blank faces whose very lack of expression shouts the mockery of the ritual that is enclosed not only in Ana's participation, but in the acting out of the ritual by the whole town. In a description worthy of Larra, the scene becomes spectral, a dance of death, a satanic mockery, pointing up at this moment of Fermín's apparent political, social and religious triumph, the emptiness of his endeavor, the hollowness of his inner life:

> En los cristales de las tiendas cerradas y de algunos balcones se reflejaban las llamas movibles; subían y bajaban en contorsiones fantásticas, como sombras lucientes, en confusión de aquelarre. Aquella multitud silenciosa, aquellos pasos sin ruido, aquellos rostros sin expresión de los colegiales de blancas albas que alumbraban con cera la calle triste, daban al conjunto apariencia de ensueño. No parecían seres vivos aquellos seminaristas cubiertos de blanco y negro, pálidos unos, con cercos morados en los ojos, otros morenos, casi negros, de pelo en matorral, casi todos cejijuntos, preocupados con la idea fija del aburrimiento, máquinas de hacer religión, reclutas de una leva forzosa del hambre y de la holgazanería. Iban a enterrar a Cristo, como a cualquier cristiano, sin pensar en Él; a cumplir con el oficio. (II. 365)

The face of the Virgin, Dolorosa of the procession, is similarly death-like, conjuring up in its reflections the appearance of Doña Paula in Chapter 11 as an "amortajada" (I. 413), or as a looming dark figure at the opening of Chapter 15 (I. 541). Yet although the description of the Virgin here explicitly links her to the suffering

Son (the Virgin and Christ, Paula and Fermín evoked in terrible two-step), a doubly-oriented passage merges the suffering Virgin (Paula?) with the suffering because self-exposing Ana, who has adopted the role of Dolorosa, formerly the domain of Paula. While ostensibly an evocation of the statue of the Dolorosa in the procession, the passage calls up in depersonalized yet horrific form the agony of Ana who has placed herself in this grotesque exhibition, and who can only escape it by feigning a death-like lack of expression: "Detrás venía la Madre. Alta, escuálida, de negro, pálida como el hijo, con cara de muerta como él. *Fija la mirada de idiota en las piedras de la calle* la impericia del artífice había dado, sin saberlo, a aquel rostro la expresión muda del dolor espantado, del dolor que rebosa del sufrimiento" (II. 366, emphasis mine). Lest the resemblance should escape us, the following paragraph signals Ana's face as the blank one of the statue: "También Ana parecía de madera pintada; su palidez era como un barniz. Sus ojos no veían" (II. 366). Here she is not even accorded the ex-humanity of the skull, having become merely the painted head of a provincial statue. And at this point, reduction is all, so that all her efforts are concentrated on the vain attempts to conceal her feet from the eyes of the crowd.

The whole town turns out to watch Ana in the Easter procession, all gathering to look at her foot, her "bajos," while the experience for her is that of mortification. In the making public of what is not only the symbol of sexuality, but also of the sexual shame of the woman, and to boot, the feelings of the priest about his own disowned femininity, and the replacement for the disowned and rejected powerful femininity of his mother, we observe the town participating in an act of multiple, communal voyeurism. Ana in displaying herself to their gaze is also, finally, doing what they have tried to make her do from the start, namely, to join with the rest of them in the breaking of sexual and moral boundaries. In their displacement onto her of the sense of shame, and the existence of the object of voyeurism, they enact for themselves, or rather have her enact for them, the repudiation of their own desire for sexual exhibitionism, which in its turn is arguably their defense against their suspicion that they may, after all, have nothing to exhibit.

The procession does not end well, in that Ana does not continue to be the public slave of Fermín. In his final rejection of her in the Cathedral, however, he is able to complete his perverse ritual. The strategy of perversity has as its intention the reversal or rectification of earlier trauma. For Fermín, this is his subjection to a series of feminine powers, from which he is unable to detach himself (he cannot leave either the church or his mother, and certainly not his shared history with the latter which taints him with her "mancha"). But in his rejection of Ana, rectification is accessible. Kaplan (1991: 128) notes that the requirement of the perverse strategy is as follows: "a reversal of roles so that a once abused and traumatized child now assumes the role of the abusing parent. the sexual partner, the 'loved one', is treated to the humiliation of being excluded, cast away, abandoned." A Pyrrhic victory.

CONCLUSION

> Nevertheless, despair is veritably a self-consuming, but an impotent self-consuming that cannot do what it wants to do. What it wants to do is to consume itself, something it cannot do, and this impotence is a new form of self-consuming, in which despair is once again unable to do what it wants to do, to consume itself. (Kierkegaard, *The Sickness unto Death*)

> But in another sense despair is even more definitely the sickness unto death. Literally speaking, there is not the slightest possibility that anyone will die from this sickness or that it will end in physical death. On the contrary, the torment of despair is precisely this inability to die. Thus it has more in common with the situation of a mortally ill person when he lies struggling with death and yet cannot die. Thus to be sick *unto* death is to be unable to die, yet not as if there were hope of life; no, the hopelessness is that there is not even the ultimate hope, death. (Kierkegaard, *The Sickness unto Death*)

The question of "oceanic feeling" spoken of by Freud in *Civilization and Its Discontents* arose through a letter received from a friend, who commented on a feeling that he called "a sensation of 'eternity', a feeling as of something limitless, unbounded – as if it were 'oceanic'" (Freud 1930: 251). Freud responded by speaking of "oceanic feeling" in the context of two positive experiences: the state of being in love which produces this oceanic feeling, and the state of the infant at the breast who "does not as yet distinguish his ego from the external world as the source of the sensations flowing in upon him" (Freud 1930: 254). Both of these associations are linked to a sense of boundlessness, of melting, of a flow which can barely be said to occur, given that there is no clear sense of the places from which and to which it moves. But Freud's first association to the issue raised in the letter was apparently quite different. He speaks of security: "If I have understood my friend rightly, he means the same thing by it as the consolation offered by an original and somewhat eccentric dramatist [Grabbe] to his hero who is facing a self-inflicted death. 'We cannot fall out of this world' " (Freud 1930: 252).

If there is a hole in the text of *La Regenta*, a gaping lack, it is in the form of a total absence of the reassuring container implied in "We cannot fall out of this world." The text of the novel, permeated with the sense of boundlessness, of limits that will not hold, and of defenses that will always be breached, signally lacks the sense of security of Freud's first association. Its discomfort, for the reader, derives from the degree to which that security is sought, and will always be denied. This occurs at divers levels. For the reader, what is denied is the ease of the familiar adultery story, a story which presupposes, as is evident to the characters of the novel who engage in hysterical flight into it, that there are boundaries around the self and around gender which make the events of the story (union and betrayal) possible. For the characters, engaged in their hysterical flight, what is denied is any possibility of either escape or satisfaction.

One of the central myths unconsciously subscribed to in the course of the narrative is that the entry into the mechanics of plot will affirm identities and boundaries, that is to say, that change can come from outside the self. Ana tries to imagine her condition as other, yet simultaneously voices for herself the very reason why it will never alter. She figures herself as the motherless child, and, locked into this mentally adopted (if materially accurate) representation of herself, she looks for rescuers, improvement, and ultimately the security of someone who wants her. Thus to perceive herself as the object of Álvaro's desire (however perfunctory in the habitual seducer this may be) is to imagine that something may change because someone else will intervene in her condition. At no point is there the sense that Ana, as character, has self-knowledge, since there is no sense of a self to have that knowledge.

The high profile of mechanical imagery in the novel signals two crucial facts. First, the absence of life or desire. If Álvaro "desires" Ana, or anyone else, it is a mechanical response, a part of his Don Juanesque repetition compulsion, a type of perversion into which he is locked as firmly as is Fermín into *his* particular forms of perverse substitutions. Ana's misadventure of being caught in a hunting trap speaks not simply of her role as object in a patriarchal world, but speaks even more emphatically of the mechanical nature of the masculine "desire" which traps her. This is, moreover, a trapping which, as with the *humane* traps favoured by Víctor, ensnares but will not kill, will not give her the ending that would proclaim her integrity of identity, while indicating that the one trapping probably has no desire to consume anyway (a lack of desire, or of taking the object seriously that is conjured up by the image of Víctor's abandoned cigar). The second function of mechanical imagery is to highlight the interrelatedness of strategies engaged in during the course of the novel. At one level there is a simple handing on, a sending down the line, of desires, frustrations, appetites. Ana in particular is handed on, and while we may focus on her trajectory, we could also pay attention to the gesture which initiates that handing on – a sense of impotence, helplessness, not being able to "handle" the situation, the gesture transformed eventually into Fermín's desperate clasping at his own neck at the end of Chapter 30. No-one can "handle" Ana, neither her first confessor, nor her second, neither her husband, nor Álvaro, and it should be recalled that since Ana is habitually the substitute object, the failure to "handle" her will denote the failure to "handle" other things. Fermín's failure to handle her is thus his failure to handle either his mother or himself. And we should not lose sight of the possibility that Álvaro, while believing that he is the promoter of the adultery plot, is arguably in the same situation as Ana is. In a very obvious manner he is Víctor's substitute, but in a more sinister manner he is that of Fermín. Although it is apparently his desire for Ana that sets the final infidelity in motion, the concentration in the dénouement upon Fermín and Ana confirms Álvaro's function as that of a type of catspaw, in that he has provided for Ana and Fermín the possibility of acting out an adultery narrative which for them was prohibited. He has thus functioned, as it were, as the perverse object of their collective desire. If there is a lack of attainment in the novel, beyond the appeasement of Celedonio's impersonal and unsavoury curiosity, it is because throughout the characters have engaged in a wilful misrecognition of their condition, and sought to bring about ends for which the necessary component part, the existence of the self, has been irrevocably absent. A dance of death in which the release by death is denied.

BIBLIOGRAPHY

Alarcos Llorach, Emilio. "Notas a *La Regenta*," in id., *Ensayos y estudios literarios*, 99-118. Madrid: Júcar, 1976.
Alas, Leopoldo. *La Regenta*. 1884-5. Ed. Gonzalo Sobejano. 2 vols. Madrid: Clásicos Castalia, 1981.
Aldaraca, Bridget. "The Medical Construction of the Feminine Subject in Nineteenth-Century Spain." In *Cultural and Historical Grounding for Hispanic and Luso-Brazilian Feminist Literary Criticism*, ed. Hernán Vidal, 395-413. Minneapolis: Institute for the Study of Ideologies and Literatures, 1989.
———. "El caso de Ana O: Histeria y sexualidad en *La Regenta*." *Asclepio* 42 (2) (1992): 299-309.
Anthony, E. James. "Hysteria in Childhood," in A. Roy, ed., *Hysteria*. Chichester: John Wiley, 1982.
Aquinas, Saint Thomas. *Summa Theologica*. Trans. by the Fathers of the English Dominican Province. London: R. and T. Washbourne Ltd, 1917.
Barnes, R. and R. F. Barnes. *System of Obstetric Medicine and Surgery*. 2 vols. London: Elder, Smith, 1884.
Bataille, Georges. *Erotism: Death and Sensuality*. 1957. Trans. Mary Dalwood. San Francisco: City Lights, 1986.
Bernheimer, Charles and Claire Kahane. *In Dora's Case: Freud-Hysteria-Feminism*. New York: Columbia University Press, 1985.
Bick, Esther. "The Experience of the Skin in Early Object Relations." *International Journal of Psycho-Analysis* 49 (1968): 484-6.
Bion, Wilfred R. *Seven Servants: Four Works*. New York: Jason Aronson, 1977. Contains *Learning from Experience* (1962), *Elements of Psycho-Analysis* (1963), *Transformations* (1965) and *Attention and Interpretation* (1970).
Boerhaave, Herman. *Aphorismi de Cognoscendis et Curandis Morbis*. Leyden: Luchtmans and Haak, 1728. Trans. into English. London: Bettesworth and Hitch, 1735.
———. *Institutiones Medicae*. 4 vols. Madrid: Villaepandea, 1796-7.
Bond, R. L. "Vying with Vision." *Renaissance and Reformation* 8 (1984): 30-38.
Brenkman, John. *Straight Male Modern: A Cultural Critique of Psychoanalysis*. New York and London: Routledge, 1993.
Brennan, Teresa, ed. *Between Feminism and Psychoanalysis*. 1989. London and New York: Routledge, 1991.
Britton, Ronald. "The Oedipus Situation and the Depressive Position." *Sigmund Freud House Bulletin, Vienna*, 9 (1985): 7-12. Repr. in *Clinical Lectures on Klein and Bion*, ed. Robin Anderson, 34-45. The New Library of Psychoanalysis 14. London: Tavistock/Routledge, 1992.

Bronfen, Elisabeth. *Over Her Dead Body: Death, Femininity and the Aesthetic.* Manchester: Manchester University Press, 1992.
Bruch, Hilde. *The Golden Cage: The Enigma of Anorexia Nervosa.* Shepton Mallet: Open Books, 1978.
Caldwell, Richard S. "The Blindness of Oedipus." *International Review of Psycho-Analysis* 1 (1974): 207-18.
Caro Baroja, Julio. "Honour and Shame: A Historical Account of Several Conflicts." Trans. from Spanish by R. Johnson. In J. G. Peristiany, ed., *Honour and Shame: The Values of Mediterranean Society,* 81-137. London: Weidenfeld and Nicholson, 1965.
Charnon-Deutsch, Lou (1989a). "Voyeurism, Pornography and *La Regenta.*" *Modern Language Studies* 19 (4) (1989): 93-101.
―――― (1989b). "*La Regenta* and Theories of the Subject." *Romance Languages Annual* 1 (1989): 395-8.
――――. *Gender and Representation: Women in Spanish Realist Fiction.* Amsterdam/Philadelphia: John Benjamins, 1990.
Cirlot, J. E. *A Dictionary of Symbols.* 1962. Trans. Jack Sage. 2nd ed. London: Routledge and Kegan Paul, 1971.
Claret, Antonio María. *Nuevo manojito de flores o sea recopilación de doctrinas para los confesores.* Barcelona, 1859.
――――. *Llave de oro, o serie de reflexiones que, para abrir el corazón cerrado de los pecadores ofrece a los confesores nuevos el Excmo. e Ilmo. Sr. D. Antonio María Claret, Arzobispo de Cuba.* Barcelona, 1862.
Collas, Ion. *Madame Bovary: A Psychoanalytical Reading.* Geneva: Librairie Droz, 1985.
Cooper, J. C. *An Illustrated Encyclopedia of Traditional Symbols.* London: Thames and Hudson, 1978.
Copjec, Joan. "Cutting Up." In *Between Feminism and Psychoanalysis,* ed. Teresa Brennan, 227-46. 1989. Repr. London and New York: Routledge, 1991.
Davis, Madeleine and David Wallbridge. *Boundary and Space: An Introduction to the Work of D. W. Winnicott.* Harmondsworth: Penguin Books, 1981.
Descuret, Jean Baptiste Félix. *La médicine des passions, ou les Passions considérées dans leurs rapports avec les maladies, les lois et la religion.* 1841. 3rd ed. Paris: Labé, 1860. Also included in Taxil, *Les livres secrets des confesseurs.*
Diccionario del uso del español, by María Moliner. 2 vols. Madrid: Gredos, 1966.
Dictionary of Moral Theology, ed. Pietro Palazzini. 1957. Trans. H. J. Yannone, S. T. L. London: Burns and Oates, 1962.
Dictionnaire de spiritualité ascétique et mystique, ed. M. Viller *et al.* 14 vols. 1932. Vol. 4. 1960.
Dictionnaire de théologie Catholique, ed. A. Vacant, E. Mangenot & E. Ammann. 15 vols. Paris: Librairie Letouzet et Ané, 1903-50.
Dollimore, Jonathan. *Sexual Dissidence: Augustine to Wilde, Freud to Foucault.* Oxford: The Clarendon Press, 1991.
Douglas, Mary. *Purity and Danger: An Analysis of the Concepts of Taboo.* New York: Praeger, 1966.
Eliade, Mircea. *The Forge and the Crucible.* 1956. Trans. by S. Corrin. 1971. 2nd ed. Chicago: University of Chicago Press, 1978.
Ellenberger, Henri F. *The Discovery of the Unconscious: The History and Evolution of Dynamic Psychiatry.* New York: Basic Books, 1970.
Ellrich, Robert. "Envy, Identity and Creativity: *Inferno XXIV-XXV.*" *Dante Studies* 102 (1984): 61-80.
Evans, Martha Nöel. *Fits and Starts: A Genealogy of Hysteria in Modern France.* Ithaca and London: Cornell University Press, 1991.

Ey, Henri. "History and Analysis of the Concept." 1964. Repr. in *Hysteria*, ed. Alec Roy. Chichester: John Wiley and Sons, 1982.

Eysenck, H. *Sense and Nonsense in Psychology*. Harmondsworth: Penguin Books, 1966.

Fairbairn, W. R. D. "A Revised Psychopathology of the Psychoses and Psychoneuroses." 1941. In id., *Psychoanalytic Studies of the Personality*, 28-58. London and New York: Routledge, 1952.

———. "Endopsychic Structure Considered in Terms of Object-Relationships." 1944. In id., *Psychoanalytic Studies of the Personality*, 82-136. London and New York: Routledge, 1952.

———. *Psychoanalytic Studies of the Personality*. 1952. Repr. with intro. by David E. Scharff and Ellinor Fairbairn Birtles. London: Routledge, 1992.

Ferenczi, Sandor. "The Ontogenesis of the Interest in Money." 1914. Repr. in id., *First Contributions to Psycho-analysis*, ed. and trans. E. Jones. International Psycho-analytical Library, 45. London: Hogarth Press, 1952.

Flaubert, Gustave. *Madame Bovary*. 1857. Trans. Alan Russell. Harmondsworth: Penguin Books, 1950.

Fontane, Theodor. *Effi Briest*. 1895. Trans. Douglas Parmée. Harmondsworth: Penguin Books, 1987.

Forrester, John. *The Seductions of Psychoanalysis: Freud, Lacan and Derrida*. Cambridge: Cambridge University Press, 1990.

Freud, Sigmund, and Joseph Breuer. *Studies on Hysteria*. 1893-5. Translated by James and Alix Strachey. Ed. James and Alix Strachey, with Angela Richards. Pelican Freud Library, gen. ed. James Strachey, vol. 3. Harmondsworth: Penguin Books, 1978.

Freud, Sigmund. "A Project for a Scientific Psychology." 1895. Repr. in *The Origins of Psychoanalysis*, Standard Edition, vol. 1, 283-391. Trans. James Strachey with Anna Freud. London: Hogarth Press and Institute of Psycho-Analysis, 1966.

———. *The Interpretation of Dreams*. 1900. Trans. James Strachey. Ed. Angela Richards. Pelican Freud Library, gen. ed. James Strachey, vol. 4. Harmondsworth: Penguin Books, 1976.

——— (1905a). *Case Histories I: "Dora" and "Little Hans."* 1905. Ed. Angela Richards. Pelican Freud Library, gen. ed. James Strachey, vol. 8. Harmondsworth: Penguin Books, 1977.

——— (1905b). *On Sexuality: Three Essays on the Theory of Sexuality and Other Works*. 1905. Ed. Angela Richards. Pelican Freud Library, gen. ed. James Strachey, vol. 7. Harmondsworth: Penguin Books, 1977. Includes "The Sexual Aberrations"(1905).

——— (1905c). "The Sexual Aberrations." 1905. In *On Sexuality: Three Essays on the Theory of Sexuality and Other Works*, 45-87. Ed. Angela Richards. Pelican Freud Library, gen. ed. James Strachey, vol. 7. Harmondsworth: Penguin Books, 1977.

——— (1908a). " 'Civilized' Sexual Morality and Modern Nervous Illness." 1908. Trans. under James Strachey, ed. Albert Dickson. Pelican Freud Library, gen. ed. James Strachey, vol. 12, 27-55. Repr. Harmondsworth: Penguin Books, 1991.

——— (1908b). "Character and Anal Eroticism." 1908. In *On Sexuality: Three Essays on the Theory of Sexuality and Other Works*. Ed. Angela Richards. Pelican Freud Library, gen. ed. James Strachey, vol. 7, 205-15. Harmondsworth: Penguin Books, 1977.

———. "Family Romances." 1909. In *On Sexuality: Three Essays on the Theory of Sexuality and Other Works*. Ed. Angela Richards. Pelican Freud Library, gen. ed. James Strachey, vol. 7, 221-5. Harmondsworth: Penguin Books, 1977.

Freud, Sigmund. "A Special Type of Choice of Object Made by Men." 1910. In *On Sexuality: Three Essays on the Theory of Sexuality and Other Works*. Ed. Angela Richards. Pelican Freud Library, gen. ed. James Strachey, vol. 7, 227-42. Harmondsworth: Penguin Books, 1977.

———. "On the Universal Tendency to Debasement in the Sphere of Love: Contributions to the Psychology of Love II." 1912. In *On Sexuality: Three Essays on the Theory of Sexuality and Other Works*. Ed. Angela Richards. Pelican Freud Library, gen. ed. James Strachey, vol. 7, 243-60. Harmondsworth: Penguin Books, 1977.

———. "The Instincts and Their Vicissitudes." 1915. In *On Metapsychology: The Theory of Psychoanalysis*. Trans. under James Strachey. Ed. Angela Richards. Pelican Freud Library, gen. ed. James Strachey, vol. 11, 113-38. Harmondsworth: Penguin Books, 1984.

———. "The Dissolution of the Oedipus Complex." 1924. In *On Sexuality: Three Essays on the Theory of Sexuality and Other Works*, ed. Angela Richards. Pelican Freud Library, gen. ed. James Strachey, vol. 7, 313-22. Harmondsworth: Penguin Books, 1977.

———. "Fetishism." 1927. In *On Sexuality: Three Essays on the Theory of Sexuality and Other Works*. Ed. Angela Richards. Pelican Freud Library, gen. ed. James Strachey, vol. 7, 345-57. Harmondsworth: Penguin Books, 1977.

———. *Civilization and Its Discontents*. 1930. In *Civilization, Society and Religion*. Trans. under James Strachey, ed. Albert Dickson. Pelican Freud Library, vol. 12, gen. ed. James Strachey, 1985, 243-340. Harmondsworth: Penguin Books, 1991.

———. *New Introductory Lectures on Psychoanalysis*. 1933. Trans. James Strachey. Ed. James Strachey and Angela Richards. Pelican Freud Library, gen. ed. James Strachey, vol. 2. Harmondsworth: Penguin Books, 1973.

Fumagalli, Giuseppe. *L'Ape Latina: Dizionarietto di 2588 frasi etc*. Manuali Hoepli. Notes by Fumagalli. Milan: Urico Hoepli, 1911.

Gay, Peter. *Freud: A Life for Our Time*. London: J. M. Dent and Sons, 1988.

Gilman, Sander L. "The Image of the Hysteric." In *Hysteria Beyond Freud*, by Sander L. Gilman, Helen King, Roy Porter, G. S. Rousseau, and Elaine Showalter, 345-452. Berkeley: University of California Press, 1993.

———, with Helen King, Roy Porter, G. S. Rousseau, and Elaine Showalter. *Hysteria Beyond Freud*. Berkeley: University of California Press, 1993.

Gullón, Agnés Moncy. "Naming in Chapter XI of *La Regenta*." In *"Malevolent Insemination" and Other Essays on Clarín*, ed. N. Valis, 155-66. Michigan Romance Studies, 10. Ann Arbor: University of Michigan, 1990.

Gullón, Germán. "Invención y reflexividad discursiva en *La Regenta*, de Leopoldo Alas." In id., *La novela como acto imaginativo*, 123-47. Madrid: Taurus, 1983.

Hinshelwood, R. D. *A Dictionary of Kleinian Thought*. 1989. 2nd ed., revised and enlarged. London: Free Association Books, 1991.

Ife, Barry. "Idealism and Materialism in Clarín's *La Regenta*: Two Comparative Studies." *Revue de Littérature Comparée*, 44 (1970): 273-95.

Jung, C. G. "Psychological Aspects of the Mother Archetype." 1938. In *Aspects of the Feminine: C. G. Jung*, 103-19. Trans. R. F. C. Hull. London: Routledge and Kegan Paul, 1982.

Kahane, Claire (1985). "Introduction: Part II." In *In Dora's Case: Freud-Hysteria-Feminism*, ed. Bernheimer and Kahane, 19-32. New York: Columbia University Press, 1985.

Keller, Evelyn Fox. *Reflections on Gender and Science*. New Haven and London: Yale University Press, 1985.

Khan, M. Masud R., *Alienation in Perversions*. The International Psycho-Analytical Library 108. Ed. Clifford Yorke. London: The Hogarth Press and the Institute of Psycho-Analysis, 1979.

King, Helen. "Once Upon a Text." In *Hysteria Beyond Freud*, by Sander L. Gilman, Helen King, Roy Porter, G. S. Rousseau, and Elaine Showalter, 3-90. Berkeley: University of California Press, 1993.
Klein, Melanie. "Early Stages of the Oedipus Conflict." 1928. In ead., *Love, Guilt and Reparation and Other Works 1921-1945*, 186-98. London: Virago, 1988.
———. "Notes on Some Schizoid Mechanisms." 1946. In ead., *Envy and Gratitude and Other Works 1946-1963*, 1-24. London: Virago, 1988.
———. "Some Theoretical Conclusions Regarding the Emotional Life of the Infant." 1952. In ead., *Envy and Gratitude and Other Works 1946-1963*, 61-93. London: Virago, 1988.
———. "Envy and Gratitude." 1957. In ead., *Envy and Gratitude and Other Works 1946-1963*, 176-235. London: Virago, 1988.
———. "On the Sense of Loneliness." 1963. In ead., *Envy and Gratitude and Other Works 1946-1963*, 300-317. London: Virago, 1988.
The Selected Melanie Klein. Ed. and with introduction by Juliet Mitchell. Harmondsworth: Penguin Books, 1986.
Klein, Melanie. *Envy and Gratitude and Other Works 1946-1963*. London: Virago, 1988. Contains "Notes on Some Schizoid Mechanisms" (1946), "Some Theoretical Conclusions Regarding the Emotional Life of the Infant" (1952), "Envy and Gratitude" (1957).
———. *Love, Guilt and Reparation and Other Works 1921-1945*. London: Virago, 1988. Contains "Early Stages of the Oedipus Conflict" (1928).
Labanyi, Jo. "City, Country and Adultery in *La Regenta*." *Bulletin of Hispanic Studies*, 63 (1986): 53-65.
———. "The Raw, the Cooked and the Indigestible in Galdós's *Fortunata y Jacinta*." *Romance Studies* 13 (Winter 1988): 55-65.
———. "Mysticism and Hysteria in *La Regenta*: The Problem of Female Identity." In *Feminist Readings on Spanish and Latin-American Literature*, ed. L. P. Condé and S. M. Hart, 37-46. Lampeter: Edwin Mellen Press, 1991.
Lacan, Jacques. *The Seminar of Jacques Lacan*. 1975. Ed. Jacques-Alain Miller. Book I, *Freud's Papers on Technique 1953-1954*. Trans. with notes by John Forrester. Cambridge: Cambridge University Press, 1988.
———. *The Four Fundamental Concepts of Psycho-Analysis*. Originally Book XI of *Le Séminaire de Jacques Lacan*. 1973. Includes "Of the Subject who is Supposed to Know, of the First Dyad, and of the Good." Ed. Jacques-Alain Miller, translated by Alan Sheridan. Harmondsworth: Penguin Books, 1979.
———. *The Psychoses: The Seminar of Jacques Lacan*. 1981. Ed. Jacques-Alain Miller. Book III, 1955-1956. Includes "The Hysteric's Question." Translated with notes by Russell Grigg. Cambridge: Cambridge University Press, 1993.
———. "Intervention on Transference." 1951. In *In Dora's Case*, ed. Bernheimer and Kahane, 92-104. New York: Columbia University Press, 1985.
Lear, Jonathan. *Love and Its Place in Nature: A Philosophical Interpretation of Freudian Psychoanalysis*. New York: The Noonday Press, 1990.
Lévi-Strauss, Claude. *Le cru et le cuit*. Paris: Librairie Plon, 1964.
Livy. *The War with Hannibal*. Books 22-30 of *The History of Rome from its Foundation*. Trans. by Aubrey de Sélincourt, ed. Betty Radice. Harmondsworth: Penguin Books, 1965.
Macleod, Sheila. *The Art of Starvation*. London: Virago, 1981.
Mandrell, James. "Malevolent Insemination: *Don Juan Tenorio* in *La Regenta*." In *"Malevolent Insemination" and Other Essays on Clarín*, ed. N. Valis, 1-28. Michigan Romance Studies, 10. Ann Arbor: University of Michigan, 1990.
———. *Don Juan and the Point of Honor: Seduction, Patriarchal Society, and Literary Tradition*. University Park, PA: Pennsylvania State University Press, 1992.

Marcus, Steven. "Freud and Dora: Story, History, Case History." In *In Dora's Case*, ed. Bernheimer and Kahane, 56-91. New York: Columbia University Press, 1985.

Maudsley, Henry. *Body and Mind*. London: Macmillan, 1873.

———. *The Pathology of Mind*. New York: Appleton, 1886.

Mazzeo, Guido. "The Banquet Scene in *La Regenta*: A Case of Sacrilege." *Romance Notes* 10 (1968): 68-72.

Micale, Mark S. "Charcot and the Idea of Hysteria in the Male: Gender, Mental Science and Medical Diagnosis in Late Nineteenth-Century France." *Medical History* 34 (1990): 363-411.

———. "Hysteria Male/Hysteria Female: Reflections on Comparative Gender Construction in Nineteenth-Century France and Britain." In *Science and Sensibility: Gender and Scientific Enquiry, 1780-1945*, ed. Marina Benjamin, 200-39. 2nd ed. Oxford: Basil Blackwell, 1996.

Michie, Helena. *The Flesh Made Word: Female Figures and Women's Bodies*. Oxford: Oxford University Press, 1989.

Minsky, Rosalind. "Reaching Beyond Denial – Sight and In-sight – a Way Forward? (Drawing on the Theory of Freud, Klein, Winnicott, Lacan, and Kristeva)." *Free Associations* 5 (3) (1995): 326-51.

Monlau, Pedro Felipe. *Higiene del matrimonio o el libro de los casados*. 1853. Revised and trans. into French as *Hygiène de la Génération. Le Mariage dans ses Devoirs, ses Rapports et ses Effets Conjugaux au point de vue légal, hygiénique, physiologique et moral*. Paris, 1885.

———. *Elementos de higiene privada, o arte de conservar la salud del individuo*. 2nd ed., revised and enlarged. Madrid: Rivadeneyra, 1857.

Moscucci, Ornella. "Hermaphroditism and Sex Difference: The Construction of Gender in Victorian England." In *Science and Sensibility: Gender and Scientific Enquiry 1780-1945*, ed. Marina Benjamin, 174-99. 2nd ed. Oxford: Basil Blackwell, 1996.

New Catholic Encyclopedia. 17 vols. Washington: Catholic University of America, 1957-67.

Nimetz, Michael. "*Eros* and *Ecclesia* in Clarín's Vetusta." *Modern Language Notes* 86 (1971): 242-53.

Olivier, Christiane. *Jocasta's Children: The Imprint of the Mother*. Trans. George Craig. London and New York: Routledge, 1989.

Palazzini, Petro, ed. *Dictionary of Moral Theology*. 1957. Trans. H. J. Yannone, S. T. L. London: Burns and Oates, 1962.

Paulino Ayuso, José. "Devorar para ser devorado: comentario sobre un arquetipo en *La Regenta*, de Clarín." *Cuadernos de investigación filológica* 15 (1-2) (1989): 25-39.

Pérez Galdós, Benito. *Fortunata y Jacinta*. 1884-6. Repr. in *Obras completas*. Ed. F. C. Sainz de Robles. 6 vols. (vol. 5). Madrid: Aguilar, 1967.

Petruccione, J. "The Persecutor's Envy and the Rise of the Martyr Cult: Peristephanon Hymns 1 & 4." *Vigiliae Christianae* 45 (1991): 327-46.

Phillips, Adam. *On Kissing, Tickling, and Being Bored: Psychoanalytic Essays on the Unexamined Life*. Cambridge, MA: Harvard University Press, 1993.

Pitt-Rivers, Julian. *The People of the Sierra*. London: Weidenfeld and Nicolson, 1954.

———. "Honour and Social Status." In *Honour and Shame: The Values of Mediterranean Society*, ed. J. G. Peristiany, 21-77. London: Weidenfeld and Nicholson, 1965.

Porter, Roy. "Love, Sex and Madness in Eighteenth-Century England." *Social Research*, 53 (2) (Summer 1986): 211-42.

Porter, Roy. *Mind-Forg'd Manacles: a History of Madness in England from the Restoration to the Regency*. 1987. Repr. Harmondsworth: Penguin Books, 1990.

———. "The Body and the Mind, the Doctor and the Patient," in Sander L. Gilman, Helen King, Roy Porter, G. S. Rousseau and Elaine Showalter, *Hysteria Beyond Freud*, 225-85. Berkeley: University of California Press, 1993.

———. "A Mind and its Meanings." Review of Francis Crick, *The Astonishing Hypothesis: the Scientific Search for the Soul* (1994). *Times Literary Supplement* 4772, 16 Sept. 1994, 6-7.

Porto-Mauricio, Leonardo de. *Directorio de la confesión general compuesto por el B. Leonardo de Porto-Mauricio*. In *Nuevo manojito de flores o sea recopilación de doctrinas para los confesores*, by Antonio María Claret, 85-119. Barcelona, 1859.

———. *Discurso místico-moral que después de la misión hacía a los señores sacerdotes confesores el B. Leonardo de Porto-Mauricio*. In *Nuevo manojito de flores o sea recopilación de doctrinas para los confesores*, by Antonio María Claret, 20-84. Barcelona, 1859.

Reich, Wilhelm. *Character Analysis*. 1933. 3rd enlarged ed. 1950. Trans. Vincent Carfagno. London: Vision, 1973.

Rogers, Edith. "Surrogates, Parallels and Paraphrasings in *La Regenta*." *Revista de Estudios Hispánicos*, 18 (1984): 87-101.

Rousseau, G. S. " 'A Strange Pathology': Hysteria in the Early Modern World, 1500-1800." In *Hysteria Beyond Freud*, by Sander L. Gilman, Helen King, Roy Porter, G. S. Rousseau, and Elaine Showalter, 91-221. Berkeley: University of California Press, 1993.

Roustang, François. *The Quadrille of Gender: Casanova's "Memoirs."* 1984. Trans. Anne C. Vila. Stanford: Stanford University Press, 1988.

Roy, A., ed. *Hysteria*. Chichester: John Wiley, 1982.

Rutherford, John. *Leopoldo Alas: "La Regenta."* London: Grant and Cutler, 1974.

———. *"La Regenta" y el lector cómplice*. Murcia: Universidad de Murcia, 1988.

Saillard, Simone. "La peritonitis de Don Víctor y la fiebre histérica de Ana Ozores: dos calas en la documentación médica de Leopoldo Alas novelista." In *Realismo y naturalismo en España en la segunda mitad del siglo XIX*, ed. Yvan Lissorgues, 315-27. Barcelona: Anthropos, 1988.

Sánchez, Elizabeth. "The Missing Mother: Locating the Feminine Other in *La Regenta*." *Romance Languages Annual* 1 (1989): 597-602.

Sánchez Pérez, F. *La Liturgia del espacio*. Madrid: Nerea, 1990.

Sedgwick, Eve Kosofsky. *Between Men: English Literature and Male Homosexual Desire*. New York: Columbia University Press, 1985.

Segal, Hanna. *Introduction to the Work of Melanie Klein*. London: The Hogarth Press and the Institute of Psycho-Analysis, 1986.

Showalter, Elaine. *The Female Malady: Women, Madness and English Culture, 1830-1980*. 1985. Repr. London: Virago, 1988.

———. "On Hysterical Narrative." *Narrative* 1 (1) (1993): 24-35.

Sieburth, Stephanie (1990a). *Reading "La Regenta": Duplicitous Discourse and the Entropy of Structure*. Amsterdam/Philadelphia: John Benjamins, 1990.

——— (1990b). "Kiss and Tell: The Toad in *La Regenta*." In *"Malevolent Insemination" and Other Essays on Clarín*, ed. N. Valis, 87-100. Michigan Romance Studies, 10. Ann Arbor: University of Michigan, 1990.

Simon, Elizabeth. "La figura de la Madona y del Mesías en *La Regenta*: un estudio a partir del color." *Hispanófila* 32 (3) (1989): 21-34.

Sinclair, Alison. "The Consuming Passion: Appetite and Hunger in *La Regenta*." *Bulletin of Hispanic Studies* 69 (1992): 246-61.

———. *The Deceived Husband: A Kleinian Approach to the Literature of Infidelity*. Oxford: Oxford University Press, 1993.

Sinclair, Alison. "Masculine Envy and Desire in *La Regenta*: the Skull and the Foot." *Tesserae* 1 (2) (Summer 1995): 171-190.

——— (1996a). "The Force of Parental Presence in *La Regenta*." In *Culture and Gender in Nineteenth-Century Spain*, ed. Lou Charnon-Deutsch and Jo Labanyi, 182-198. Oxford: Oxford University Press, 1996.

——— (1996b). "The need for zeal, and the dangers of jealousy: identity and legitimacy in *La Regenta*." In *Scarlet Letters: Fictions of Adultery from Antiquity to the 1990s*, eds. Naomi Segal and Nick Whyte, 174-185. Basingstoke: Macmillan, 1996.

Slater, Eliot. "Diagnosis of 'Hysteria'." 1965. Repr. *British Medical Journal*, 29 May 1967, 1395-99.

Sobejano, Gonzalo, ed. *La Regenta* (1884-5) by Leopoldo Alas. 2 vols. Madrid: Clásicos Castalia, 1981.

Sontag, Susan. *Illness as Metaphor*. 1977. Repr. Harmondsworth: Penguin Books, 1983.

Stern, Daniel N. *The Interpersonal World of the Infant: a View from Psychoanalysis and Developmental Psychology*. New York: Basic Books, 1985.

Stoller, Robert. *Presentations of Gender*. London and New Haven: Yale University Press, 1985.

Tanner, Tony. *Adultery in the Novel*. Baltimore: Johns Hopkins, 1979.

Taxil, Léo. *Les Livres Secrets des Confesseurs: Dévoilés aux Pères de Famille*. Paris, 1883.

Tissot, S. A. A. D. *Onanism; or a Treatise upon the Disorders Produced by Masturbation; or the Dangerous Effects of Secret and Excessive Venery*. Tr. A. Hume. London, 1766.

Tolstoy, Leo. *Anna Karenin*. 1874-6. Trans. Rosemary Edmonds. Harmondsworth: Penguin Books, 1968.

———. *The Kreutzer Sonata and Other Stories*. 1890. Trans. D. McDuff. Harmondsworth: Penguin Books, 1985.

Turner, Harriet. "From the Verbal to the Visual in *La Regenta*." In *"Malevolent Insemination" and Other Essays on Clarín*, ed. N. Valis, 67-85. Michigan Romance Studies, 10. Ann Arbor: University of Michigan, 1990.

Urey, Diane. " 'Rumores Estridentes': Ana's Resonance in Clarín's *La Regenta*." *Modern Language Review* 82 (1987): 356-75.

———. "Writing Ana in Clarín's *La Regenta*." In *"Malevolent Insemination" and Other Essays on Clarín*, ed. N. Valis, 29-45. Michigan Romance Studies, 10. Ann Arbor: University of Michigan, 1990.

Vacant, A., with E. Mangenot. and E. Amann, eds. *Dictionnaire de théologie Catholique*. 15 vols. Paris: Librairie Letouzey et Ané, 1903-50.

Valis, Noël. *The Decadent Vision of Leopoldo Alas: A Study of "La Regenta" and "Su único hijo."* Baton Rouge: Louisiana State University Press, 1981.

———. "Order and Meaning in Clarín's *La Regenta*." *Novel* 16 (1983) (1982-3): 246-58.

———. "Sobre la última frase de *La Regenta*." In *Clarín y "La Regenta" en su tiempo*, 795-808. Actas del Simposio Internacional, Oviedo 1984. Oviedo: Universidad de Oviedo, 1987.

———, ed. *"Malevolent Insemination" and Other Essays on Clarín*. Michigan Romance Studies, 10. Ann Arbor: University of Michigan, 1990.

———. "On Monstrous Birth: Leopoldo Alas's *La Regenta*." In *Naturalism in the European Novel: New Critical Perspectives*, ed. Brian Nelson, 191-209. New York/Oxford: Berg, 1992.

———. "Aspects of an Improper Birth: Clarín's *La Regenta*." In *New Hispanisms: Literature, Culture, Theory*, ed. Mark I. Millington and Paul Julian Smith, 96-126. Ottawa Hispanic Studies 15. Ottawa: Dovehouse Editions, 1994.

Viller, M., ed. *et al. Dictionnaire de spiritualité ascétique et mystique.* 1932. 14 vols. Vol. 4 (1960). Paris: Librairie Letouzey et Ané.

Warner, Marina. *Alone of all her Sex: the Myth and Cult of the Virgin Mary.* 1976. Repr. London: Picador, 1985.

Weber, Frances. "The Dynamics of Motif in Leopoldo Alas's *La Regenta.*" *Romanic Review* 57 (1966): 188-99.

Winnicott, D. W. "Primitive Emotional Development." *International Journal of Psycho-Analysis* 26 (1-2) (1945): 137-43.

———. "The Capacity to be Alone." In id., *The Maturational Processes and the Facilitating Environment: Studies in the Theory of Emotional Development*, ed. John D. Sutherland, 29-36. International Psycho-Analytical Library, vol. 64. London: The Hogarth Press and the Institute of Psycho-Analysis, 1958.

———. *The Maturational Processes and the Facilitating Environment: Studies in the Theory of Emotional Development.* International Psycho-Analytical Library 64. Ed. John D. Sutherland. London: The Hogarth Press and the Institute of Psycho-Analysis, 1965.

Žižek, Slavoj. *The Sublime Object of Ideology.* London/New York: Verso, 1989.

NORTH CAROLINA STUDIES IN THE ROMANCE LANGUAGES AND LITERATURES

I.S.B.N. Prefix 0-8078-

Recent Titles

"EL ÁNGEL DEL HOGAR". GALDÓS AND THE IDEOLOGY OF DOMESTICITY IN SPAIN, by Bridget A. Aldaraca. 1991. (No. 239). *-9243-2.*

IN THE PRESENCE OF MYSTERY: MODERNIST FICTION AND THE OCCULT, by Howard M. Fraser. 1992. (No. 240). *-9244-0.*

THE NOBLE MERCHANT: PROBLEMS OF GENRE AND LINEAGE IN "HERVIS DE MES", by Catherine M. Jones. 1993. (No. 241). *-9245-9.*

JORGE LUIS BORGES AND HIS PREDECESSORS OR NOTES TOWARDS A MATERIALIST HISTORY OF LINGUISTIC IDEALISM, by Malcolm K. Read. 1993. (No. 242). *-9246-7.*

DISCOVERING THE COMIC IN "DON QUIXOTE", by Laura J. Gorfkle. 1993. (No. 243). *-9247-5.*

THE ARCHITECTURE OF IMAGERY IN ALBERTO MORAVIA'S FICTION, by Janice M. Kozma. 1993. (No. 244). *-9248-3.*

THE "LIBRO DE ALEXANDRE". MEDIEVAL EPIC AND SILVER LATIN, by Charles F. Fraker. 1993. (No. 245). *-9249-1.*

THE ROMANTIC IMAGINATION IN THE WORKS OF GUSTAVO ADOLFO BÉCQUER, by B. Brant Bynum. 1993. (No. 246). *-9250-5.*

MYSTIFICATION ET CRÉATIVITÉ DANS L'OEUVRE ROMANESQUE DE MARGUERITE YOURCENAR, par Beatrice Ness. 1994. (No. 247). *-9251-3.*

TEXT AS TOPOS IN RELIGIOUS LITERATURE OF THE SPANISH GOLDEN AGE, by M. Louise Salstad. 1995. (No. 248). *-9252-1.*

CALISTO'S DREAM AND THE CELESTINESQUE TRADITION: A REREADING OF *CELESTINA*, by Ricardo Castells. 1995. (No. 249). *-9253-X.*

THE ALLEGORICAL IMPULSE IN THE WORKS OF JULIEN GRACQ: HISTORY AS RHETORICAL ENACTMENT IN *LE RIVAGE DES SYRTES* AND *UN BALCON EN FORÊT*, by Carol J. Murphy. 1995. (No. 250). *-9254-8.*

VOID AND VOICE: QUESTIONING NARRATIVE CONVENTIONS IN ANDRÉ GIDE'S MAJOR FIRST-PERSON NARRATIVES, by Charles O'Keefe. 1996. (No. 251). *-9255-6.*

EL CÍRCULO Y LA FLECHA: PRINCIPIO Y FIN, TRIUNFO Y FRACASO DEL *PERSILES*, por Julio Baena. 1996. (No. 252). *-9256-4.*

EL TIEMPO Y LOS MÁRGENES. EUROPA COMO UTOPÍA Y COMO AMENAZA EN LA LITERATURA ESPAÑOLA, por Jesús Torrecilla. 1996. (No. 253). *-9257-2.*

THE AESTHETICS OF ARTIFICE: VILLIERS'S *L'EVE FUTURE*, by Marie Lathers. 1996. (No. 254). *-9254-8.*

DISLOCATIONS OF DESIRE: GENDER, IDENTITY, AND STRATEGY IN *LA REGENTA*, by Alison Sinclair. 1998. (No. 255). *-9259-9.*

THE POETICS OF INCONSTANCY, ETIENNE DURAND AND THE END OF RENAISSANCE VERSE, by Hoyt Rogers. 1998. (No. 256). *-9260-2.*

When ordering please cite the *ISBN Prefix* plus the last four digits for each title.

Send orders to: University of North Carolina Press
  P.O. Box 2288
  CB# 6215
  Chapel Hill, NC 27515-2288
  U.S.A.

The Department of Romance Studies Digital Arts and Collaboration Lab at the University of North Carolina at Chapel Hill is proud to support the digitization of the North Carolina Studies in the Romance Languages and Literatures series.

www.ingramcontent.com/pod-product-compliance
Lightning Source LLC
Chambersburg PA
CBHW020652230426
43665CB00008B/403